# Pieces of a Girl

# Pieces of a Girl

by Stephanie Kuehnert

Dutton Books

**Dutton Books**

An imprint of Penguin Random House LLC, New York

First published in the United States of America by Dutton Books,
an imprint of Penguin Random House LLC, 2024

Visit us online at PenguinRandomHouse.com.

Library of Congress Cataloging-in-Publication Data is available.

ISBN 978-0-525-42975-3 (hardcover)
ISBN 978-0-147-51771-5 (paperback)
1st Printing

Printed in the United States of America

LSCC
Design by Anna Booth
Text set in Chaparral Pro

This is a work of nonfiction. Some names and identifying details have been changed.

*For Scott*

# CONTENTS

[Introduction] *The Girl in the Story* .................... 1

[Part 1] *Weirdos* .................... 9

[Part 2] *Become What You Are* .................... 27

[Part 3] *Boys Will Be . . .* .................... 67

[Part 4] *True Bad Romance* .................... 83

[Part 5] *Girls Will Be . . .* .................... 115

[Part 6] *Live Through This* .................... 131

[Part 7] *Writer Grrrl* .................... 151

[Part 8] *Dig Me Out* .................... 197

[Part 9] *Some Girls Wander by Mistake* .................... 235

[Part 10] *She's Lost Control* .................... 253

[Part 11] *Follow the Music* .................... 277

[Epilogue] *The Writer in the Story* .................... 299

# Pieces of
## a Girl

# The Girl in the Story

**IF I COULD . . .**

If I could write a book when I grow up, this is what it would be about: Me Me and my life

I've always wanted to tell stories. For as long as I can remember. Made-up ones were fun. I was pretty good at that—creating elaborate histories for my dolls, coming up with new episodes of *The Smurfs* or *Voltron* for my brother and me to act out.

But I wanted to tell real stories. Stories about my life.

The first books I remember being obsessed with was Laura Ingalls Wilder's Little House series.

When I was five, six, and even seven, I'd tie my doll's bonnet around my neck, put on my winter boots and a long, floral-patterned, hand-me-down dress that looked like something Ma might make with a new bolt of fabric from the general store and a bit of lace that she'd traded hand-churned butter to get. I'd run around like this and make everyone call me Laura.

I wanted to be Laura so badly, it's embarrassing now.

Those books are problematic. They are racist. My parents read them to me, but I remember them stopping and pointing this out. My mom, the main bedtime reader, would pause and stumble a bit during certain passages when Laura's family encountered Native Americans or Black folks. She'd clear her throat and say, "The way they are talking about people who don't look like them is wrong." I don't remember if I asked questions, but I saw the words she wouldn't say when I read the books to myself. My dad, whose hair was not as long as it had been when I was born, or earlier, when he'd protested the Vietnam War, read on the nights when Mom worked. He'd close the book after he finished and fix me with a serious gaze to say, "That land Laura's family is building their house on? It didn't really belong to them. It was taken away from the Native Americans. That's not fair, is it?"

I shook my head, but I still loved Laura, and they let me. The fact that these books—my first literary obsession—led to a dawning awareness of societal injustice and a very clear sense of where my family stood on it is something I reflect on a lot now, but at the time, what gripped me about the Little House stories was that they were about a real girl from a long time ago. A girl with tangled, mousy-brown hair like me who lived through a lot and went on to tell all about it. A girl who'd authored her own story.

My next obsession was with another little brown-haired girl, Ramona Quimby. She was fictional, but her more modern life shared similarities to mine. Smart and quirky, sometimes mischievous and misunderstood, distinctly herself even while desiring to fit in—I was Ramona without even dressing up. Maybe, just maybe, this meant that my life would be story-worthy, too.

But my life did not seem as interesting as the books I read. I remember mentally narrating it in third grade: *She walks to her locker. At this new school, they have locks, and she struggles to remember her combination* . . .

There were no panthers, no blinding scarlet fever like Laura. Not even any incidents with egg in my hair like Ramona.

By nine years old, I doubted I'd ever have any *real* stories, any interesting, book-worthy ones like Laura or Ramona. So I started writing about cows living on Mars and girls with mysterious ailments in space prisons. Someday, when we made it to space—"the final frontier," as they said on *Star Trek*—then life would be worth documenting again. But the present? The age I was living in? The life of *this* little brown-haired girl? Nah.

Secretly, though, I kept hoping. I thought, *Maybe when I'm a teenager, things will pick up, get interesting and real* . . .

At ten, I fought my brother for control of the TV whenever PBS aired new episodes of *Degrassi Junior High*. I idolized Spike. I could tell from her eyebrows she had been a brown-haired girl until she bleached that hair and sculpted it into those spikes that provided her with the coolest nickname. "Can I bleach my hair?" I asked my mother, who had only recently allowed me to get my ears pierced. "Can I shave half of it?" The answer was no, of course. "No," with a smile because she knew I wasn't really serious. Not when I was still trying so hard to fit in with the popular crowd at school. When I asked for a blond streak in my hair at fifteen, she immediately gave permission, provided that I paid for it. But at ten and eleven, all I could do was gel my bangs into little points like Winona Ryder in *Beetlejuice*. I never left the house like that, though, and not because my mom told me I couldn't.

In fifth and sixth grades, I was still torn between the paths I saw toward a storied life: There was Spike, who had a baby in eighth grade with a guy who jumped off a bridge while doing acid, and then there was Brenda on *Beverly Hills, 90210*, a brown-haired girl from the Midwest who moved to California, made a lot of rich, blond friends, and fell in love with a brooding surfer/motorcycle rider who looked like James Dean. I could be an outsider or an insider. Or, I supposed, I could be an insider who is really an outsider and burns it all down with another brooding, motorcycle-riding, rebel-without-a-cause boyfriend like Winona Ryder in *Heathers*.

By thirteen, though, I was just the outsider with a couple of complicated friendships and an unrequited crush on the tall dark-haired boy in my gym class who wore a Sex Pistols shirt and was actually nice to me. I was also still the voracious reader. The same girl who documented her trips to the library in her *Beezus and Ramona Diary* with great zeal and won every summer reading challenge because she was either reading mysteries by the side of the public pool or holed up in her parents' air-conditioned bedroom with the books she pulled off their shelves—Shakespeare, Stephen King, and Leslie Marmon Silko, all of which she was probably too young for, but no one in her house believed in putting restrictions on reading.

In eighth grade, English class was always the best part of my day. Everything we read that year was amazing and seemed to speak to my soul. *The Outsiders*, *Lord of the Flies*, *Romeo and Juliet*, and above all else, our poetry unit, which gave me my new literary heroine:

Sylvia Plath.

I knew that Sylvia had killed herself—our teacher told us right off the bat—but that only made me idolize her more. Her words hadn't saved her; they'd just kept her alive long enough to tell her story and write some searingly beautiful poems so the world that had been too cruel to keep her would never be able to forget her. That, I felt, was something to strive for. As a thirteen-year-old who had already started taking out her feelings on her own skin with safety pins and razor blades, it seemed like the best possible hope I had.

I started writing poetry. It wasn't good (*yet*, I thought), but it was real. And it seemed even safer than journaling. I could lay my feelings bare but hide the meaning or claim I wasn't writing about myself.

At fifteen, I wrote my junior theme—our high school's penultimate research paper that most students wrote in junior year, but honors students wrote a year early—on Sylvia and another one of my biggest influences/sheroes, Courtney Love. Courtney was the frontwoman of the band Hole, but most famously in 1995, she was Kurt Cobain's widow. In the paper, I compared Sylvia's poems and Courtney's lyrics. The way they wrote about the female experience, about motherhood, about their own pain, was markedly similar, which is perhaps unsurprising because Sylvia was one of Courtney's influences. Sylvia was a template for a lot of us artistic (and often white) girls. But Courtney brought edge and anger. She punctuated her pleas for her baby with a scream of "FUCK YOU!"

*Is this,* I asked in my paper, *what kept her going? What allowed her to pack up her baby daughter and take her on tour just six months after her husband's suicide instead of putting her in her crib and sticking her head in the oven like Sylvia had?*

I wrote that paper because I desperately wanted to know the magic formula—what allowed one girl to survive her story, and the other . . . not? Courtney was, of course, still a ticking time bomb. She could overdose. She could give in to the many awful voices urging her to blow her brains out, too. But I didn't think she would. Her story would be long, wild, very much worth telling, and ultimately triumphant.

I wanted that. With so many more scars from deep, self-inflicted razor cuts, I didn't think I stood a chance, but I still wanted that.

I survived high school with Courtney's music as my soundtrack. The longer I lived, the more biting and fierce the music I loved got. Bikini Kill. 7 Year Bitch. Heavens to Betsy. Sleater-Kinney. I wrote manifestos about my angry, bloody girlhood and xeroxed them. Handed out these zines at my high school and mailed them in trades across the country. I was bleached blond then. Like Spike. Like Courtney. That little brown-haired girl I'd been was buried deep beneath the pain and rage. She still wanted me to tell her story, though. Our story.

By the end of my adolescence, which for me was more like twenty-four than eighteen, I knew I'd collected a few tales that might be worth sharing, but I wasn't sure I wanted to—not without hiding them in metaphor in poems, or spitting them through venom in zines, or assigning reimagined versions of them to fictionalized characters.

My panthers were three-headed girl-beasts. Those brooding boys who looked like the rock stars I worshiped had done things that shattered me. The kind of trouble I got into didn't just lead to me being called a pest or a nuisance like Ramona, but to principals and therapists and EMTs being called. Instead of blinding scarlet fever, there was blind drunkenness, blind rage, blistering pain as I puked off fire escapes, lashed out at other girls, carved my ex-boyfriend's initial into my thigh. Then I tried my damnedest to black it all out.

These were not the kind of stories that eight-year-old me ever thought I would have. They were not the kind of teenage adventures I daydreamed about after watching *Degrassi* or *90210*. They did not wrap up neatly at the end of an episode or even a season. They did not build into the triumphant backstory of a heroine. They weren't even the tales of a quirky but loveable kid who became a rebellious but whip-smart adolescent. They did not make me feel wise or good or strong.

Above all, I knew it would hurt like hell to retell them. It would be like picking up the shards of glass of one of the mirrors I accidentally-on-purpose smashed and reassembling it. What would I look like in there, through all the cracks, the bloodstains?

But I have to do it.

For Laura; for Ramona.

For Spike; for Brenda.

For Sylvia; for Courtney.

For the Stephanie who wanted so badly to be all of them, and above all, wanted to be the girl in the story.

# PART 1

Weirdos

We moved to Oak Park, Illinois, from St. Louis, Missouri, the summer I turned eight.

A couple blocks north of our house, you could stand on the bridge over the Eisenhower Expressway and see the Sears Tower. Downtown Chicago was only ten miles away.

The park down the street from us had the biggest and best-looking sledding hill I'd ever seen . . . which turned out to be built atop toxic waste from a gas plant. Two years after I graduated high school, they put a giant white tent over the whole park while it was "remediated." It took six years to clean up the deep wells of poison that we'd played on year-round.

Maybe that poison explained Liza/Brooke/Dani, the three-headed girl-beast that ruled Washington Irving Elementary's class of 1991.

Liza was the leader, but Brooke and Dani had glommed on so tight they'd all become one. There wasn't room for any more heads on that Electric Youth–scented, Gap-clad, Keds-hooved body, but almost every girl tried and sometimes they believed they'd succeeded. That included me, even though my first encounter on the playground with them at the beginning of third grade went like this:

"Is that a YKK zipper?" Liza asked, grabbing the front of my coat and leaning into examine it. She was all perfect dark brown waves, thin, freckled cheeks, and an icy smile made extra threatening by her long canines. When she concluded, "It's not," Brooke and Dani pounced.

"Do you shop at Kmart or something?"

"She's wearing generic sneakers, too!"

I felt like a field mouse surrounded by hyenas. I didn't know what to say. Having the right letters on your zipper, the right blue rubber tag affixed to the back of your shoe, hadn't mattered at my old school. My closest friend in second grade occasionally got her clothes from the free box, always got free lunch, and could only visit the little school store to buy the Now and Later candies and giant pickles that we both loved at the beginning of the month.

While Liza/Brooke/Dani circled and cackled, I pressed my tongue to the roof of my mouth. This was a trick I'd taught myself to keep from crying. I had a lot of practice with that.

According to my mother, I'd potty-trained early because I was so eager to start preschool, but despite how badly I wanted to be there, I cried every morning when she dropped me off. She sent me with one of her handkerchiefs to help me get through each day until I adjusted.

I stayed at that school through kindergarten, but I was a wreck all over again when I started first grade.

Now I was starting third grade at a new school in an entirely new state. I had a little pink handkerchief with clowns on it in my backpack, but I never took it out. I couldn't imagine the ridicule from Liza/Brooke/Dani. Worse, I'm sure, than over the clothes or when the students in the gifted program were announced. More cackling ensued then, and whispers of "Nerds!" I hadn't expected this either. In St. Louis, being part of the gifted program was a point of pride.

*Stiff upper lip! Stiff upper lip!* I told myself, pressing my tongue to the roof of my mouth. That was the advice my parents had given me in second grade when I hadn't liked the teacher in my gifted classroom. Compared to my previous grandmotherly teachers, she was a drill sergeant, and the books and projects she assigned were too hard.

*Stiff upper lip!* meant be strong and walk tall like Smurfette striding into the office marked PRESIDENT on one of the posters in my bedroom. (GIRLS CAN DO ANYTHING! the caption on the bottom declared, and back then, I thought I could.)

*Stiff upper lip!* meant HANG IN THERE! like another of my posters read—the one with the kitten dangling from a tree branch by its claws. (That was how every day at Washington Irving Elementary School felt.)

*Stiff upper lip!* got me through until fifth grade, when I became best friends with another girl who couldn't quite cut it with Liza/Brooke/Dani.

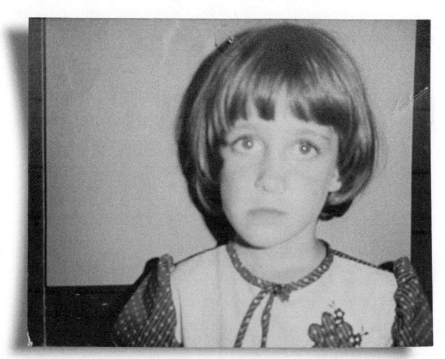

**Me on the first day of first grade, trying not to cry**

Juliet and I liked to say that we'd been best friends since third grade, but that wasn't actually true. I had three other best friends before we got close: One was a neighbor who was a year older than me so we never saw each other at school. The other two were classmates, but one had strict parents who never let her hang out after school, and both of them ended up moving away before the end of fifth grade.

I know that Juliet was around through all of this, but the only image of her that I can conjure up from before we were ten is long brown hair and a pastel-colored sweater. She is silent and still, not very Juliet-like at all. Because it is not a memory, it's our third-grade picture.

The real Juliet memories are anything but still. In them, she's always smirking, crossing her eyes, cartwheeling, handspringing, hugging, shoving, running, skating, and especially laughing. Juliet is the only person whose laugh I hear in my mind whenever I think of her—loud, unrestrained, sometimes on the verge of turning into a cough—and hers is the only phone number besides my own that I remember from childhood. So I don't think it matters that she wasn't the first (or last) girl that I shared halves of a BEST FRIENDS necklace with, because she was so much more than that.

We signed our notes and letters to each other *LYLAS*.

*Love. You. Like. A. Sister.*

Sometimes strangers thought we *were* sisters. We liked that.

Juliet was the only kid in a house of adults—her grandmother, grandfather, and the basement-dwelling uncle we hardly ever saw. Her mom lived in the city, so we saw her even less, and the only things Juliet knew about her father, the man who'd given her his Puerto Rican blood and last name, were that he'd died when she was young and he'd been a lot older than her teenage mother.

I had a mom, a dad, and a little brother whose hair Juliet and I gelled into a mohawk during sleepovers, but I'd always wanted a sister. Maybe a few, like Laura had, but definitely an older one like Ramona had. However, as much as I liked that people thought Juliet and I were sisters, I hated that they always thought she was older. I wished puberty would hurry up so our sizes would match the way so many of our other features did.

We both had brown hair (though mine was a half shade lighter) and hazel eyes (though mine were more green with an orange ring around them that Juliet repeatedly told me was "so cool"). But the difference in our height was so drastic that Juliet could casually lean her elbow on my shoulder. She also needed a bra and got her period two years before I did, which I silently envied.

At the beginning of fifth grade, Juliet and I had been paired up in science class. Hanging out after school to make a tornado that churned inside of a plastic two-liter and a volcano that spewed baking soda lava led to hanging out on a regular basis as well as eating dinner at each other's houses.

I liked dinner at Juliet's house better than at mine because we ate in the living room: Grandpa in his recliner, Grandma on the love seat she shared with stacks of paper and cartons of cigarettes, Juliet and me on the couch. Grandma's food was always delicious and always ready in time for *Star Trek: The Next Generation*, a show I'd never seen before, but was soon as addicted to as Juliet was. We loudly recited Captain Picard's "Space, the final frontier" introduction, emphasizing his British pronunciation of the word "civil-*i*-zations," and then when the music kicked in, we sung along with it—"Dun-dundundun-dundundun!" Grandma shook her head, and Grandpa eventually said, "Okay, pipe down, you two," but unless he'd had a really shitty day at work, he'd be smiling.

Sometimes there were weekend marathons of *ST:TNG*, and we'd plan a sleepover, preferably at Jules's house, because even after her grandparents fell asleep—Grandma on her love seat and Grandpa in the recliner, most of the time—we could watch it on the little TV in Juliet's room with no one to tell us to go to bed. But at least when we were at my house, we didn't have to fight my brother Dan for the TV during *Star Trek* because we'd gotten him hooked, too. In fact, after I informed Dan that at Juliet's we ate dinner in front of the TV so that we could see it, we lobbied for the same privilege, but were denied.

Juliet didn't seem to mind missing *Star Trek* to eat with my family, though. She would happily tell my parents what was going on at school while I sighed, rolled my eyes, and fidgeted in my seat, waiting for the moment when I could say, "Can we *puh-leeease* be excused?"

I didn't get along with either of my parents back then, especially not my mother, whom I blamed for making it hard for me to fit in with Liza/Brooke/Dani. She was the mom who always had to "think about it." There were several occasions when I was invited to a sleepover or party and had to *beg* her not to call and interrogate the host's parents. We also had regular screaming matches about her refusal to buy me clothes from the Gap like everyone else. She couldn't see why I needed her to pay double for a cardigan at the Gap when we could get a perfectly good one at Kmart. She told me if I wanted those clothes I had to save my allowance, even though that was another issue: every other kid in my grade seemed to earn double what I did, meaning I had to save for a month for one lousy pocket tee.

Thankfully, Juliet helped me out. Not with money—her allowance wasn't that much more than mine—but whenever she outgrew a shirt or a sweater, she gave them to me, and even though they were too big, I eagerly accepted.

We didn't talk about it. Why I needed those clothes. Why we were both so desperate to fit in with Liza/Brooke/Dani, to belong. So desperate that we let them ~~copy~~ borrow our homework and ~~burn our foreheads with a curling iron~~ curl and rat our bangs, and pretended not to know that they called us "weirdos" and "lesbos" behind our backs because we liked *Star Trek* and spent so much time together. Being in on the note-passing, the jokes, and especially the invitations to all the slumber parties made it all worth it.

The biggest, most important of all slumber parties was the one for Liza's birthday. In addition to serving cake and opening presents, Liza's chosen activities for the evening were playing with the Ouija board and watching a documentary on exorcism. In it, the possessed girl puked up chicken feathers and spoke in tongues while a priest tried to cast the evil spirit out. Liza/Brooke/Dani watched with wide, delighted eyes while I tried to cover mine whenever I thought I could get away with it.

Afterward, Liza said, "It was like *The Exorcist* but even cooler because it was real."

I murmured in agreement with the rest of the girls even though I'd never seen *The Exorcist*. My parents wouldn't let me watch anything R-rated—a rule that usually infuriated me, but when it came to stuff I knew would give me nightmares, I was secretly relieved.

While everyone else continued to rehash the highlights of the show, I slipped off to the bathroom, feeling sick to my stomach.

*Are there feathers in there?* I worried. *Could I be possessed?*

Someone in the documentary had said that the devil could find his way in if you weren't thinking good, godly thoughts. I realized that I wasn't really thinking any sort of thoughts while I sat on the toilet. Afraid I was leaving room for the devil, I mentally recited, *Hate the devil. Love god*, over and over again, trying to ignore the fact that, having hardly ever attended church, I knew nothing of the devil or god.

My fear only worsened after our Ouija board experience.

The board was set up on top of the pull-out couch that Liza and her chosen friend (presumably Brooke or Dani, but possibly no one if she didn't feel like sharing) would use later while the rest of us slept on the floor. Candles were lit, the lights shut off, and all six or eight of us crowded onto that mattress in a circle around the board.

We summoned the spirit of George Washington. I'm not sure if he was the only dead person we could collectively think of or if he just showed up. All I know is that someone asked if he lied about chopping down that cherry tree and then the bed collapsed. Everyone screamed. A few girls claimed to have seen a flash of green in the mirror above the couch—"Like the dollar bill!" Liza laughed.

The lights went on and the candles were blown out. Girls spread out on the floor, telling stories about the Ouija board. The sister/aunt/mom who had one and tried to throw it in the trash, but the next day it was sitting on their porch. How you could get possessed if you didn't envision yourself surrounded in white light.

Then Liza/Brooke/Dani started asking everyone if they were baptized, which apparently warded against demon possession in most cases.

Liza's lips curled as she zeroed in on Juliet. "That doesn't surprise me. You probably can't be baptized since you're a bastard."

This was not something that Juliet regularly shared. She'd told me about her parents after the lights went out during a sleepover that was just the two of us, and she'd probably told Liza under the same circumstances. There was a period when Juliet and Liza had seemed so tight that I thought for sure that she'd join or possibly replace Brooke/Dani. Apparently, Juliet had done something to blow it. She never told me what—she might not have even known—and she also never told me the secrets that she could have used to hurt Liza back. She just told me that there were some, and she didn't even share that much for months. At Liza's birthday party, Juliet played along.

Liza laughed, so we all laughed, Juliet loudest of all. That was her trick to keep herself from crying.

The subject changed eventually. To boys. To our recent sex-ed lectures. Liza/Brooke/Dani demanded that everyone get in their sleeping bag and wiggle around, pretending to be sperm and eggs.

After that we finally went to bed. I couldn't sleep thanks to a worried stomachache, but going home was out of the question—one girl had left after the Ouija board incident, and Liza/Brooke/Dani had been calling her a baby all night. I tiptoed off to the bathroom to sit on the toilet and mentally chant, *Hate the devil. Love god.*

"Are you okay?" Juliet whispered when I returned. I lied and said yes. I don't think we talked any further that night because it wouldn't have been safe in Liza's house, but later she said, "I don't care that I'm not baptized, do you?"

Until I'd become aware of demon possession, I hadn't given a single thought to not being baptized, and if Juliet couldn't be baptized just because her parents weren't married, that was stupid. So even though I was still freaked enough that whenever I caught myself not thinking I filled my head with *HatethedevilLovegod*, I told her that I didn't care about being baptized either.

Despite both of us not caring, the Weirdo Religion was born. It had its own written language that was meant to look like Egyptian hieroglyphs, but was more like squiggles on a page that we pretended to know how to read. I don't remember the mythology we invented, but since we loved *Star Trek*, I'm sure it involved aliens. We made scrolls out of construction paper and had ceremonies where we dressed up in sheets and carried candles around my basement (unlit per Mom's rules) while listening to Weird Al Yankovic. We baptized ourselves, my brother, our pets, and a couple of other friends that we deemed weird enough. Not Liza/Brooke/Dani.

With junior high approaching, coolness was paramount, and that was something they knew we could never achieve, so they stopped letting us hang out with them. We told ourselves we were okay with it, even though it hurt like hell. At least that's how I felt, and I assumed Juliet felt the same. We didn't talk about that either. We laughed, goofed off, provided distractions. That was how we always took care of each other. We were weirdos, and weirdos are best at being weird. And that was fine.

At least it seemed to be.

It got us through grade school, and stupidly, I thought the hardest part was over.

**From my gymnastics team days, sixth to seventh grade**

As soon as I got my schedule, I knew seventh grade was going to suck.

Our seventh-grade class was divided into two teams. Juliet and I had a fifty-fifty shot of being on the same one. We had bad luck. We had no classes together. None. Not even lunch.

This made our outside-of-school time even more sacred. Our main activity besides watching *Star Trek* was gymnastics. I'd spent most of my childhood switching back and forth between dance classes and gymnastics lessons, but at some point in fifth or sixth grade, Juliet and I had decided to take gymnastics together. I racked up a couple of trophies at the regional meets, but I had a bigger collection of ribbons from when I didn't quite make it to the top five. Juliet almost always stood a step or two above me on the winners' platform.

It stung, but I was happy for her. She was a lot more competitive, so her celebrations often involved a blow-by-blow dissection of how she excelled and I failed. I couldn't land back walkovers as well as she could. My form on the bars was never as solid. We were pretty evenly matched on trampoline, and usually I did better than her on beam and won *something*, but at the regional finals in seventh grade, I wobbled on the beam and my flips on the trampoline were too loose. Meanwhile, Juliet placed in both trampoline and the floor event. She was going to the state competition in Springfield. Neither of us had ever made it that far before. I hugged and high-fived her. Then I listened to her relive her glories in the car on the way home . . .

Sort of. After a while I tuned them out to stew, to make a decision that had been coming for a while: gymnastics was not my thing.

It had become painfully clear that despite my small size and all the time I spent glued to the TV watching Olympic gymnasts, I would never be a champion. And I didn't like things that I couldn't seem to dominate no matter how hard I worked—it didn't make for a triumphant story.

Juliet wanted me to come to Springfield with Grandma to watch her compete. My mom told me she couldn't justify the expense. I didn't fight her too hard. I was proud of Juliet, but I was over gymnastics.

I made the mistake of telling Juliet both things at the same time—that my mom said I couldn't go to Springfield *and* that I was quitting gymnastics—over the phone.

"You get straight As. You *have* everything! Why can't you let me have this one thing and be there for me?"

"My parents can't afford to send me to Springfield when I'm not competing. And they can't afford to keep paying for gymnastics when I suck!" I made up that last part. My parents had never said anything like it to me, but since money was always an issue, it did seem like a waste.

"You do suck," Juliet shot back. "You're a loser. A quitter. You suck as a gymnast and especially as a best friend. I HATE YOU!" She slammed down the phone.

I called back three times, and every time she picked up and hung up until she finally said, "Stop fucking calling here. My grandmother is going to get pissed at me. Do you want us *both* to hate you?"

*No, no, no.* The last thing in the world I wanted was for either of them to hate me.

Juliet didn't speak to me for almost an entire weekend.

I cried so hard I hyperventilated. I couldn't eat because my stomach was in knots. My mom tried to comfort me, but in the process she got angry at Juliet, saying, "I'm not so sure you two should be friends if she's going to treat you this way."

I lost it then. "You don't understand! She is the only one who understands me! I can't lose her! I can't! Can't! Can't! Can't!"

I kept screaming some version of this over and over again until my mom yelled back, "Fine! Then I'm calling her grandmother, because you two need to work this out."

"No! You can't do that! I'll look like a baby!" I argued, but I didn't argue that hard. Partially because I was exhausted. Partially because even though it wasn't a good solution, it was *a* solution.

Also even though I told my friends I hated my mom for holding me back—even though we had stupidly ugly battles where I yelled melodramatically, "I'm going to call DCFS!" and she yelled back just as melodramatically, "Fine! They can take you! You're too hard to live with anyway!"—our battles always ended with her saying, "Make me the villain."

My mom knew what girls were like: brutal, bloodthirsty creatures who regularly forced one another to walk through fields rigged with land mines.

"It's so much worse now," she'd say when our fights would come to a lull, when we'd both screamed and cried ourselves to exhaustion and I curled up in her bed, where she stroked my sweaty hair. "I don't know why you're so mean to each other. And I don't know why you think you have to be friends with such mean girls, but if you have to, tell them it's my fault. Tell them you hate me."

She didn't think Juliet was mean, not like Liza/Brooke/Dani, but that's still what she advised me after talking to Juliet's grandmother, who demanded that Juliet ride her bike over to my house and fix things with me.

Juliet wouldn't come inside, so we talked on the corner. She straddled her bike, ready to ride off at any second, and glared the way she glared at Grandma's back after she'd gotten lectured. I hung my head, unbrushed tangles falling into my face. I apologized, deflected blame onto my mother, but Juliet didn't take the bait.

She crossed her arms over her chest and said, "I can't come inside your house because you made your mom hate me and that's—" Her voice cracked, and her hand darted up to scrub away the tears that she couldn't prevent from falling. "You don't understand how much that sucks," she concluded, trying to sound vicious and angry, but it came out as a whisper.

"I do understand, and I'm sorry. But she doesn't hate you. Why would she call your grandmother to get you over here if she didn't want us to be friends?"

Juliet shrugged, her face slack.

I continued to apologize, told her that she was right. I was a quitter. I didn't like things I wasn't good at, but I was proud of her. She just stared at my house as if trying to will my mom to come out. I offered to go inside and get her, but Juliet said bitterly, "She'd just be doing it for you. Your mom will do anything for you."

*Unlike mine,* were the unspoken words that hung between us. We talked about how cool Juliet's mom was when she took us into the city to ride the double-decker bus, how much more fun and less strict she was compared to my mom or Juliet's grandma. But we never talked about why Juliet didn't live with her. Instead of focusing on her absence, we filled our lives with her presence: listening to the classic rock that she loved and wearing tie-dye and crystals.

"I'm sorry," I repeated.

She shook her head like I didn't get it.

And I didn't. Because we weren't just talking about her mom in some coded way. That was only part of the reason that Juliet needed my mom's approval so badly. Why our friendship wasn't really fixed until the next day when, instead of letting me walk home from Juliet's, my mom picked me up and came inside to personally invite her to dinner at our house.

My mom had seemed thrown at first when I'd gotten angry at her after the meeting she'd arranged with Juliet.

"*You* have to talk to her," I insisted. "She won't forgive *me* because she thinks *you're* mad at her."

"I *am* mad at her," Mom replied before repeating what she'd said about Juliet not acting like a real friend.

But ultimately she agreed. Juliet was right: my mother would do anything for me.

She loved Juliet, too, though. I saw it when she made the dinner invitation. When her brow creased with those same worried lines that appeared when I was hurting. When her hazel eyes softened as she told Juliet, "I've missed you." My mom wasn't an actress or a good liar; she couldn't say anything she didn't mean.

Things went back to normal after that, but only briefly. Then the truth came out. The real reason why Juliet had gotten so mad about Springfield and gymnastics:

Her grandma was sick.

Really sick.

It seemed to progress so quickly. By spring, when we went over to Juliet's on the weekend, we'd find Grandma shrunken into her love seat with a colorful scarf wrapped around her head, the table beside her cluttered with pill bottles and a foam mannequin head displaying the light brown wig she wore to work. The chemo had taken her hair. Chemo to fight the lung cancer from the ever-present cigarette that dangled from her lips.

I don't remember who told me first, Juliet or my parents. I do know that Grandma called my parents. She told them, so they could talk to me and we could all be there for Juliet. I have a vague recollection of my nurse parents in professional mode, explaining cancer, asking if I had questions even though they couldn't answer the only important one: Would Juliet's grandmother die?

I don't remember my conversation with Juliet at all except that she sobbed really hard, which I'd never seen before. I was the one who cried. Juliet sniffled sometimes. She fought frustrated tears like during our blowout about gymnastics or embarrassed ones like when her puppy raided the bathroom trash and left maxi pads all over the house. But she never sobbed like she did in seventh grade.

I held her when she broke down. Or I tried to. She didn't want that for long. She turned to anger quick. Or jokes. Or both.

Juliet wasn't just losing her grandmother, she was losing her home. Her grandfather couldn't care for Grandma plus Jules, so it was decided that before eighth grade started, Juliet would move upstate to live with her aunt.

Best friends forever. Soon we were split in half just like the necklace. It would only last two years, Juliet's stint up north. Then her aunt didn't want her anymore and bounced her to her mom, who rented an apartment in Oak Park. But we were never the same. Two years is an eternity when you are a teenage girl, an entire lifetime. Our paths diverged just enough. We were both wounded by the separation, and in response, sometimes we hurt each other in the ways only girls can. We healed apart, bearing different sets of scars.

Love You Like a Sister. That remained true. We weren't best friends anymore, though we both refused to admit it for years, decades even, until we silently and mutually agreed to drop "like a" from the phrase.

Love you, sister. Weirdos forever.

# PART 2

Become

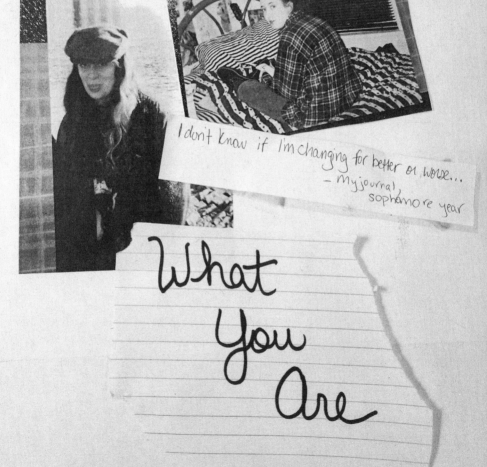

I don't know if I'm changing for better or worse...
— my journal,
sophomore year

What
You
Are

So we all know the story of the hungry caterpillar, right? It eats a ton. Then it stops. Makes a cocoon and emerges a beautiful butterfly. Of course, what's not in the kids' book is that the caterpillar actually digests itself in the cocoon. That's part of how it makes this radical transformation. That's how it becomes what it is.

I get it. I feel like I went (*or am still going*) through a similar process.

I remember I didn't sleep at all the night before eighth grade started.

I got up. Peed. Went back to bed. Realized I was thirsty. Got up again. Drank water from one of the little Dixie cups in the bathroom. Went back to bed. Tossed. Turned. Looked at the clock. Counted the dwindling amount of time I had left to sleep. Worried about that. Worried about not seeing Juliet. Worried about how different everything was going to be. Told myself to stop fucking worrying and get some sleep. Squeezed my eyes shut. Realized I had to pee again . . .

The same cycle repeated until my alarm went off. I went to school feeling raw. Like if someone so much as brushed up against me I would scream. Like I was shedding and regrowing my skin—becoming something. That's pretty much what all of junior high felt like. I devoured music like food and tried desperately to turn beautiful colors and grow wings. Sometimes I still wonder, did I ever come out of that cocoon? Was I a butterfly? A moth? Or did I just eat myself alive?

Whatever happened, I guess this is my account of the transformation.

# Grunge

*Seventh grade has just started, and I'm in my friend Kendra's bedroom, which has always seemed so much more sophisticated than mine. It's her arty touches—the brightly colored boxes she leaves sitting out, the collages made of pictures clipped from fashion magazines. With her sharply angled bob and the scarf wrapped around her long neck, she looks like she's stepped out of a fashion magazine herself. She always has. Liza/Brooke/Dani never cramped her style like they did mine. For the past two years, the only distinctive things I dared to wear to school were my earrings—giant peace signs, wooden zebras, black-and-white balloons, electric-blue lightning bolts, neon-pink female stick figures that dangled all the way to my shoulders. I'm sure Liza/Brooke/Dani thought they were weird, but it had taken me so long to convince my mom to let me pierce my ears, I couldn't give them up. I'm reclaiming my true sense of style now. Today Kendra and I went shopping at the vintage store by my house and I bought a pair of white boots from the sixties that look like ice skates. I'm sure Liza/Brooke/Dani and their new friends will make fun of them even more than my Converse, but I don't care.*

*In addition to her incredible fashion sense, Kendra has always been on top of it when it comes to music. We met three summers ago, when we were nine and our brothers were on the same T-ball team. We went back to her* house and she introduced me to MTV. Now Kendra flips through a shoe box of cassettes, explaining that she heard about this band from Seattle. They had a new album, but she couldn't find it, so she bought their first one. She pulls out a tape with black, white, and gray cover art and puts it on—side B because she doesn't feel like rewinding. The guitars are fast and sludgy-sounding like someone starting up a piece of heavy machinery over and over. The singer screams, high-pitched and somewhat off-key, about being a negative creep. During the chorus, he yowls, "Daddy's little girl ain't a girl no more." After the song ends, Kendra turns it off and asks me what I think of Nirvana.

I tell her to turn the tape back on.

## JANUARY 1992

Juliet and I house-sit for a friend of her grandmother's during winter break. We're spending the night all by ourselves. My mom was a little bit nervous about that, but since we'd recently learned that Grandma is dying and Juliet is moving, she went along with it. I'm actually not sure how I'm going to sleep tonight because the scent of old-man cologne is so thick in the air that I can taste it in the microwave popcorn we're eating while watching Saturday Night Live. It's giving me a headache, and I'm feeling totally nauseous until the SNL musical guest comes on. It's the band that Kendra played me. I still haven't gotten around to buying anything by them yet, but I see their "Smells Like Teen Spirit" video on MTV all the time now. It's pretty good, but the live version is even better. Harder. Faster. I'm immediately reminded of how much I loved listening to them in Kendra's room.

Then the second song they play starts with the bassist shrieking a line from "Get Together" by the Youngbloods, which I recognize because part of me still wants to be a hippie like my dad was. It ends with the band smashing everything on the stage. I have forgotten the old-man smell, my nausea, and my headache. I have officially discovered my favorite band of all time—a band that actually belongs to me and my generation, not my parents' or Juliet's mom's. I want to stand up and cheer . . .

But I don't because Juliet turns to me and says, "That sucked! And why the hell did they smash everything?"

I have officially discovered my favorite band of all time and in the exact same moment, I have officially discovered that my very best friend in the whole wide world and I are growing apart.

## AUGUST 1992

In the morning I sit on my front steps and tighten the laces of my Rollerblades. I do this carefully because in the afternoon I won't have time to make adjustments. As soon as camp ends, I'll have to slip into them and skate for my life.

The thought makes me queasy, so I pop a tape into my Walkman.

My headphones have become my armor. When the girl-beast shouts "Freak!" in the hallways because I'm wearing the wrong shoes or the boy-beast in my gym class reminds me that I look like the guy from the Black Crowes—ugly, flat-chested, and greasy-haired—I blast Hole's Pretty on the Inside, side B, Courtney Love shrieking, "Is she pretty on the inside? Is she pretty from the back?"

I prepare for camp with Faith No More's The Real Thing, side A.

I am thirteen and in love with Mike Patton, the lead singer of Faith No More. He has long brown hair like mine, and when he headbangs in his music videos, you can see that it's shaved underneath.

I nod my head in time with the driving guitar riff, slap the sides of my peach-and-gray skates, and push off. As my hair blows out behind me, snarling in the wind, I decide to shave the underside of my head, too. It's too hot to have long, thick hair clinging to your neck.

(Especially when being chased by a pack of girls who have nicer Rollerblades and longer limbs.)

"You want it all, but you can't have it," Mike Patton croons into my ears—to me it is crooning; others might view it as shouting. In the video for this song, he stomps around, swinging his hair and glaring at the camera. I don't just love Mike Patton because he's one of the hottest guys on MTV. He knows how I feel.

*All I wanted a torment-free summer. To forget about seventh grade. It was supposed to be my time to shine at the theater camp open to students from both of Oak Park's junior highs. Since Liza/Brooke/Dani and their boy-beast counterparts weren't there, I actually tried out and got a role in* Grease *instead of hiding behind the scenes on stage crew.*

(I hadn't known that the beast from Emerson, the other junior high, would be worse.)

*I arrive at camp with the angry "Surprise! You're Dead!" blaring in my ears. The drums rat-a-tat-tat like machine-gun fire, and Mike Patton screams about torturing someone who wronged him. For a moment I feel strong enough to stand up to anyone, but then I meet the blue eyes of the Barbie doll that leads the Emerson girl-beast. I scurry inside and try to enjoy the day, rehearsing my beloved* Grease *songs and forcing smiles at the few castmates who don't hate me.*

*I eat lunch with my stage crew friends and plan to go home with one of them after camp. She has Rollerblades, too. I warn her that last week up to six girls chased me to Juliet's house every day. She believes that since there are two of us, they'll leave us alone, but I'm prepared.*

*My Rollerblades are already laced, and I have a tape in my Walkman: the Sex Pistols'* Never Mind the Bollocks, *side A. I saw an old live video of them on MTV's* 120 Minutes. *Johnny Rotten is not pretty like Mike Patton, but his snarl makes up for that.*

*Sure enough, four cackling girls pursue us. They all have shampoo-commercial hair and curves like high school cheerleaders. I look like a third grader by comparison, but at least I'm fast and so is the music that keeps me moving. Instead of worrying about what will happen if they yank me to a stop with their manicured claws, I picture the kids in the Sex Pistols video slam dancing in big, black boots and the safety pins shoved through Johnny Rotten's ears. I can barely understand his lyrics because his rage is even thicker than his British accent, but I think Johnny might understand me even better than Mike Patton does.*

*"Wow, Steph," my friend says breathlessly as we clomp through her front*

door on our skates. "Those girls really hate you. You should have just done stage crew."

I shake my head. Maybe it would have helped me avoid the beast, but my intrusion into the pretty, popular girl territory of acting isn't the only reason it's after me. The blue-eyed Barbie doll thinks she's sticking up for a friend of hers who I had a disagreement with last year. She has no interest in my side of the story. I don't think her minions even know the story at all. They're just chasing me because I'm small and weak and it's fun. That's grounds enough for making my summer a living hell.

Before Juliet left, she said, "Don't let them ruin this for you. If they do, I'll come back and kick their asses. No one fucks with my Stephie-Lou."

We laughed. Even though we knew that neither of us could fight them. All I could do was run.

Or skate.

The beast twirls in delicate circles on the sidewalk in front of my friend's house. It catches sight of my pale, sweaty face in the window and laughs before skating off.

I carefully wind the cord of my headphones around my Walkman, still thinking about Johnny Rotten.

I've decided that I will get big, black boots and wear safety pins as earrings.

And forget my old stiff upper lip mantra, I will learn how to snarl.

## DECEMBER 1992

I borrow two of my dad's flannels and never give them back. I raid his toolbox for sandpaper and use it to make holes in the knees of all my jeans. At least, Mom says, I got them at thrift shops. I don't think she knows how to react when I cut the hood off my favorite Gap shirt from elementary school, the one I'd saved up so many weeks of allowance for. It's navy blue and I'm both pleased and fascinated that the fabric turns a purplish pink when I intentionally splash it with bleach.

I'm not completely over name brands, though. I just want different ones. When I open the box of fake Doc Marten shoes for Christmas, I force a smile and plan to start saving for real Doc boots. It will be a slow process because whenever I go to Clark and Belmont in the city, I blow my money on more jeans and flannel at Ragstock, vintage clothes at Hollywood Mirror, fishnets and striped tights at Pink Frog, and T-shirts at the Alley. They have all the cool band shirts there. I couldn't even decide what to buy the first time I went, so I got one of their many logo tees. The one I chose said NO ANIMAL TESTING in giant letters.

I have a few vegetarian friends and they've started asking me why I eat meat—especially since I've been boycotting companies that tested on animals since I saw a Degrassi episode about it in fifth grade. Aren't cows, chickens, and pigs as worthy of my compassion as the monkeys, bunnies, cats, and dogs subjected to cruel tests? Isn't killing an animal even worse?

I debate this for a while, weighing the tastiness of meat against the animals, who didn't have a voice, couldn't say they were in pain.

One night my family has steak for dinner and I can taste the blood. My parents say it's just "the juices."

I take another bite. Chew it.

Flesh, I think. I'm chewing flesh. And even though what I'm tasting isn't technically blood, this was a cow who bled. For me.

"I can't do this anymore," I blurt. "For my New Year's resolution, I'm going vegetarian."

I waffle a little bit on the particulars at first—I eat fried chicken once while visiting Juliet—but then I firmly decide that I will not eat anything that had a face, and I never look back.

## APRIL 1993

It's my first flight ever (if you don't count the one when I was a baby, which I don't). We're going to Florida, to Disney World, for spring break. I probably would have appreciated it more if I'd been two years younger. The magazine store in the airport is more exciting to me now than the Mouse. I buy an issue of Spin *that provides an A-to-Z guide of alternative music. It features everything I love and a few things I haven't heard of yet. I plan to cut out the pictures of Winona Ryder, Evan Dando, a pair of* Ren *and* Stimpy *boxers, and a Converse sneaker ad, and use them to start my own collage like the ones in Kendra's room.*

*My brother and I convince our parents to sit through a sales pitch for time-shares so that we can get free passes to Universal Studios, which we've heard has better rides. We're especially excited to try the one based on* Back to the Future. *It proves to be the highlight of the trip—the ride and the sibling bonding. It's been a while, since we're at different schools now and will be until my senior/Dan's freshman year.*

*I'm not quite sure how to bridge the growing gap between us. We both still love science fiction, but I don't love baseball anymore. I never loved it the way he and my dad do; in fact I mainly loved it because it was a way to spend time with them, to speak their language. My new language is music, and my brother tries to understand it, but he is more enthusiastic about Weird Al's cover of "Smells Like Teen Spirit" than the actual Nirvana tape I give him. Though when I suggest that maybe he'd like the band Devo, describing them as "weird like us," he brightens.*

*I know he misses the Weirdo Religion, the* Star Trek *marathons, maybe even the way Juliet and I used to mess with his hair. I want to say I'm sorry, that I miss it, too, but I don't know how. Just like how I don't really know how to be a big sister. One time in grade school I threatened a kid who was picking on him, but I think that just embarrassed him and now he hears all my fights with my parents, so he knows about my trips to the guidance counselor and the summer-camp girl-beast . . .*

*That realization shuts me down. Dan doesn't need a crazy, messed-up older sister. And I can never give him back what we used to have—him, Juliet, and me.*

*Especially because when we return from Florida, I find out that while I was gone, Juliet's grandmother passed away.*

When I walk into my room after school, the phone is ringing.

I pick it up to hear Juliet cackling. "Kurt Cobain is DEAD! He won't be making any more crappy music!"

"No, he's not! That's just a rumor," I counter, thinking—hoping—that she's just heard about his overdose in Rome last month and is trying to rub it in my face because she has a constant need to remind me how much she hates Nirvana. But deep down I just know.

"He's DEAD! He SHOT HIMSELF! Turn on Q101, turn on MTV, if you don't believe me!"

I hang up the phone and run over to my stereo. "All Apologies" is ending, and then the DJ announces: "It has now been officially confirmed: Kurt Cobain is dead."

Kurdt Lives Forever!
We miss you Kurdt.

4-8-94
Kurt Cobain has shot himself. Kurt Cobain is
dead. Why do people take their lifes? Kurt, I never
thought you were like that I never thought you were
so "Dumb" Did you consider your wife or child?
Why'd you do it Kurt? April 8th will always be a day
of mourning

My reaction to learning of Kurt Cobain's death as scrawled in my journal

# Real Teenage Life

In eighth grade, a girl named Robin became my next best friend. "Next best" as in she came next chronologically *and* she was next best to Juliet by comparison. Needless to say, that second part created some tension.

While no one ever mistook Robin and me for sisters—even though we were the same height, Robin's eyes were brown, her hair much darker and skin much paler—sometimes I felt like I had more in common with her than with Juliet. Especially when it came to music. Robin was as hungry as I was for new bands. Loud bands. Metal, grunge, punk, indie rock, we loved it all. We watched *Headbangers Ball*, *120 Minutes*, and *Alternative Nation*, bonding over MTV the way Juliet and I had over *Star Trek*. And this music—I couldn't tell Juliet this, but it mattered more. Trips to the record store were like trips to the library. It was that sacred.

Robin lived with her dad and her older brother. Her parents were divorced, and her mom lived in a small town a few states away. Her dad spent most weekends at his girlfriend's house. Her brother sometimes tried to throw parties, but while he played sports, he wasn't super popular, so mostly he went out . . . wherever semipopular preps went, maybe those keggers in Thatcher Woods that I would hear blond girls talk about in the bathroom when I got to high school.

Anyway, what this meant was that whenever Robin and I went to her house we were usually left to our own devices, so we had a lot more sleepovers at her house than at mine. My mom would later tell me that she had remorse about this, mom guilt, for letting her young teenage daughter spend so much time in a house alone with men. I waved this off. Robin's dad and brother were nice, harmless, and hardly ever there. I'd always been safe at Robin's house—well, at least at her *dad's* house, and at least until sophomore year, and that's when I started bringing my own trouble with me everywhere.

In eighth grade, Robin and I were just testing the waters. Like we stole her dad's cigarettes sometimes and tried to smoke them without choking—he smoked Marlboro Reds, after all. Once we took a can of beer that had been either her dad's or her brother's, but the first time we got tipsy had actually been at my house. My mom was working night shift, and my dad wasn't paying attention, so we poured cheap wine left over from some family party into plastic cups. We even went back for seconds, sneakily watering down the bottle. We barely drank the beer from Robin's house. It was so gross that we just tried (and failed) to use it to start a fire.

We were pretty obsessed with fire in those days, being big *Beavis and Butt-Head* fans and all. In fact, that is kind of who we were, except the smart girl versions. We mostly just watched MTV, but sometimes set fires and once tried to get high by smoking a mixture of herbs from Robin's kitchen in a pipe we'd shoplifted from Walgreens. Okay, I guess we weren't that smart, but it was a step up from Beavis and Butt-Head, who tried to lick frogs after hearing it would make them hallucinate.

As much as we loved grunge and metal, Robin and I were fascinated by hippie culture. We overused the word "groovy." We made miniature clay busts of hippies in Applied Arts class (and somehow the joints in their mouths always mysteriously broke off in the kiln). We listened to Jimi Hendrix alongside Nirvana and Alice in Chains, and I'd always loved the Beatles. My dad's Jefferson Airplane tape and *Woodstock* soundtrack lived in my room in eighth grade.

It wasn't just Juliet who tried to connect to a missing parent through their culture. Unlike Juliet's mom, my dad lived under the same roof, but he worked long hours and was attending grad school. His attention felt rare and fleeting. I did my history project on the Vietnam War protests so that I could interview him. He was my folk hero. He had stories worth telling—the kind I aspired to—and he'd started living them in high school! There were black armbands and picket lines as well as allusions to drug use. He made *I didn't inhale* jokes in reference to our president, Bill Clinton.

I'd already taken to raiding my dad's bookshelf, and after I interviewed him for my project, I read *One Flew Over the Cuckoo's Nest* and *The Electric Kool-Aid Acid Test*. Robin and I had a massive fight on the walk to school one day when I mused about trying acid someday. Our fake weed was one thing, but that was a bridge too far for her.

"That's crazy!" she screamed. "You could *go* crazy! You could be locked up in a mental institution because you refuse to lie down because you think you're a glass of orange juice and you're going to spill if you lie down."

I laughed and told her that was an urban legend. She rattled off more urban legends that she claimed to have heard from her brother. When I refused to take her seriously or retract my desire to do acid, she crossed the street, shouting at me not to follow her.

We made up later that day, but this was one of the key differences between Robin and me: she was a lot more content to live vicariously through music and books and TV. I still wanted to be in the story, even if it was a little bit scary to think about the things that Juliet was doing an hour and a half away.

Jules jumped into teenage life feetfirst at her high school. She started smoking pot and had a serious boyfriend. Meanwhile, I spent my freshman year wondering when Real Teenage Life was going to start. Though I knew the movies and shows I watched *weren't* real, I expected that once I hit high school my experience would at least somewhat reflect what I'd seen on TV. You know, parties, boys, a whole gang of friends.

Or something.

Anything that would snap me and Robin out of the same pattern we'd been stuck in: Afternoons watching MTV or playing *Sonic the Hedgehog* or *Ecco the Dolphin* on Sega Genesis. Friday and/or Saturday nights ordering Chinese and rewatching *The Shining* and *Wayne's World* . . . and sometimes *Beauty and the Beast* and *Aladdin*. (*Disney movies? What the hell! We're in ninth grade. We're not nine!*) Messing around with the Ouija board in her bedroom, calling up our favorite spirits. *(Seriously? Shouldn't we be making real friends instead of making up imaginary ghost friends? Are we four or fourteen?)*

As part of my quest for a more storied life, we tried out the classics of the Normal High School Experience:

## THE PEP RALLY

Attendance was actually required at the first fall pep rally because it took the place of ninth period. "You can just leave, though," my friend Jo told me at lunch. "That's what my brother says. It's so crowded, they can't keep track of everyone."

In an attempt to hide my uncool, *I can't possibly ditch* side, I took a contemplative drag from the Camel I'd bummed from her. To escape the cacophony of the cafeteria—so many hoots, hollers, and whistles, plus the occasional football whizzing over your head—I'd started going out for a cigarette with Jo in the parking lot between the soccer field and the football stands, the only place on school grounds where smoking was still allowed.

I liked the taste of Jo's Camels a lot better than Robin's dad's Marlboro Reds. Though she didn't mind supplying me, Jo told me where I could buy cigarettes, a store that didn't card, but I was too scared to try.

I was also too scared to leave school before I was technically dismissed. I shrugged and said, "I think I'll go anyway. Just to see what it's like."

Jo dropped her cigarette and ground it out with her all-black Converse high-top. "Everyone says the upperclassmen throw pennies at the freshman."

"Yeah." I took one last drag, waiting for her refute this with evidence from her brother. Robin's brother wouldn't tell us if it was true or not, but he was a prep, not one of us (or what we were trying to be) like Jo's metalhead brother.

Jo shook her head, her dyed-black curls bouncing off her cheeks. "I don't want to experience that indignity."

*Great,* I thought, *so it probably is true. Please let it be like in* Dazed and Confused *where getting hazed leads to becoming friends with the cool upperclassmen.*

As it turned out, there was no hazing. The drill team did a routine to some pop song. Guys in uniforms ran around the field house. It was a total bore, and I probably could have ditched because Robin came to sit with me and her homeroom teacher didn't notice.

## THE FOOTBALL GAME

Even though we both hated football, Robin and I got up on Saturday morning and walked to school on the day of the homecoming game just to see if it would be life-altering. It might have been if we'd been willing to fork over the five bucks each to actually sit in the stands, but that money seemed better spent on cheese fries. We stood in the parking lot, where Jo and I smoked and craned our necks, squinting to see if we recognized anyone in the stands.

I turned around and looked at the empty parking lot, longing for the usual lunch crowd—the metalheads, the stage crew kids who wore all black even when they weren't working a production, and the stoners. Some people stayed there through all three lunch periods, chain-smoking and kicking around a hackysack. Jo and I usually only had one cigarette before heading back inside, but it was my favorite part of the day. It felt like real high school. A place where something could actually happen. Where courage might strike like lightning and I'd talk to that senior guy with wavy brown hair as long as mine and my entire life would change . . .

But it hadn't yet. And it wasn't going to while the parking lot was empty.

I turned back to the stupid football game and said irritably, "I don't know why we're here."

Robin's shoulders sagged. "I don't either."

We were both lying. We didn't want to admit that we hoped one of our crushes might be there and ask us to the homecoming dance at the very last minute. Even though we'd have to wear our dresses from the eighth-grade dance. Even though Baby Kurt Cobain from my Spanish class or the grungy blond in Robin's algebra class probably wouldn't be caught dead at a football game. We scanned the stands one more time before bailing to get those cheese fries.

In addition to formal dances like homecoming, our school also had informal ones called "morps."

"Prom" spelled backward—get it?

The name alone made me want to vomit, but a couple of weeks after homecoming, Robin and I were talked into it by some of our friends from junior high.

The morp took place in the student center, a large, open space just inside of the school's main entrance where people killed time before school or during lunch. Usually, the student center was bright and airy even when crowded, but they'd dimmed the lights and brought in some strobes, attempting to create a nightclub vibe. It was sweaty and loud, and pressed up against a wall, I felt thoroughly out of place and uncomfortable. "Smells Like Teen Spirit" came on, and the kids who made fun of me for wearing Converse sneakers two years ago ("stupid preppy shits," as Jo would have called them) actually tried to start a mosh pit.

Robin and I exchanged disgusted scowls. This was even worse than the pep rally and the football game. I was about to tell Robin that we should leave when a guy with shoulder-length green hair came up to us, grabbed my black crystal necklace and studied it, then took Robin's necklace—a blob of colorful clay that had been melted into a screaming face—and studied it even more closely before looking from her to me to her and proclaiming, "Penile implantations!"

He ran off, leaving us somewhere between mortified and laughing hysterically.

Our junior high friends chirped: "What the hell?"

"Oh my god, was he high?"

"That's Jeff. He hangs out at Scoville Park. Definitely high."

I watched Jeff's green hair fly out behind him as he sprinted out of the student center and down the hall. Then he was gone. Off-screen, wherever he'd run to, Real Teenage Life was probably happening, but I was too scared to follow.

# Nevermind

I first bonded with Baby Kurt when we had a substitute in Spanish. We were watching a stupid movie about bullfighting, and Baby Kurt started singing Nirvana songs under his breath. I glanced over him, and he raised his eyebrows. An invitation. A dare. I started singing, too.

When the sub tried to get us to shut up and pay attention, I objected, "I don't want to watch this. I find it disturbing, and I fundamentally disagree with it."

Baby Kurt slapped his desk and declared, "Yeah!"

"Well, please stop singing," the flustered sub said.

I felt a twinge of guilt but kept singing anyway, knowing that the social benefits would far outweigh any academic consequences.

Sure enough, the class just got a beleaguered lecture from Señor Mackey about cooperating with subs. Baby Kurt smirked at me and from then on, instead of being the girl that he only talked to when he needed to borrow a pencil, I was the one he gave cigarettes to—Winstons, which I liked even better than Camels—and high-fived on his way to his desk.

But there was no high-fiving on the Monday after Kurt Cobain died. Baby Kurt walked into class right at the bell, wearing all black and looking extra pissed. He met my eyes. His were bloodshot, presumably from smoking weed at lunch like he'd told me he did sometimes. Mine were, too, but because I'd spent the whole weekend crying while watching the tribute footage on MTV.

He gestured at my Nirvana shirt and nodded.

I bit my lip and nodded back.

"Such a fuckin' waste."

"Yeah." I nodded again.

"I was at Scoville when I heard," he told me as he sat down, ignoring the instructions that Señor Mackey was yapping in Spanish. "This kid came running up to me and my friend saying Kurt was dead, so I pulled out my Walkman. Then a car drove up with Nirvana on the radio. One of the dudes threw open the door so we could all hear the announcement. I fuckin' smashed my Walkman in the street and went home." He knocked his book off his desk as if to demonstrate.

Señor Mackey cut his eyes at Baby Kurt, picked up the book, and muttered something in Spanish about class having started and no more talking except "en español."

Baby Kurt glared at him but went silent.

I sat there wishing I'd been at Scoville, surrounded by people who understood what it was like to love Nirvana so much that you needed to smash things—or scratch KC into the skin above your ankle with a safety pin as I had done.

Then while Señor Mackey droned on about verb conjugations, Baby Kurt started chanting the chorus of "Sliver":

"Gramma take me home! Gramma take me home! Gramma take me home!"

I turned around and stared at him with everyone else. I was on the verge of laughter—of joining in because it reminded me of that day with the substitute—but Baby Kurt looked entranced, like Danny from *The Shining* screeching, "Redrum!"

He continued chanting those lyrics until Señor Mackey shouted, "Go to the dean's office!"

Baby Kurt shot out of his chair and through the door. As soon as he stepped out of the room, he grinned back at me like Kurt Cobain exiting the stage after Nirvana thrashed it during the 1992 Video Music Awards.

I knew he wasn't going to the dean's office to be reprimanded. He was going to leave school, maybe go to Scoville Park and ditch the rest of the day. And why not? Kurt Cobain had killed himself. The world was a fucked-up, sad place.

Oh well, whatever, nevermind.

# Mixtapes and Marijuana

I recognized Greta as soon as she sat down across from me in algebra at the beginning of freshman year. From theater camp. She'd played Rizzo, but unlike her character, she hadn't been leader of the gang, the head of the girl-beast who chased me home on Rollerblades every day. She'd only chased me once or twice, but still she was their friend, and I thought she would remember me because I remembered her. When she tapped me on the shoulder with her pencil, my stomach twisted like a pretzel.

*Why, why was freshman year going to have to be like that horrible summer?*

"Hey, I like your shirt," she said. "Did you go to that concert?"

I was wearing my Soul Asylum tee. "Yeah, it was amazing," I replied, because it was. So amazing that the words spilled out despite my fear that any second she would recognize me, any second she would hate me.

"Yeah, it was! Did you see Screaming Trees open? Oh my god, they were the best."

I nodded in honest agreement, though my smile was forced because I was waiting for the other shoe to drop. But she seemed too swept up in talking about the music.

Eventually, she stuck her hand out across the aisle, grinning widely. "I'm Greta, by the way."

*I know.*

"Stephanie." I shook her hand, trying not to flinch. If she was going to remember . . .

"Cool to meet you."

I could finally smile for real. "Yeah, you too."

Our teacher called for everyone's attention then, so we both faced forward, but I continued to study her out of the corner of my eye. Freckles spilled across the bridge of her nose, and she had kinky, dark brown hair worn up in a bun—features that set her apart from the girl-beast I'd associated her with, made up of "all-American" white girls straight from the pages of a teen magazine. I tried to remember what Greta wore two summers ago. Had she been as preppy as her friends? Now we were dressed almost identically, aside from the bands on our T-shirts. Also, she had the regular black Doc Martens. My Docs had square toes, which was probably the reason they'd been on clearance, the only way I'd been able to afford them.

Greta lived on the north side in a big house. She was on the drill team. She was still friends with some of those girls from theater camp, and even though they dressed in Docs and flannel now, too, they still had shampoo-commercial hair and played sports. I should have hated her. I should have thought she was a poseur. But I couldn't and she wasn't. She knew about more bands than me. Our friendship was born of mixtape exchanges and Greta pouring her heart out about her first romance . . . which happened to be with the guy I'd spent eighth grade crushing on. I never told her that. I kept my old feelings secret like my summer-camp memories, but somehow we were close anyway.

A month before our sophomore year started, Greta called asking if I wanted to get stoned. I said yes without hesitation and ran downstairs to innocently ask my mom for a ride to her house.

The hesitation caught up with me after I got there, when the guy that Greta and I had waited over an hour for finally pulled up in a battered white van, the kind of vehicle I'd been told *not* to get into since I was five.

"How do you know this guy again?" I asked.

"He's a friend of a friend of my brother."

The dude honked his horn—we'd waited an eternity, but thirty seconds was too long for him to waste on us.

Greta smiled at me. Kind as always. Not at all pushy. Her brown eyes glittered like they had earlier that summer when we found each other at Lollapalooza right before Smashing Pumpkins went on. She wanted us to have this moment. "Shall we?" she asked, offering me her hand.

I wanted us to have this moment. I grabbed her hand and we ran down the steps toward the van.

Greta got into the passenger seat next to the dealer, Todd. I got into the back, which was covered with so many candy bar wrappers, Slurpee cups, and empty cigarette packs that it looked like a 7-Eleven had exploded. Smelled like it, too. Todd glanced back at me. Just a cursory glance, thank god. Not the hungry up-and-down that I'd learned back in junior high both to expect and to fear. He was a skinny dude with sweaty blond hair and a barely-there mustache. His struggle to grow facial hair made me think he was just old enough to drive, but then he said we had to go to his apartment, so he must have been at least eighteen.

Going to his apartment had not been part of the plan. According to Greta, he'd drive around the block, we'd give him some money, and we'd get out of the van with a plastic baggie of pot.

"Wait, you don't have the stuff?" Greta asked as we sped away from her house, tires squealing, muffler not muffling.

I glanced nervously out the windows, certain someone was going to call the cops because this van did not belong in Greta's neighborhood.

"I just came from work," Todd squawked, gesturing to his Kiddieland shirt. "I went out of my way to pick you up. Do you want weed or what?"

"Yeah, of course, no problem," Greta said. Then, to smooth any ruffled feathers, she smiled and asked, "How was work?"

Todd shrugged. "It was okay. You know, a job."

"Do you ever get to ride the rides?"

I tried to tune out their small talk and the classic rock on the radio to focus on what Oak Park looked like from a car that did not belong to my parents or

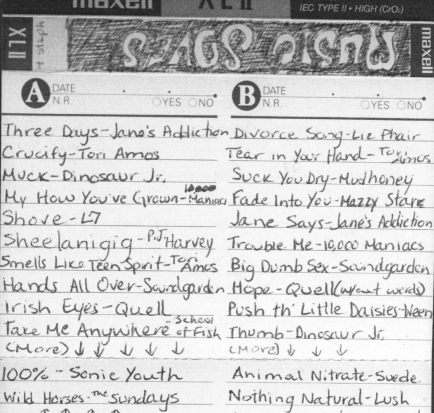

**maxell XL II** POSITION IEC TYPE II · HIGH (CrO₂)

XL II + steps · maxell

Music Saves

**Ⓐ** DATE · · · N.R. ○ YES ○ NO
**Ⓑ** DATE · · · N.R. ○ YES ○ NO

| A | B |
|---|---|
| Three Days—Jane's Addiction | Divorce Song—Liz Phair |
| Crucify—Tori Amos | Tear in Your Hand—Tori Amos |
| Muck—Dinosaur Jr. | Suck You Dry—Mudhoney |
| My How You've Grown—10,000 Maniacs | Fade Into You—Mazzy Star |
| Shove—L7 | Jane Says—Jane's Addiction |
| Sheela-na-gig—P.J. Harvey | Trouble Me—10,000 Maniacs |
| Smells Like Teen Spirit—Tori Amos | Big Dumb Sex—Soundgarden |
| Hands All Over—Soundgarden | Hope—Quell (w/out words) |
| Irish Eyes—Quell | Push th' Little Daisies—Ween |
| Take Me Anywhere—School of Fish | Thumb—Dinosaur Jr. |
| (More) ↓ ↓ ↓ ↓ ↓ | (More) ↓ ↓ ↓ |

| | |
|---|---|
| 100%—Sonic Youth | Animal Nitrate—Suede |
| Wild Horses—the Sundays  | Nothing Natural—Lush |
| (sorry, the last one ran out at the end) | Classic Girl—Jane's Addiction  (sorry this one rang out too) |

**Ⓐ**          **Ⓑ**

Music Saves: the mixtape Greta gave me during our freshman year one of my friends' parents. I was setting off in a modern-day covered wagon on a Real Teenage Life adventure; I had to document it, even if only for myself and only with my brain.

The sunlight seemed different, warmer maybe, like the moment was setting itself up to be viewed through hazy, sepia-tinged nostalgia. And worry was replaced by the electrifying feeling I'd had when I first rode the roller coaster at Kiddieland—the one that Todd was saying was no longer exciting because he worked there and "it's not Six Flags or anything."

The worry returned when the van started sputtering as we crossed over the expressway.

"Goddammit!" Todd hit the steering wheel and pumped the pedal. "It will be fine," he told us, even though we hadn't asked.

The van kept moving, its stale cigarette smell overpowered by noxious exhaust. I managed to ignore it as we passed my grade school because I needed to look at it through almost-adult eyes. It seemed smaller, I thought with satisfaction.

We coasted into a Shell station, and Greta asked, "Did you run out of gas or something?"

"Or something," Todd muttered. "My house is around the corner from here. We'll walk."

Todd lived in a dark basement apartment that was about as clean as his car, but at least it wasn't about to explode. However, when we got there, he informed us that we'd have to wait for *his* guy, because apparently he was just a low-level dealer.

It was an awkward, nerve-racking hour because I still felt like I was breaking every rule I'd learned in kindergarten. I was setting myself up to be held hostage, maybe even murdered. But eventually we got our weed and decided to walk the two miles back to Greta's rather than wait to see if Todd could fix his death-trap van.

Greta rolled a couple of expert joints on Todd's coffee table before we left, and we stopped in an alley a couple blocks from Todd's building to smoke the first one. As Greta pulled it out of her purse, my heartbeat quickened and I asked her if she was sure it was safe to smoke out in the open. She said that all you had to do was keep walking.

"You're going to cough," she warned me. "But so am I. Do you want me to go first?"

"Yeah." I carefully observed what she did so I could imitate her. She inhaled more deeply than she would have from a cigarette and held the smoke longer. Sure enough, when she exhaled, she started coughing.

Clearing her throat and dabbing at her eyes, she handed me the joint. I put it to my lips and took a deep drag. The smoke was harsh, worse than five Marlboro Reds. My lungs wanted to force it back out, but I fought that instinct, focusing on the herbal tang I tasted. I liked it better than cigarette smoke. I exhaled, coughing harder than Greta had, but managed to continue walking. I handed the joint back, trying to assess if I felt anything besides rawness in my lungs.

As if reading my mind, Greta said, "It will take a few hits before you feel anything. I didn't feel anything at all my first time." Then, registering my disappointment, she added, "But that was probably because I didn't really hold in the smoke."

*Hold the smoke. Get high, get high, get high,* I told myself every time I inhaled. By the third hit, I felt the muscles in my face relax. By the last hit, we were both giggling like maniacs.

Then we set off on our trek across town. I basked in air that seemed so humid and sticky earlier, but now felt fresh and light. The world seemed more vibrant, too—and even trees, even the dry grass were a brighter green. We stopped for cigarettes (buying my first pack of Winstons was nothing after smoking my first joint) and chips and candy (you've got to have both salty and sweet foods when you're high, I discovered). When we approached a park near Greta's house, she asked if I wanted to smoke the other joint.

I did. I wasn't even nervous about being in public anymore. We smoked under a tree, then stretched out on our backs and let the sun wash over our skin. I'd never felt so relaxed in my life, and I never wanted it to end.

*This is it,* I thought. *Real Teenage Life!* I was living it. I was *enjoying* it. And I was determined that sophomore year would be the year of this feeling.

# Scoville Park

After I got a B in biology freshman year—the only B I had gotten or would get in anything aside from gym class—I decided to drop out of the honors science track and take regular chemistry sophomore year.

My dad argued with me about this. I wouldn't be challenging myself or living up to my potential, blah, blah, blah. I cried in genuine fear of another B and ranted in genuine self-hatred about how stupid I felt. The B had proved to me that I was good at English, not science and math. Though my tears were real, I was also strategically playing the do-not-put-pressure-on-your-fragile-daughter card.

Fortunately, I won, because if I hadn't moved down to the regular chemistry class, I never would have met Mel, who'd recently moved to Oak Park. Mel, who finally asked me the question that it felt like I'd been waiting my whole life for:

Mel nodded and exhaled. We'd stuck a pencil in one of the school's side doors so we could grab a smoke during the break between lecture and lab. "I was gonna go with Jeff."

She meant *that* Jeff. Penis Jeff, as Robin and I called him. Mel and Jeff had gym together and when she'd described him, I knew exactly who she was talking about even though his hair was orange now instead of green.

"Jeff has early dismissal," she continued. "So I was gonna ditch ninth period. What do you have ninth period, Stephanie Kuehnert?" She grinned at me. For some reason she loved saying my full name. Maybe because when I'd taught her how to pronounce it—*Key*-nert—she'd gotten it right immediately and I'd told her that was rare.

"I have Spanish."

"Spanish." Mel took a long drag off her cigarette as if mulling it over. "Well, Stephanie Kuehnert, you want to ditch Spanish, get stoned with me and Jeff, and go to Scoville Park instead?"

It meant I'd get detention, but my answer was an automatic "Yes."

Scoville Park sat almost literally in the middle of town. It was three blocks from my high school, but in the opposite direction of the way that Robin and I walked home.

I thought it was the center of the universe. If there was a big bang that would set my Real Teenage Life in motion, it would happen there. The stories I'd heard (that's where you go to buy and do drugs; if you hang out there, your name goes on the school's regular locker search list) and the people I associated with Scoville (Baby Kurt; Penis Jeff) had me convinced it was mythical.

I had long dreamed of walking up Lake Street, past the football field, the gas station where you could buy cigarettes if the right person was working, the bread store that gave out free slices of bread after school (perfect if you were high or starving, and we were usually both), and across Oak Park Avenue to the park entrance, where there was always a weird combination of old people waiting for the bus and sketchy kids waiting for their dealers to call back on the pay phone.

Inside, it was a sea of flannel and band shirts and dyed hair and wallet chains, but there were nuances that distinguished each group. The skaters wore their jeans extra baggy and hung out by the statue at the top of the hill practicing ollies and kickflips. The hippies wore a lot of color, kept their long hair down, and played hacky-sack in the sun. The metalheads wore a lot of black, kept their long hair up in ponytails, and hung out on a brown-painted wooden sculpture, aptly dubbed "the brown thing." And these were just the obvious differences, the ones you could see walking in. Once you started hanging out there, you saw the subtler divisions. The larger groups that appeared to be sitting together but were really in two different circles. They might party together or smoke pot in someone's garage or cohost a show in someone's basement, but at the core they were separate groups. Some of this was based on which junior high people had gone to or what extracurriculars they did—stage crew or theater or band or sci-fi club—because that was how friends met and bonded, but a lot of this was also based on music. The industrial kids who listened to Nine Inch Nails and My Life with the Thrill Kill Kult were friendly with but not actually part of the same group as the indie rockers who listened to Sonic Youth and Pavement and who sometimes played the same shows as the artsy kids who were not quite hippies but maybe sort of beatniks and into jazz.

This, I think, is part of what made Scoville Park so overwhelming to me. I was a shapeshifter. I was still in my cocoon, trying on identities. What color would I be when I emerged? Did I decide that? Did I have to choose? Hippies and punks were supposed to hate each other, but there were things I admired about both subcultures. What if I liked Pantera and Nirvana? Nine Inch Nails and Sonic Youth? Because I did. At my core, I liked all of it, but more urgent than anything was the need to belong *somewhere* at the park.

In retrospect, I had a lot of options. So many paths, and down them, so many different stories that I could have lived (and that I would, years later, in my creative writing classes).

Juliet was dating one of the guys in the metalhead crowd. She moved back to Oak Park right before sophomore year started and was living with her mom in an apartment building across the street from Scoville. I often stopped by there to smoke a bowl before heading to the park. She, too, was friends with

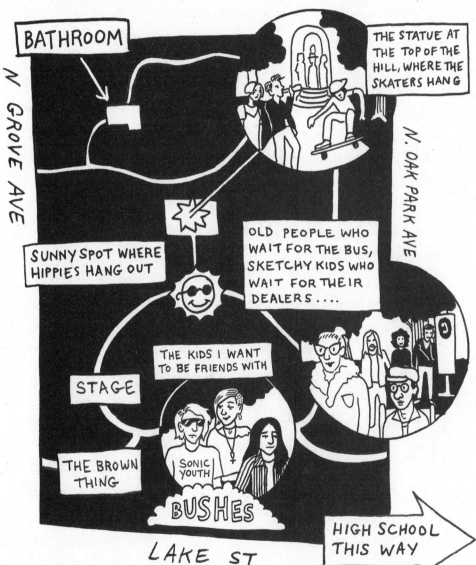

Mel and Penis Jeff. I could have followed Jules and Mel to the brown thing, and then wandered off with Mel to the hacky-sack circle. In fact, I am sure I did this once or twice. If Juliet and Robin had gotten along better, maybe I would have done it more.

Penis Jeff was actually the person that Robin and I were most comfortable around at first. He was bubbly and free-spirited. He always had pot and was happy to share, but he never had a bowl. "Do you have anything to smoke with?" he'd ask. "I can make a bowl out of anything. A Coke can, an apple. What do you have in your backpack?"

The weekend after our first trip to Scoville, Penis Jeff invited me and Robin out with him and Mel. He was not clear on what we'd be doing. "Just give me your address. I'll pick you up. We'll drive around and see what's happening."

And that's exactly what we did. He dropped Mel off at some point. There was a guy she liked, a stoner metalhead who sometimes sat on the brown thing and sometimes played hacky-sack in the sun. He smoked a lot of pot and was perfect for her. Penis Jeff loved setting people up, romantically or platonically—for him, those lines blurred anyway. Our first mission was to find where this guy was hanging out. Once we did, Jeff was ready to move again. Did Robin and I want to come? Oh, hey, he'd gotten a page. I didn't have a pager. My dad had one for work, but my parents thought that the only reason kids my age had them was if they were drug dealers. This wasn't entirely true. Jeff's pager pinged with secret messages that told him who was looking for him, where they were, and what was happening.

His pager was our guide that night, leading us to a couple of different houses. I only remember the last one, which belonged to one of Penis Jeff's stage crew friends. She was a junior and her parents were out of town. There had been a party at her house, but by the time we got there only a few people remained. They were all on acid. The girl hosting the party was lying on her living room rug naked. She greeted us that way. Penis Jeff screamed, "Naked party!" and immediately began to strip. Robin and I declined, which the hostess and Jeff were cool with. It was awkward, the nudity, since we barely knew Jeff and had just met the other naked people, but it wasn't sexually charged or scary.

People were just hanging out, high and naked. There was no peer pressure to join them. Jeff asked if there was acid left, but there wasn't.

After a while, Robin started to get antsy about getting back to her house, and I was getting bored and tired—hanging out with people who are on drugs when you aren't wasn't the most fun thing, as it turned out. The night ended when Penis Jeff, who was, for some reason that I think had to do with both of them laughing at his penis, standing above the hostess, who was still on her back with an ashtray on her chest, jumped and the ashes all flew into her mouth. She had braces. It was a gross mess that, fortunately, because she was on acid, she found hysterical.

Back at Robin's, we didn't know what to make of the night. It was weird. Robin wasn't sure she wanted to do it again. I was just disappointed that none of the houses we visited that night had contained the people I wanted to see—a group that Penis Jeff had brought me to on my first day at Scoville.

On that first afternoon I would have followed Mel and Juliet to the brown thing, but Jeff had grabbed my hand and said, "Let's go see my friends."

He pointed at a group of six or eight kids sitting in a loose circle on the side of the hill. They wore ripped jeans, Converse, and T-shirts for bands like Sonic Youth, Nirvana, and Veruca Salt. One of the girls had short blond hair that was shaved at the sides, and the other wore glasses and a so-ugly-it's-cool shirt. I recognized a couple of the boys from junior high. They'd been geeks like me, but now they were in a band called Acetone.

I wanted to thrift-shop with the girls. I wanted to see the guys jam in someone's basement. I wanted to share in their inside jokes, to speak in their language of music and dry wit. This was it. This crowd that Robin and I would dub simply "Acetone," even though only four of them were in the band, was the one that I wanted to belong to, that I'd daydreamed about finding since junior high.

However, after a lukewarm hello when Jeff introduced us, Robin and I were mostly ignored for the rest of the afternoon.

"Can we just hang out at my house tomorrow? I don't want to go back there. No one was nice except for Jeff," Robin said as we walked home from Scoville that first day.

I was disappointed—devastated, actually. I hadn't expected to leave Scoville Park, and especially a group of kids who liked all of the same things as me, feeling like I had around Liza/Brooke/Dani. But, I rationalized, they'd probably had their own beasts, and I knew that made it hard to open up to new people. Robin and I had barely spoken either. Our shyness might have presented as standoffishness, too.

"We just have to get to know them," I insisted before reciting my new mantra, which I would say to myself even more often than I said it to her in the weeks ahead: "I want to go back."

# *Acacia*

A week or two after I started hanging out at Scoville Park, I was trapped in a house where a bunch of dudes were sitting around playing (and supposedly teaching Robin and me) Magic: The Gathering.

This was something I would have been into in grade school or junior high, but now I was pretty sure I was missing something big, something *real*, at the park. Annoyed, I dragged Robin out for a smoke, ready to insist that we bail, but we found another girl standing on the porch. She wore an Anthrax T-shirt and black jeans, multiple chains hung from her wallet, and she had a Marlboro Red between her lips. Despite being barely five feet tall, she gave off the vibe of a nightclub bouncer. Flipping long black bangs out of her face, she looked up at us.

"Oh, there are . . . girls here?" she said, brown eyes narrowing in confusion—very legitimate confusion considering the card-playing guys inside. Then her eyes widened in recognition as she scanned my face. "North Riverside Mall," she stated, and she even remembered, "Stephanie?"

Back in eighth grade I had a shoplifting phase. Juliet and her Next Best Friend did it, so Robin and I did, too. There were a lot of things I ~~wanted~~ needed and didn't have money to buy. Earrings from Claire's. Incense from Spencer's. A horoscope book from Waldenbooks. I had some sense of morality in that I only took from chain stores. However, the thrill quickly eclipsed any ~~wants~~ needs and I ended up taking random things like a book of baby names and a giant tie-dyed peace sign flag just because I could. It all came to a grinding halt when Robin and I got caught at Walgreens with a pen (me) and a pocket full of lighters (her).

But the day I stole the stupid tie-dye flag, I met this girl at the mall. She was a seventh grader who went to the other junior high, a friend of a friend. She managed to get a couple of badass skull chokers out of the locked jewelry case at Spencer's, a move that impressed me so deeply that even though we never hung out again, I remembered her instantly almost two years later.

"North Riverside Mall," I confirmed. "Acacia."

And when she said, "Cool," extending her Zippo to light my cigarette, I had this feeling that I'd finally found what I'd been looking for.

Since I thought Real Teenage Life was supposed to be like a movie, I kept waiting for my costars to walk on screen—the people who would play the roles of My Cool New Best Friend, My First Boyfriend, and the members of My Gang of Misfits/Ultimate Friend Group. Then, I thought, the action would finally begin.

But what high school was really like most of the time was a series of small but significant moments. I wrote them out in my diary like they were epic. I revisited them in poem after poem. I replayed them when I couldn't sleep. I waited anxiously for the next one.

These small but significant moments starred people like Greta and Jo, Penis Jeff and Baby Kurt. Cameo players. If my life was a TV show, there would be an episode about them and then they'd fade into the background. A couple of them might fool you, like Baby Kurt. (*Is he auditioning for a boyfriend role?* you might have wondered. Nope, I was too shy for that freshman year, but stay tuned for another Kurt wannabe. No shortage of them in the early nineties!) For the most part, you'd see them in the hallway and go, *Oh, I think I remember that girl . . .* Then they'd pop back in for a short but essential scene in season three (junior year) and you'd go, *Oh yeah, that's the girl who Stephanie smoked with freshman year. What was her name? Something with a J, right? She let some junior that her brother knew pierce her nose in the bathroom at lunch while Stephanie watched in shock and admiration and wrote diary entries about how she wished she could be that effortlessly cool.*

Actually, if life were a TV show, they'd probably be compiled into one cool girl—the new best friend who changes everything. Maybe life is like a TV show for some people, but it wasn't for me. Instead, there were girls who weren't my best friends, who popped in and out of my life or were around only briefly, and their sparkling appearances shaped me in some crucial way, preparing me for the place I was trying to go, the role I was trying to land.

And then there was Acacia.

Caci was not there to make another cameo. Her appearances may have been sporadic at first because she was a self-described "floater." She didn't belong to any particular group at Scoville. She'd started hanging out with metalheads in sixth grade. She was dating a guy from Acetone that day she showed up on the porch and lit my cigarette, and she was there because Will, the guy hosting the Magic: The Gathering card game, was the closest thing she had to a best friend. She hadn't spent a lot of time there lately, but she would start showing up more because I was there. Similarly, I agreed to keep hanging out at Will's because she might be there.

Acacia and I were drawn to each other in a way that cannot really be described.

"This is weird," she would remark early on, while hanging out with me and Robin. "I'm not usually friends with girls. They don't like me."

Girls hurt her and used her. They didn't like the way she got along with guys, and they spread rumors about her. Acacia expected betrayal the way I feared abandonment, and yet somehow we knew that we could trust each other.

Acacia wasn't just the Cool New Best Friend either. She hadn't simply arrived to step into the role that Juliet had vacated and Robin had taken on as understudy.

We were different. We were more. We were girl soulmates.

# Out of the Nest

"Go, go, go, go now

Out of the nest, it's time . . ."

—TORI AMOS, "MOTHER"

Dear Mom,

I've been thinking about my first concert, the one you took me to for my eleventh birthday. Janet Jackson at the World Music Theatre.

You splurged for seats. They were in the back, but still, it was incredible to be that close to Janet and her dancers and the lights and the explosions.

It was also very loud. Painfully loud. So loud that it seems funny to me now that I stand right up front at much smaller indoor venues. I guess I had virgin ears back then.

You hadn't anticipated this issue, which makes sense. I know you like Janet better than Madonna, but this was my music, not yours. You go to folk concerts, those wine-bottle-and-picnic-in-the-park affairs.

So you hadn't brought earplugs and were apologizing for it by the end of the first song, when you saw me grab my ears while trying to smile and sing along. I made it through four songs. I had to see Janet do my favorite, "Black Cat," but after that the pain was so excruciating I couldn't keep from crying.

You took me to the bathroom, grabbed toilet paper, and told me to shove it into my ears. You said we could try to sit on the lawn if it was still too loud in our seats.

I shook my head. Even with the toilet paper, even all the way by the bathrooms it was still so loud that my ears were throbbing. I broke down in tears. I was so angry that I was going to miss Janet, and more than that, I was angry at myself. That concert was supposed to be the best day of my life, but I couldn't handle it. I'd wasted your special birthday present—the best present I'd ever gotten. And what would my friends say when I had to confess to this huge failure?

"No one ever has to know but you and me," you told me.

The amphitheatre was in the town you'd grown up in, so you said we could drive around to kill time. You'd show me everything you remembered. That way not even Dad or Dan would know we left early.

So that's what we did. You drove and told me stories. Since the concert was so loud, we could still hear Janet in the background.

You were right: not all had been lost by walking away.

"Mother, the car is here,
Somebody leave the light on . . ."

Lately we've been watching that show together, My So-Called Life. It premiered right around when I started hanging out at Scoville Park. The main character, Angela Chase, is a sophomore like me. Her old best friend reminds me a little of Robin because she wants things to stay the same way and she's really jealous of Angela's new best friend, Rayanne Graf.

Rayanne is like Scoville Park but in girl form—exciting, daring, a little bit dangerous, a whole lot of real. At the end of the pilot, she spins around Angela and says, "We had a time, didn't we?" And that moment sums up everything I want:

A time. Please, let me have a time!

I catch you sneaking glances at me a lot during the show, like you know My So-Called Life is My Real Teenage Life—or at least, what I want it to be. You're the kind of person who talks to the TV when she gets really into something; I am the kind of person who watches quietly and reacts later, privately.

"I am nothing like her," you'll say of Angela's mom.

I think you are waiting for me to tell you that I am exactly like Angela Chase. To confide about my crush, my Jordan Catalano. To talk about my Rayanne. Or maybe you're afraid that I am becoming Rayanne; we have the same hair after all, blond-streaked and full of baby barrettes.

You told me those stories about your teenage life while we drove around, just the two of us, Janet's music coming through the window. Now you want me to share mine as we sit in the living room, just the two of us, the TV in the background.

The truth is that I am an Angela—an Angela who is still seeking her Jordan—but I wish I was a Rayanne. Then I would fit in at Scoville, no problem.

Of course I don't tell you any of this. I just nod and reassure you that you are not like Angela's mother, because you aren't.

Angela and her mom fight a lot, which we don't do as much anymore. The only time Angela's mom reminded me of you was the episode where she saved Rayanne's life when she ODed. You would do that. You're the kind of mom I could call when things get scary. You're the kind of mom that I can crawl into bed with and cry to like Angela does in the pilot.

And I want to crawl into your bed like that. I want to wrap my arms around your neck and cry into your nightgown. I want to tell you how much I secretly hate Scoville Park.

Instead, I lie awake, trying not to cry and telling no one how I feel. Not you. Not Robin, who I drag to Scoville every day even though I really want to go back to her house, too, because the life I'd imagined for us while sitting on her couch watching music videos was so much better than this reality.

I can't even admit it to Juliet. I don't really hang out with her at the park all that much, and when I do see her, we're never alone.

I wish we were.

*Hell, I wish we were in fifth grade again, watching* Star Trek *on her grandparents' couch. I wonder if she does, too. When I ask her about Grandpa and her dog, who is still living with him in her old house, her face lights up, so maybe she does, but I can't bring myself to take it one step further. To ask,* Do you miss it like I miss it? The way we used to be? And is it worth it? The way we are now? The way we're trying to be?

*To ask Juliet those questions or to cry to you would be to surrender, to fail. And I can't do that.*

No pain, no gain, Stephie-Lou *is what I tell myself that Juliet would say, because as much as I yearn for childhood, I've been yearning for this since childhood. A place where I belong, where I can live out stories worth telling. I can't go back to the days when my nose was stuck in a book or my eyes glued to the TV. I can't keep living* through *the stories I love, I need to live like I'm* in *them. So I'll have something to write about one day, like Laura (or more likely, Sylvia), before I die.*

Stiff upper lip *is what I pretend you would say if I crawled into your bed because you can't fix it like you did the Janet Jackson concert. You'll just tell me that if I hate it, I shouldn't go. I don't have to. I'll find something else.*

*But I won't.*

*This is it, Mom. Scoville is where I belong.*

# PART 3

What are little boys made of, made of?
What are little boys made of?
    Frogs and snails
    And puppy-dogs' tails,
That's what little boys are made of.

Boys Will Be...

What are young men made of, made of?
What are young men made of?
    Sighs and leers
    And crocodile tears,
That's what young men are made of.

# FROGS AND SNAILS AND PUPPY DOG TAILS

In fifth grade, I carved SK + SK into a tree in a park near my house. The other SK was Steve Kennedy, the boy that I'd told Liza/Brooke/Dani that I liked.

I did not actually like Steve. He was not as funny or interesting as other boys in my class, and while I wasn't totally sure that any boys were "cute," I didn't think he was. He had a Charlie-Brown-sized head, and his crew cut did not help matters.

I'd panicked when they asked me which boy I liked. I could not understand why all the other girls suddenly had this need to be paired off Ken-and-Barbie-style, but they did, and I didn't want my lack of a crush to be another mark against me.

I chose Steve because:

A. Alphabetical proximity meant I sat near him so I thought of him quickly.

B. I knew that the crew cut fit the preppy-boy mold that Liza/Brooke/Dani had determined was boyfriend material either instinctively or via the teen movies that played on cable constantly.

C. I knew instinctively that Steve's large noggin put him on my level. It was a fine line to walk—finding a boy who met Liza/Brooke/Dani's standards, but wasn't so perfect that one of them would want him.

When my choice of Steve was deemed acceptable—SK + SK is so cute!—I decided to commit to it and went *by myself* to carve that adorable matching set of initials into that tree in the park by my house. I'm not sure if I did it because I thought this act would somehow make me fall in love or because I was afraid my "friends" would find out I was lying and then I could point to the tree and ask, *Would I go* that *far if I didn't actually want Steve Kennedy to be my boyfriend?* I also regularly tore out all of the pages I'd written in my diary about potential crushes and whether something was wrong with me if

I didn't *like*-like anyone. My diary had a lock on it, but it seemed flimsy, like something that Liza/Brooke/Dani or even Juliet could easily break into while I was in the bathroom or something. I put these pages into envelopes with my cousin and regular pen pal Becca's name on them, figuring that should something happen to me, my parents would give them to her and she would know to destroy them.

Fortunately, my "crush" was never questioned, nor was I pushed to actually pursue Steve. I was informed, however, that a boy named Kirk liked me. He expressed this "like" by mocking how short and unathletic I was and intentionally kicking the kickball *at* me during recess. Once I actually retaliated. I don't remember what exactly he'd done to torment me that day, just that I'd snapped while we were standing in line against the chain-link fence and I reached up and scratched him, my pinkie fingernail making a little ragged tear next to his eye. He howled as if I'd actually scratched his eye out, an exaggerated attempt to get me in trouble. Our teacher didn't fall for it, simply telling us to get into alphabetical order, which effectively split Kirk and me up. Liza/Brooke/Dani cackled at Kirk. Juliet congratulated me. For one brief moment, the whole class seemed in awe of me—the smallest gazelle who'd managed to pull one over on one of the lions. This did not embolden me, though. By ten years old, I already knew the way of things. He was a lion. I was a gazelle. He was predator. I was prey. This was why I didn't understand why I was supposed to like boys.

The number of Kirks multiplied when I got to junior high. White boys with gleaming smiles, often blond and blue-eyed, but there were some dark-haired ones, too. They were named Adam and Nick and Patrick and Brett and Jamie and Jamie and Jamie. So many named Jamie. An ungendered name that had probably seemed so sweet and innocuous to their parents.

*My Jamie certainly wouldn't tease girls about their lack of tits 'til they cry.*

*My Jamie is a kitten, not a lion snatching at bra straps with his claws.*

*Oh, he did? Well, certainly he didn't mean it.*

*After all, boys will be . . .*

The summer between eighth grade and freshman year, I went with Robin to visit her mom. She lived in a small town in Pennsylvania that Robin described as the sort of place where everyone worked in factories and coal mines and the happening weekend spot was the bingo hall (well, if you were sober or a kid). We were determined to make it fun, though. An adventure.

Robin's mom was a cool mom like Juliet's. Presumably because she missed Robin and would do anything to anything to make up for her absence, she let us drink wine coolers and set us up with the sixteen-year-old twin boys down the road. In theory, this was awesome, but it quickly turned less cool when we discovered that the twins had long, curly mullets. Hair metal still reigned in the Rust Belt; grunge was for . . . the f-word that I made them apologize for using.

Despite their many, *many* flaws, we decided to hang out with them because they were the only people close to our age. Also they promised to take us to a pool hall and the cemetery where *Night of the Living Dead* was filmed, and we'd get to ride in the back of their pickup truck, something we'd never done before.

The situation went from uncool to straight-up Not Okay when one of the twins (the other had a girlfriend, as it turned out) copped a feel while showing me how to hold my pool stick. Then in the truck, their friend put his hand up my cutoffs to "see how loose" they were. Meanwhile, the twin I'd rebuffed in the pool hall asked Robin out, and she agreed to it, not able to think up a nice rejection fast enough. (I pretended to have a boyfriend modeled after my eighth-grade crush, though my decision to tell them he was on the wrestling team was likely inspired by sitcoms where situations like this were played off as funny.)

He shoved his tongue down Robin's throat in the cemetery while his friend kept finding reasons to touch me, especially my legs and butt. Things got even scarier when we got back to Robin's mom's house, found that no one was home, and couldn't get rid of the guys. Eventually, the less sleazy twin convinced the others to leave.

We stole Robin's mom's cigarettes and smoked them while listening to Metallica really loud and trying not to cry. Robin eventually broke down, though. We'd both been groped, but that was her first kiss.

"It doesn't count," I reassured her, holding her close.

The next morning we told Robin's mom that we didn't want to hang out with the twins anymore. When she asked why, we just rolled our eyes and shrugged. They were obnoxious, not our type.

I didn't tell my parents about them at all other than mentioning the *Night of the Living Dead* cemetery to my dad. We were fellow horror buffs and had watched *Night of the Living Dead* together on New Year's Eve. That was such a good night. The occasions when Dad and I had fun instead of arguing were practically nonexistent, so the main reason I'd been so excited to go to the cemetery was to have a story to share with him. Though it had been ruined for me, I didn't want to ruin it for Dad, so I told him a version where I got to explore the tombstones and imagine myself fending off zombies instead of unwanted boy hands.

The only person I told what actually happened was Juliet. She wouldn't tell me until years later that she'd been through worse. Instead, she acted like the only problem was that the twins were ugly and the rest was no big deal. Like Robin and I overreacted and just didn't know how to handle ourselves around boys the way she and her Next Best Friend did. That's why they had boyfriends and we didn't.

Those boys were just being boys, and you know how boys will be . . .

## ONLY MAKE-BELIEVE

In October of my sophomore year, Derek Manning asked me out on the lead singer of Acetone's front lawn. We'd been trying to play football, of all things. No one knew the rules. Most of us were stoned. First we'd played girls versus boys. Then the girls—me, Robin, Acacia, and the two Acetone girls, Marcy and June, whom I'd been trying to befriend since I'd started hanging out at Scoville a couple weeks earlier, decided to be cheerleaders instead. I was really, truly, *finally* starting to feel like part of the group. Marcy and June were actually talking to me that day, mostly about how great Derek was. He'd been through some shit, they said. And he deserved to be happy.

Yes, I knew he'd been through some shit. He and I had been talking on the phone. Robin, who was in history class with him, had given him my number. The first time that she and I had actually had a good time at Scoville was with him. He was sitting with Acetone, and unlike everyone else, he talked to us the entire time while playing with a pair of purple John Lennon shades. We weren't high that day, but he was. He made us laugh a lot, and he laughed even more—his big, freckled cheeks turning bright red.

The next day Robin informed me that Derek had said something I'd never ever thought a boy would say about me: "Stephanie's a babe."

I wished I could return the sentiment, but with his strawberry-blond hair and freckles, he was more little-brother cute.

We had some pretty intense phone conversations, though. They would start out about music—he introduced me to a couple of metal bands I hadn't heard of—or goofy childhood stories and end with confessions about too much drinking (him) and cutting (me). I really loved getting to know him . . . as a friend.

I'd tried to make that clear in our conversations and through Robin, but after that game of lawn football, when my mom arrived to pick me and Robin up, Derek ran up and stopped me before I could get into the passenger seat.

"Stephanie, will you go out with me?" he blurted.

I stared at him, shell-shocked.

I didn't want to hurt him. Not after our conversations, not at all. Not in front of an audience—particularly not *this* audience of Robin and June and Marcy, who'd all been telling me, "He's a really nice guy," and were clearly rooting for this relationship to happen.

Besides, I wanted a boyfriend, right? Maybe if I went out with Derek, I would magically develop romantic feelings—even if that hadn't worked when I carved the initials of my "crush" into a tree in fifth grade.

So I said yes. In front of everyone, including my mom, who blinked a few times and said, "Well . . ." when Robin and I got into the car.

Robin looked at me and started giggling. Then I started giggling and we said, "Oh my god," back and forth a bunch of times.

A couple days later, she was going out with Derek's best friend, Will, and then we were best friends dating best friends, a situation that we'd fantasized about since eighth grade . . . except it wasn't like my fantasies at all.

Mostly we just hung out with a bunch of other people at Will's since it was getting too cold for Scoville (despite being the epicenter of everything, Scoville was pretty much useless as a hangout spot from November until sometime in April depending on how brutal winter was) and Will had a car, a disgustingly trashed basement, and parents who didn't care if his friends, even girls, were there at all hours.

There was one Friday night that we decided to get pizza just the four of us. Like the proper sort of "date" that happens all the time on TV. This was the first and only one I ever went on in high school and I don't even remember the actual date part, just the two disastrous moments that bookended it.

My parents insisted on meeting Derek and Will before Robin and I went on the date. This was ridiculous because we were already hanging out with them after school every day and riding around in Will's car, but it was the only way to appease my dad, who at that point, only seemed to appear to say, "Absolutely Not!" to things like later curfews, going to concerts, and hanging out with boys.

When Derek and Will arrived, they chased my little brother around the living room pretending to pick lice out of his hair and eat it like monkeys. By the time we left my house, I didn't know who I was more annoyed with—my parents or the boys.

The night ended with another crushing disappointment. Derek and I were in the backseat of Will's car, and as we pulled up in front of my house, he leaned over and laid one on me. My first kiss. This was exactly how I'd always hoped my first date would end . . . except it felt all wrong. Derek's mouth was a lot wetter than the kisses I daydreamed about, and it tasted like an ashtray.

But I kept kissing him for three weeks. Conveniently, he spent one of those weeks with his family at Disney World. He brought me back a set of Mickey Mouse ears. I almost swooned over that. It was the kind of gesture I'd always wanted/never believed a guy would make for me. For a moment, I believed we could have a Real Teenage Romance that I would journal about fondly when I was older.

That little spark didn't ignite, though. Everyone but Derek could tell I was faking, and one day Will dragged me into his father's workshop—a separate room in the basement that I remember as quite hot and quite bright—and demanded to know what I really thought of Derek. It felt like a police interrogation. I confessed immediately that I didn't like Derek the way he liked me, and Will insisted that I had to break up with him. Pretending was only going to hurt Derek worse in the long run.

I smoked a bowl to steady my nerves and told Derek that it wasn't him, it was me—I was too depressed to have feelings for anyone. And I really meant it when I said it . . .

A few weeks later, on New Year's Eve Eve, Derek, who was drunk and still a year away from having his learner's permit, got behind the wheel of one of our older friend's cars and drove it into a tree. It was just a sapling—a rare and expensive one, apparently—that had been planted earlier that year on that strip of grass between the street and the sidewalk in front of Marcy's neighbor's house. The sapling got wedged beneath the car, so Derek could go no farther. He threw open the door and ran off into the snowy night as people came out of Marcy's to see what was going on.

Will was called. He drove around looking for Derek and then came to get Robin and me, bringing us back to Marcy's to help clean up the scene of Derek's crime. Mercifully, the owners of the tree were out of town, and no cops had been summoned to the scene. Someone located Derek and confirmed that he was okay, physically. Emotionally, however . . . Several pairs of eyes cut over to me.

I was the girl who'd broken his heart.

I shouldn't have said yes to him on that other lawn even though "no" wouldn't have been the right answer either.

I shouldn't have tried so hard to like him, or I should have tried harder.

I shouldn't have broken up with him even though his best friend told me to.

I shouldn't have fallen for one of his other best friends, and I certainly shouldn't have acted on those feelings, even though that boy did.

Even though Derek had a new girlfriend now, there were still so many things I should have or shouldn't have done to prevent this night and Derek's pain. Not to mention that once again I was at fault for damage to a poor helpless tree. Me. Not any of the boys, because you know how they will be . . .

## ACE OF DIAMONDS

Brandon Harris was my second boyfriend.

(Kind of.)

(Not really.)

I met him the same day I met Derek. As we were walking out of the park, we came across a couple of kids puking in the bushes.

"Dude, you guys are *so* wasted. What the fuck did you do?" Derek asked a Black boy in a trench coat who was rolling around in the dirt, his dreadlocks nearly landing in a vomit puddle.

"Whiskey," the boy groaned.

Derek burst out laughing. "You are so fucked up!"

The boy on the ground laughed, too. Then his bloodshot brown eyes landed on me and he slurred, "Duh I know yew?"

I shook my head, but couldn't help grinning. Couldn't help thinking, *Maybe from my dreams*, because even though he had leaves stuck to his hair and puke on his coat, he was really fucking hot.

"This is Stephanie and Robin," Derek said to him. Then he told us, "This drunk-ass motherfucker is Brandon."

Brandon laughed again before groaning and crawling off to puke some more.

A couple days later, Brandon came up to me at Scoville with hazy recognition in his heavy-lidded eyes. Wearing a big grin, Derek reminded Brandon of our first encounter—lording it over Brandon as if he wanted to shame him, to trip him up. I could see that then, but I wouldn't realize why until I'd watched them compete for a couple of years, with Brandon regularly winning the girl just because he could.

The problem with Derek's approach—perhaps in general, but definitely when it came to the puking incident—was that Brandon couldn't be shamed or tripped up. That part of his brain where he cared about what people thought was completely shut off, like to the point that, as Brandon would later tell me, a few shrinks had thrown around the words "sociopath" and "borderline personality disorder." I envied that—the attitude, I mean, not the diagnoses. It was one of the main things that made me want him. Because maybe by being with him, I would learn how to be *like* him.

Of course, the other thing that made me want him was the way I felt when he looked at me and said, "Stephanie," in a smoky voice before Derek could reintroduce us. His lips curled like my name was a dare, and while I'd had a few crushes by then and had even considered myself hopelessly in love with a few of them, that was the moment when I understood why people had sex. I didn't *like*-like Brandon, I *wanted*-wanted Brandon, and the way he stared deep into my eyes, the fact that he remembered my name (and not Robin's) after his whiskey bender, told me that the feeling was mutual, which was an even greater thrill.

But a few days later, Derek asked me out, and then Brandon was just his friend, just a guy we hung out with. He had to be. Because I'd made a commitment, and I wasn't the kind of person who could break that kind of commitment.

(No, I was the kind of person who tried really hard not to hurt others by putting up a dam around my real feelings—a dam that would eventually leak. Or burst.)

The week after Derek and I broke up, there was a show in Will's basement. Acetone and a bunch of other bands made up of random combinations of Scoville dudes. Derek was so excited about the new band he was drumming for. He told me that they were going to blow me away.

And I was blown away . . . when Brandon strolled up to the microphone and filled the stinky, sweaty basement with his presence like Jim Morrison. Well, if Jim wore a black trench coat over a T-shirt emblazoned with an anarchy symbol, which he might have if he were sixteen in 1994. Brandon didn't really sing, more like read poetry over the noise. And I felt like he was staring at me, but it was kind of hard to tell with his locs hanging in his face. Either way, as I listened to that dark poetry full of swirling imagery about shattered souls that I wished *I* could have written, I started to suspect that I'd lied to Derek. I was capable of having feelings, just not for him.

This was confirmed a few days later, when a group of us went to the movies and Brandon and I walked out holding hands.

He had taken my hand in the dark at some point. His palms were dry and calloused, but as soon as he touched me my stomach flipped in that good way, the way I'd never felt with Derek no matter how hard I tried, the way I'd honestly started to believe I was too depressed to ever feel.

I thought that Brandon would let go once we were out in the light and everyone could see us, because Derek was there and we'd just broken up and Brandon was his friend and there was probably some sort of code . . . but Brandon only squeezed my hand tighter, and that awesome stomach-flipping, butterflies-and-fireworks feeling spread all the way down to my toes. It wasn't even dampened by the deep frown on Derek's face, which turned pinker than usual when he noticed that I was holding hands with Brandon.

Brandon never officially asked me to go out with him like Derek had. He staked his claim when he took my hand.

I told myself that I didn't care if we used the terms "girlfriend" and "boyfriend" because we connected on a deeper level. Everyone thought it was just physical because we were always making out—on top of the washing machine in Will's basement, in the backseat of Will's car with our friends crammed in next to us—but they didn't know about the notes and the notebooks of poetry we exchanged or our phone calls. I'd put out matches against my wrist while I talked to Brandon and tell him that I was practicing being numb. He never stopped me from cutting or burning my skin because he did it, too. He got me in ways no one else had, and I trusted him with the darkest parts of me.

Brandon also shared things with me that he usually kept hidden. Like how it felt to live in two different worlds—the Black one, where he was interrogated about why he had white friends and listened to white music like industrial and punk, and the white world, where he got to like the things he wanted to like without being questioned, but he'd always be the outsider. The Black world didn't get the kind of poetry he wrote, but the white world never heard his real voice. Just like it had never seen the boy in the junior high photo that Brandon gave me randomly one day.

"I found this. I thought you would think it was funny," he said of the wallet-sized image of him with close-cropped hair, dressed in a suit and tie.

When I didn't laugh, he did. That laugh I heard all the time when we were stoned, the one that didn't match his deep voice or his black-trench-coat personality. A childish giggle that hadn't grown or changed with the rest of him, the last trace of that boy in the picture.

"It's fucking stupid," he said, trying to snatch it back.

I pulled away, pressing the photo to my chest. "No, it's not, and I'm keeping it."

He shrugged and let me put the boy he used to be in my chain wallet with my library card and my razor blade. I took it home and taped it into my journal.

On New Year's Eve, I taped a playing card in there, too. The Ace of Diamonds. Brandon had picked it up off the ground and handed it to me. We were buzzed on pot and champagne and a midnight kiss that had seemed to last for hours. Someone had thrown the cards up in the air like confetti. Maybe they'd thrown them at us to make us stop kissing. It worked. Brandon laughed when that card hit him in the cheek, then he bent down to retrieve it. I promised myself that I

would never forget the way he grinned when he gave it to me. That moment would be etched into my brain—and my notebook—forever.

Brandon made me feel more alive than I ever had. Colors intensified. Loud music soundtracked our world. The scent of him—of shea butter and cigarettes—enveloped me. We inhaled each other even more deeply than the pot smoke that we both always tasted of.

But touch was my new favorite sense. Our tongues battled. We sucked on and bit each other's necks. We raked our fingernails down each other's stomachs.

I wanted Brandon. Bad.

And I also didn't want to be a virgin anymore. At fifteen, I felt like the last one on earth. Juliet had done it. So had Robin. Even Acacia, who was a year younger than me, had done it with her boyfriend, Greg, the drummer of Acetone. All of them were part of "official" couples, though. Robin had lectured me several times that I shouldn't have sex with Brandon until he said he loved me or at least referred to me as his girlfriend. I didn't see what the big deal was—I'd been making out with Brandon for about as long as she'd been making out with Will before they did it. She told me there were rumors that Brandon used girls, had no respect for them, but that wasn't us—that wasn't *me*—I was sure of it.

(Boys will be . . . Boys will be . . . Boys will be . . .)

One night in Will's basement, Brandon and I were rolling around on the bottom bunk of an old bunk bed with Nine Inch Nails blaring at an earsplitting volume. His hand ran across the top of my bra. He squeezed my breast, and it ached in a good way. His other hand went up my thigh and landed between my legs. It was on the outside of my jeans, but he undid the button this time with his thumb.

I was ready. I would've had sex with Brandon. Then and there. But instead of unzipping my jeans, his hand came to rest on my stomach. The other one released my breast and slid around my side. He kissed my neck one more time and then passed out on top of me.

Later I would wonder if he'd already started snorting heroin then. People said he was, but people also said we were having sex, and we weren't. At the time I thought it was the weed. We'd smoked a lot of it, and I felt weird, too. Like most of me was numb, but my heart was pounding as hard as the music. Soon, I was suffocating beneath Brandon, beneath that blanket of noise from the Nine Inch Nails album that had been recorded in the house where the Manson murders had taken place. And the sun was rising. And I'd never sleep, not with that fucking CD on repeat.

Halfway through the album's second play, I couldn't handle it anymore. I pushed Brandon off me. He made a slight murmuring sound, but fell right back to sleep. I went upstairs to the den, where Brandon's best friend Trevor was curled up on a couch, blue eyes glued to the TV.

I've convinced myself that we had a conversation about Brandon that night, Trevor and me. That Trevor told me that I was different than the other girls, that Brandon was different with me. I'm pretty sure that was something I made up in a fictionalized version of my life later, though. In the years to come, I wrote a lot of stories about Brandon, trying to figure out what it meant, that month we were . . . whatever we were.

It ended a couple of weeks later, on the Tuesday after Martin Luther King Jr. Day. I'd gone out of town over the long weekend and when I got back, I found out that Brandon had hooked up with another girl at a party. (Boys will be . . . !) I told everyone who pulled me aside to whisper about it that I didn't care. Brandon and I were not officially, exclusively together, and he could do whatever he wanted. He always had and always would.

It was true. I'd never told him he couldn't be with other people, but I realized then that I couldn't handle it if he was. Even though I'd told him and myself again and again that all I wanted was to be numb, I'd developed feelings. And I couldn't pretend they weren't there, so I walked away.

I didn't confront him. I didn't tell him that whatever we'd had was over. I didn't say a word, and presumably since he knew that I knew about the other girl, neither did he. Our relationship ended exactly as it had started: unspoken, undefined.

Over the next two years, I watched him date more than one girl at the same time. They knew about each other. They tolerated it. They still slept with him.

I never did, though sometimes I thought about it. We'd see each other at the park, at parties. We'd talk as easily as we always had. We exchanged books we loved and pages of our own writing. And the air between us always felt like it does right before a summer thunderstorm—electric.

"You were the coolest girl I ever dated," he would tell me the summer I turned nineteen, when we wound up working together at the same telemarketing business. We'd hang out after work, both getting drunk, him doing harder things that I turned down.

"We never dated," I corrected.

He flashed a Cheshire cat grin and laughed that same stoned giggle. "You were the coolest girl I *never* dated, then."

I just shook my head.

*You were my first love,* I didn't tell him then or any of the other times when he would randomly drop back into my life. We'd both happen to show up at Scoville on the same night, though I had not hung out there in years. Or he'd call my mom's house out of the blue because he'd never forgotten the number and she'd hold out the phone to me, stating his name, "Brandon?" like a question she didn't think she'd like my answer to.

Brandon *was* my first love, though. We were only sort-of-kind-of-not-really together for a month, and it would take me years to put together what he'd really meant to me. In our very short time together, he'd given me a taste of his power—the one that he had and I wanted. The power to not care what anyone else thought, to just live, just be me. When I silently ended our not-really-relationship, it was a personal declaration. No more faking. No more make-believe. No more selling myself short. I was finally right there, on the verge of it. That cool girl I aspired to be, she was on the horizon. Rising, rising . . .

And then.

And then came the next boy, and, well, you know how boys will be . . .

# PART 4

# I.

My very first impression of Greg was that he was kind of an asshole.

I met him on my first day at Scoville Park, sitting with the rest of Acetone, emanating that cooler-than-thou vibe. He'd gone to junior high with me, but I didn't remember him until Robin pointed it out, and even then, only vaguely. Back in eighth grade he had brown hair that was just starting to grow long on top, more baby fat on his cheeks and under his chin, and he regularly sported Metallica shirts. In the fall of our sophomore year, he wore a brown leather trench coat that hung to midthigh. Very seventies, but worn with nineties alternative-rock irony. He also had big, black-rimmed sunglasses and his hair was dyed, chin-length, and dirty like a nineties rock star. More specifically, like Kurt Cobain.

(In my memory of that day, his hair is bright red, but Acacia says it probably wasn't. That it was either reddish brown or black. It's probably just stop-sign red in my memory because I wish I could go back and warn myself: *Stop. Danger. Pain.*)

He was in a mood my first day at Scoville. He chain-smoked, kept his sunglasses on, and barely talked, especially not to me and Robin, the unproven new girls. He got in some sort of argument with Marcy, the Acetone girl with the glasses, and stalked off without saying goodbye to anyone. Yeah, diagnosis: asshole. Not impressed.

A couple months later, at the end of an Acetone show, Greg came out from behind the drums, snatched the bass out of his bandmate's hands, and ran out to the alley to smash it. Everyone stood in a circle lit yellow by a bulb outside a nearby garage. It was like a grade-school playground fight except boy versus defenseless instrument. Some people, including the other Acetone members, looked distressed at first, but instead of stopping him, they joined in. Guy after guy took their turn with that bass, bashing it into splinters of wood and chunks of metal. Maybe it was the allure of destruction. Maybe it was the power of a bully.

(He was a bully, and the look in his eyes scared me that night. How did I let myself forget that?)

When I started hanging out with Acacia, she was dating Greg. They broke up in December, and I didn't see or think about Greg after that. I had no reason to. Acacia was my friend; Greg and I had barely exchanged two sentences.

Then, one night in the middle of January, a call from Caci changed every-thing.

"Greg likes you" were the first words out of her mouth. The two of them hadn't spoken in a couple of weeks, but he'd phoned out of the blue to smooth things over. And ask about me.

"I thought he was dating Megan."

"They broke up."

"That was fast. What, like a week?"

"He likes you," Acacia repeated. Deadpan. But she was always deadpan, and even though she was fast becoming my best friend, I didn't know her well enough to gauge if, in this case, deadpan was just deadpan or hiding hurt. I also still didn't know much about relationships, but I did know that there was a girl code.

"He's your ex."

"Yeah, *ex*. I don't care. I think you should go for it."

I held out for about a day, but she was insistent. He must have been really fucking persuasive on that phone call.

(Persuasive. Magnetic. Charming. He was all of those things. Guys like him have to be. That's how it works.)

When she finally admitted that she liked Greg's best friend, it made a little more sense. If Greg went out with her best friend and she went out with his, it was a fair trade. No broken codes. I wanted it for her, for me, for both of us. Best friends dating best friends hadn't worked out with me and Derek and Robin and Will, but that was because Derek wasn't really my type. Greg was. I'd thought he was hot all along. Even when I thought he was an asshole. At least I told myself so. I don't actually know anymore because my whole relationship with Greg involved so much rewriting.

(Rewriting and rewiring.)

When Greg invited me via Acacia to the next Acetone concert, I rewound the tape. I recorded over the episode where we met at Scoville Park and the one where he smashed the bass guitar. I decided that this is where our story actually begins:

## II.

End of January, my sophomore year of high school. One hour before the Acetone show in Greg's basement. Acacia, Robin, and I are about to have dinner with my parents, but we're as hopped up as Beavis on *Beavis and Butt-Head* when he has too much caffeine and becomes Cornholio. We pace in circles in a way that puts my poor black-and-white dog on high alert. She watches with wide eyes as we chant, "BUTT! BUTT! BUTT!" like third-grade boys who've been given crank. Then we transform back into teenage girls, cackling in such perfect sync that we would have been burned as witches back in 1600s Salem.

The dog whimpers, and my dad remarks, "Jesus Christ, how much sugar have you had?"

Our eyes meet, and the chant changes to "SUGAR! SUGAR! SUGAR!"

"Oh my god," Dad groans.

Mom simply shakes her head. She knows, no doubt, that our bizarre hyperactivity isn't the result of too much sugar or caffeine or even drugs. It can only be about a boy.

At the end of the concert Greg comes out from behind the drums to play guitar and sing on a cover of Nirvana's "Aneurysm." Until that point, the night had been amped and jumpy, but this is the scene in the movie where everything and everyone else in the room goes fuzzy and slows down, where I realize that I have never wanted a guy more—or if I did, the memory of it (that other concert where that other boy impressed me just two months earlier) dissolves the moment our hazel eyes meet.

He's looking right at me. I don't even question it, even though there are like twenty sweaty kids in this basement and I've always questioned if a guy is really looking at me, even if he's a guy that my friend says has a thing for me. But now I know.

Now my life has transformed into a lucid dream. I know what is going to happen next. My future with Greg is written, and it is everything I fantasized my ultimate teenage romance would be.

DUDE. HE WANTS YOU.

I know he's going to come up to me after the song ends and we are going to go outside for a cigarette. I know we're going to go to an isolated corner of his snowy backyard and he's going to ignore his friends and I'm going to ignore mine. I know we're going to talk and smoke for so long that I'll be shivering but I won't actually feel the cold.

I know he will ask for my number before I leave. I know he will call me the next day and we will talk for hours and at the end he will say, "So, uh, will you go out with me?" And I will say yes, and when we meet in front of the auditorium at school the next morning, he will take my hand and my stomach will cartwheel.

I know that by the end of that day, he will kiss me chastely on the lips, and by the weekend, we will be making out under the table in Robin's living room. I know that under the table, hidden from our friends' eyes by the tablecloth, he will push up the slip I am wearing as a dress and run his thumb back and forth over my bra and then he will slide his hand into the long underwear I am wearing as tights and glide his finger into my panties. My heart will race like it never has before, and I will wonder if this is too fast because we've been together for six days and have already done more than Brandon and I did in a month. Before

I can wonder about it too much, our friends will whine, "Let's go already!" and we will emerge flushed and grinning.

I know that we will continue to talk on the phone for hours every night, baring our souls to each other. He will write me little notes during school with lyrics that remind him of me.

I know that he will tell me he loves me after we've been dating for two weeks.

I know that we will have sex on our one-month anniversary. That my parents will be out and I will give my brother ten dollars to stay downstairs while I lead Greg up to my room and put on Urge Overkill's *Saturation* album (which I still can't listen to). He will be wearing a Nirvana shirt (which I still have), and he'll smell like a combination of sandalwood incense, unwashed hair, the cheap cigarettes he steals from his mom, and an aftershave I never knew the name of (but still recognize, and smelling it triggers panic attacks now). I will not question then if one month is too soon because we are head over heels in love and have talked about getting married and having purple-mohawked babies.

I know that we're going to be together forever.

At least I think we will be.

I'm wrong about that.

Wrong about a lot of things.

The wrongness is hazy and hard to decipher. There are no punches thrown. No black eyes or bruises to hide. Just these moments where Greg does or says something that *feels* like he socked me in the gut, or during the worst of it, like he kicked me in the ribs and shoved me down the stairs. But that is *just* an internal feeling, and I am thoroughly convinced that I've done something to deserve it.

As it turns out, there are a lot of things I do not know. Or I do, but I can't let myself. Not even while they are happening.

## III.

By the end of February, Acacia wasn't hanging out with me, Greg, and Robin quite as often. Her thing with Greg's best friend only lasted a couple days, and she'd started dating another guy who, while not a member of the band, was definitely part of the Acetone group. Meanwhile Greg had quit Acetone, and he said he did it because of me.

"They're saying awful things about you," he told me, explaining that Marcy had started it, but now all of them were talking. About how I moved from Derek to Brandon to him. That I was a druggie like Brandon and a . . . It took him a minute to get the word out. He made a face like I had that time when I was eight and a bee flew into my mouth.

"A whore," Greg finally spat. "God, I hate that word."

Since he'd turned his back on the people he'd been best friends with for years, he didn't understand why Acacia, one of *my* best friends, wouldn't cut ties with them since she'd only met them when she started dating him.

Caci said she hadn't heard anyone talking shit about me—maybe the girls were, but they never really talked to her—and if she did, she'd say something. I trusted her, and I also knew that she was spending most of her time with her boyfriend. I didn't care that she split her time between me and him and who-ever else. Acacia was and would always be a floater. But Greg didn't like it.

When Acacia called while Greg and I were on the phone, he'd make some sort of snippy comment like "She wouldn't have to cut into *our* phone time to catch up with you if she wasn't hanging out with *them* all day" (*he* was actu-ally cutting into what used to be my phone time with *her*) or "Don't you think she's copying you, the way she bleached half her head blond?" (I didn't—I'd even taken her to my stylist to do it).

He was still nice to Acacia when she was around, though. I assumed that he was doing it for me, but Greg only played nice when he wanted something. In this case, his ring.

It was a silver spoon ring that belonged to his grandmother. (Or so he said. Greg knew how to tell a good story.) He gave it to all of his girlfriends. Well, not Megan, because they'd only dated a week and Acacia still had it. She'd taken it off as soon as they broke up, but it got lost in the abyss of her room along with some other unmemorable things that Greg wanted back. It took Caci a few days to locate it all, but she gave it to him as soon as she did, and Greg presented me with the ring.

It was so hyped up, the receiving of this ring. It was like an old-fashioned promise ring or something, making it clear to the world that we were courting. But I don't actually remember the day he gave it to me, like where it happened or what he said. All I remember was that the ring was big—it only fit on my forefinger, not my ring finger. And it turned my skin green. I had sick zombie flesh under that ring, but I didn't dare take it off, not even when I was sleeping, for fear that I would forget to put it back on in the morning because I was consistently overtired from talking on the phone with Greg past midnight and then doing my homework.

I don't remember receiving the ring, but I do remember giving Acacia her stuff back from Greg. Acacia asked him for it a couple of times, and then as things got icier between them, she asked me to ask Greg, which I dutifully did even though it upset him. Acacia wanted only two items from him: a chain that she attached to her wallet and sometimes wore around her neck and a pink stuffed duck that she'd gotten for Easter or something and had left at Greg's house.

I can't remember what happened with the chain. I can't unremember the duck.

It happened between second and third period, near a stairwell where we usually passed Acacia. "Oh, I brought the duck!" Greg proclaimed. He was smiling, and I was, too, until he pulled it out of his backpack. Then he was laughing and I was fighting the urge to puke.

He'd defaced the poor thing with a black Sharpie and a lighter, singeing off patches of pink fur.

I spotted Acacia, shuffling down the stairs in her black combat boots, black-and-blond hair in her face. She hadn't seen it yet. She wouldn't until she got to the bottom of the steps, pushed her hair out of her eyes, and looked up. I tried to shove the duck back into Greg's bag, while he foisted it into my hands, insisting, "Give it to her. She wanted it back, right? You both asked me a million times."

"No, I can't," I stammered.

Greg was still smiling—his post-make-out-session/kicking-ass-at-Sega-Genesis-*NHL-'94*/smashing-his-bandmate's-bass smile. "Jesus, Stephanie, it's just a joke." He flicked one of the duck's many new Sharpie tattoos, SKUNKHEAD written over the top of its head. "Because that's what her hair looks like. And that's what she gets for copying you."

I couldn't squeak out an objection that she wasn't copying and that this wasn't funny. I couldn't even shake my head. It wasn't a joke. It was a test, and when I shrank away from it, he glared at me in a way that made me feel ant-sized, like he could crush me under his sneaker. His eyes asked, *Who do you care about more? Her or me?*

Then the duck was in my arms. Nothing stinks worse than burnt stuffed animal.

Acacia flipped her bangs out of her face and saw me. Saw it. She was two steps up from the hall. I was two feet from the staircase. We couldn't stand there. We couldn't run. We weren't girls who ran from things—at least she wasn't. We walked toward each other like we were trudging through quicksand. The duck was so heavy in my arms, I wished it would sink me.

I could feel Greg's eyes on me, watching the painful exchange—me giving Acacia the duck, her giving me a curt nod that said she knew we couldn't be friends anymore.

She tucked it under her arm like a football and continued down the next flight of stairs. I turned and stumbled back to Greg, on the verge of tears.

"God, you both need to lighten up," he said, taking my hand and leading me along our usual path. Like nothing had happened. Like he hadn't just ordered me to deliver a message Mafia-style, by handing one of my best friends a mutilated duck.

## IV.

In March, the small glaciers of sooty black snow that had been around since December were finally melting. It was probably forty-five degrees out, but after a long Chicago winter, forty-five feels like summer. Time for girls like me to swap corduroys, long underwear, and Doc Martens for high heels, fishnets, and their favorite skirts—in my case, the gunmetal-silver one with a layer of tulle underneath that I'd found in the kids' section at the mall. Time for douchebags with red convertibles to put the top down and whistle at girls in skirts, whooping, "HEY, *BAYYY-BEEE!*" even if they're walking down the street with their boyfriends.

Greg was big enough to be imposing, almost six feet and thick—it was fat, not muscle, but that wasn't apparent unless you were up close. Plus, he had ripped jeans and multicolored hair. He was obviously punk rock. And I thought an obviously punk-rock boy would come to the aid of his obviously punk-rock girlfriend and participate in screeching, "Fuck you!" and trying to kick the car as it drove off.

When I turned to look at Greg, he was silent, but his fury showed in his clenched jaw and curled fists. I thought he was going to chase them. Desecrate that shiny red car. But that rage was for me. I started to say what assholes those guys were, and he interjected, "They wouldn't have been shouting at you if you weren't dressed like *that*."

Like *that*.

He'd made a similar statement when we were watching Hole perform on *MTV Unplugged* together—well, not really *together*, because he was grounded, so we were talking on the phone while we watched.

"I love her dress," I'd said of the black lace baby doll that skimmed the middle of Courtney's thighs.

"You would," he scoffed.

"What does that mean?"

"That dress is slutty. It barely covers her ass."

The words slashed through me. It was one thing when jock assholes at school made comments like that; it pissed me off, but I expected it. Greg had said one of the reasons he admired Kurt Cobain was his respect for women. I couldn't imagine Kurt calling Courtney's clothes "slutty." And if he had, Courtney would have punched him in the face.

But I hadn't known how to respond on the phone when Greg insulted me via insulting her, and I *really* didn't know how to react in person when he told me it was my fault that I'd been catcalled.

The lyrics to Courtney's song "Asking for It" were in my head, but I couldn't channel her toughness.

"They don't have the right to yell at me like that, no matter how I'm dressed," I mumbled. All my bluster, all my fuck-you evaporated. Greg had sucked it right out of me. Absorbed it like a self-righteous sponge.

His jaw unclenched as his lips curved into a vicious sneer. "If the wind blows hard enough, you'll be flashing the world. Is that what you want?"

He tossed me over his shoulder, and I gasped, but *not* in the happy, surprised way I'd always imagined I would if a boy tossed me over his shoulder. This was like accidentally springboarding *into* the vault instead of over it during gymnastics.

And then I felt a breeze. A really cold breeze. At first I thought it had blown my skirt up over my hips, but Greg was holding it there, displaying my underwear to the busy street. He paraded me partway down the block before finally setting me down in a parking lot.

My legs were shaking so badly—from the humiliation, not the cold—that I had to sit down on the curb. Wiping hurt tears from my eyes, I asked, "Why the hell did you do that?"

Greg glared down at me. Glared and smirked. "Because it was funny. Lighten up."

An order. I recognized that from The Duck. But it reminded me of something else, too. In grade school, there was this girl, Paulette, who was short and round, like a kickball. Like me, she was quiet, unathletic, and at the mercy of Liza/Brooke/Dani. Sometimes during lunch recess, they made Paulette run around the baseball diamond that was painted on our asphalt playground.

"Go, Paulette, go!" they mock-cheered, struggling to breathe because they were laughing so hard.

Paulette was struggling to breathe, too. And there were tears in her eyes, but she kept running for as long as they told her to. When they finally let her stop, she forced herself to laugh with them. With *us*. Because I laughed, even though I knew it wasn't funny.

And now I fought tears and laughed at myself with Greg. It wasn't funny, but I could either laugh or cry. Crying would lead to a fight, possibly a breakup, and I couldn't risk losing Greg. Aside from Robin, he was all I had. He mentioned that on the phone every night, making some comment about how everyone hated us or it was us against the world. And I knew it was true. Liza/Brooke/Dani had been right all along—I wasn't cool enough, not even for the other misfits at Scoville Park. I was lucky to have Greg, lucky the boy-beast hadn't been right, too, and I wasn't completely unloveable. But if Greg ever stopped loving me . . .

No, I couldn't even think about that. I would do anything to keep that from happening.

Fortunately, my laughter pleased him. He took my hand and we headed down the alley, back toward my house. As my heels clicked against the bricks, I silently reassured myself, *He didn't mean it. Didn't mean it. Didn't mean it. He loves me. Loves. Me. Loves. Me.*

My mom was home when we got there. She walked out of the kitchen, took one look at me, and recognized my trying-not-to-cry face.

"Is everything okay, Stephanie?" she asked, tucking a gray-streaked wave of hair behind her ear.

"Yeah, fine," I muttered.

Her eyes, a darker hazel than mine, and her furrowed brow called out my lie. She was trying to figure out how to press me without pushing me too far. She'd learned to be more subtle since the Liza/Brooke/Dani era—or she was more afraid of upsetting the delicate balance with Greg than she had been with the girl-beast.

I tried to appease her with a partial truth. "There were these assholes in a car, like, yelling, 'Hey, baby,' at me." I rolled my eyes. Trying to play it down so Greg wouldn't get worked up again. It *was* a delicate balance.

"I'm sorry, sweetie," Mom said and for a second I thought it was okay. But then . . .

"Don't feel sorry for her. She set herself up for it. I mean, look at her tights!" Greg gestured at my fishnets, which had several big holes in them. They'd caught on a chair at school and torn. I was pissed at first, then decided it looked cool and tore them some more. "I know you probably told her not to leave the house like that," Greg continued, batting his long eyelashes. He did this whenever he ate dinner at our house and rejected vegetables by saying, "Anything green passes by me." My mom usually fake-chuckled at that, but this time she was stone-faced.

I actually thought that she was going to side with him because she *had* told me several times, "I wish you wouldn't wear those tights." We'd also had several squabbles about the slips I wore as dresses—"It's *underwear*, Stephanie!" being her exasperated argument. And now she had someone who agreed with her. Someone who had real influence over me.

But instead she shook her head. "It's her choice how she dresses." She met my eyes briefly. "I'm sorry those boys harassed you."

Triumph flared up inside of me—of course she recognized it as harassment; she'd taught me how to identify harassment—but then fear overpowered it. Greg wasn't going to like this.

He ignored the second part of her comment, though, worked a teacher's-pet grin, and said, "Well, she should make better choices."

When we got up to my bedroom, he decided to help me make those choices. First, he found a pair of jeans for me to put on and told me not to wear those fishnets out in public again. Then he turned to my closet and shoved past my T-shirts (they were all big on me, so they were okay) to inspect the slips and dresses that I'd been collecting since junior high.

"Nope," he said to my latest favorite, a vintage red velvet dress with a lace collar that I'd scored at Salvation Army for five dollars, probably ruling it out because it was short. I didn't bother asking. He was high on his power trip. Better that than angry. Besides, I reasoned, it was getting too warm for long-sleeved red velvet. But it was the perfect weather for the crocheted black dress and the flower-print baby doll that he also gave a resounding, "Nope!"

Next, he pulled out one of my slips. The blue one I'd worn during our first serious make-out session under Robin's dining room table. It went past my knees, but it was a slip. He smiled slyly, no doubt remembering that first make-out session like I was—well, like I was trying to.

*He loves me. He's smiling. This is a game. He's not doing it to be mean. He's being protective. He loves me.*

"Only for me. Only on weekends. Only when we're alone," he said with an exaggerated wink.

"Okay," I told him, forcing a wink back.

## V.

He found my journal. I don't remember how. Like if it was sitting out (probably not) or he caught sight of it under my bed (more likely). He might have even found it that day he was going through my closet, yea-ing or nay-ing my dresses. My closet was a convenient hiding place since I tended to pile rather than hang my clothes. I kept my razor blades and other sharp things there. (Though not during Greg. Greg thought the cuts were ugly—"You're beautiful, but you're making yourself ugly"—and secretive—"You can tell me everything, so you shouldn't need to cut"—and since he saw me naked, I really had no choice but to stop.) I hid my old diaries in my closet. The current one very well could have been in there that day he rummaged through my clothes, and he very well could have found it. But the bad all tends to blur together, and he made (still makes) it hard to trust my brain.

It doesn't really matter what day it was or what we were doing before it happened. All that matters is what we were in my room and he picked up a green, spiral-bound notebook and waved it at me, asking, "What is this?" and everything stopped.

It said exactly what it was on the cover: MY JOURNAL. DO NOT FUCKING TOUCH!!!! A message directed at my family, but meant for anyone. Seeing it in Greg's hand felt like being doused with gasoline and set on fire. I lunged at him, tearing it out of his hand.

His jaw dropped. "What the fuck, Stephanie?"

I pressed the notebook to my chest. He'd have to wrestle it away from me. "This is just . . . It's personal."

"But I thought we shared everything," he whined.

We did. My cigarettes were our cigarettes even though I paid for them and he smoked twice as much I did. The Manic Panic that I bought was our hair dye, even though all of it went on his head while Robin colored a rainbow in my blond streak with markers, which I told myself looked cooler anyway. The CDs I bought were our CDs—that's why he got to take them home and decide, before *I* even listened to them, that *we* didn't like them and sell them to buy cigarettes for us.

I was willing to share all of that, but not this . . .

"Greg, please," I said.

"What, you don't trust me?"

"No, I just—"

"You don't trust me." He pushed his red-blue-purple hair out of his face. "I can't believe you don't fucking trust me. I've told you everything. I haven't kept a single secret from you." He kept his voice low enough that my mom wouldn't hear, but the redness that spread from the tips of his ears down to his neck showed his anger.

The problem was that giving him the notebook would only make it worse. There weren't secrets in there—he knew about my previous relationships and most of my crushes—but there were feelings. Reading them would upset him, and if he made fun of them, it would upset me.

"I don't have any secrets either, but this notebook goes back to freshman year," I explained. "My writing is so embarrassing. That's why I don't want you to read it." On the floor next to my bed, I found my saving grace. Another notebook. I put the green one behind my back and picked it up. "I'd rather you read this. My poetry. It's *way* more personal than any stupid journal entry, but it's less embarrassing. And I've never let anyone see it. Not Robin, not Brandon."

He took it. I knew that "not Brandon" would get him—and hopefully he wouldn't find out that Brandon *had* seen it.

"Take it home with you," I suggested, "so you can take your time reading it. I really want to know what you think of my poems."

He agreed to this, and stupidly, I thought it was over, but the discussion about my journal started up again that night on the phone.

"I've told you everything," he implored. "Secrets you could use to hurt me."

"But I wouldn't!"

"You have, though. By not trusting me. That hurts so bad that I want to break up with you so you can't hurt me more, but if we broke up, I'd be so alone that I'd die." He choked up. "God, I want to die."

I buried my head under my sheets so my parents wouldn't hear and sobbed that I loved him, that I couldn't live without him. *Please don't leave me and please don't die. Oh my god, please don't die!*

He insisted the only thing that could fix us, and thereby prevent his suicide, was reading my journal, so I promised to bring it to him at school the next day.

We were on the phone until one a.m., and instead of doing my homework, I spent the rest of the night carefully tearing out pages (starting with the one containing Brandon's picture and the Ace of Diamonds card he'd given me) and writing fake entries to replace them. I hid some of the real ones I couldn't part with (the Brandon one), but threw most of them away in the dumpster across the alley from my house. Keeping them was too dangerous.

I held on to the fake journal for years. I'd meant to re-create my old entries after Greg and I broke up, but had only gotten around to fixing some of them. As time passed, I didn't know what was real and what was rewritten. He'd taken my history and jumbled it. Worse, all the entries that followed the fake ones were emotional lies because I didn't know when he might ask to read it again. Pop quiz! Hand over your soul.

One day, more than a decade after Greg, I couldn't take it anymore; the notebook was too much of a reminder. It was garbage day. I heard the trucks coming, so I ran out and threw that green notebook in the trash. Let it go to the landfill, where the real pages were, and supposedly, where my poetry had ended up as well.

Greg never said a word about those poems. He'd obviously only seen them as a stand-in for my deepest, darkest secrets. But he kept that poetry notebook, claiming he was reading it slowly. He still had it when we broke up, and I went to his house three times to demand it back, but he told me he couldn't find it. Finally, he concluded that his mom had thrown it away.

My words. Two notebooks full of them. My deepest thoughts and feelings from freshman and sophomore years. All gone. All taken by him. Aside from Brandon's picture and playing card, a few lines that I copied into later journals, and my entry about Kurt Cobain's death that I saved in a scrapbook, the only thing that remains, preserved but altered for a zine I made before throwing the green journal away, is a lie. One that I was telling to both him and myself at this point: that his very worst acts were all my fault.

4/11/95 | I let him down again.
I cant believe he forgave me so easily

# Dear Boy, maybe I

I added to his pile of problems/let downs instead of relieving them.

I want to take him away somewhere & make up for everything he's been through    I love him so much.

## was

but all I can do   is give in & buy him   anything he wants. I just wonder if after awhile it loses its meaning to him. I dont know what I'm saying I just have so much to give him, but I dont know how to.

pain   I & others caused. I just have doubts in my power

# wrong

I just want to   relieve the

to do that since ___. I'll give everything he wants though, me, money, CDs, whatever. Just so I can have someone as special as him in my life so he can see all my love for him. Today he told me I dont

# maybe    you

I just love the idea of being in love.

That hurt really bad. I felt I hadn't proved myself enough. I gave him the one thing that I can only give once in my lifetime. & also I did the one thing I thought I'd never do

never on

# didnt from break

because I realized there was someone better out there. Hurting him these two times are 2 of the 3 things I've regretted most in my life, the third of course was betraying & scaring him to shoot up. Realizing I hurt & hurt me more than anything ever before even

# my ♡♡heart

that time he swung at me   (he never hits anyone)

of course he was high at the time & the next day he apologized over & over again &

gave me my necklace I made for him for Christmas   back saying he | wasn't worthy

Anyway to think I hurt ~~sore~~ sore   me up all I could see was

black & the pain   ripping me   millions of

# BUT YOU

razor blades   digging in to me   & ripping me to shreds

So I started going crazy again   but I deserved it

# Shattered

Every ounce of pain I cause him I deserve it back double

I just want him to be happy & be proud of me,   cause he's so special

& wonderful.   It means so much to me   that he's mine, & still isn't

fully realized what he is.   I don't know

# my

when it will be, but

# mind

I love him so much now

X

& I'm so sorry   I hurt him   fuck you,
Stephanie

April . . . *Fuck, I can't.*

*Okay, deep breath.* April 11 . . .

*Seriously, breathe.* April 11, 1995 . . .

*"April is the cruellest month . . ."*

April 11, 1995. It rained. A torrential downpour. Definitely not ideal spring-break weather.

Someone dropped me and Greg off at Robin's. Probably my mom. Maybe his dad. We treated whoever it was like a chauffeur, insisting on sitting in the back together so we could hold hands. (Yeah, it was probably my mom.) Greg's hands roamed a little. Traced teasingly up my thigh.

"Let's sneak into Robin's garage and fuck," he whispered as we pulled up to her house.

I imagined the garage, cold and extra damp because of the rain. And what if Robin's brother or dad came home? I shook my head, whispered back, "We can't."

We said goodbye to the parent, opened the door, and I started to run for the front steps. Greg grabbed my hand, trying to redirect me toward the back gate. I saw Robin at the window and shouted at Greg over the loud, loud rain. "Come on! We really can't."

(It was the first time I said no.

It was the last time I said no.)

Greg stormed into Robin's house, slammed the *NHL '94* game into her Sega Genesis, and started playing while we watched. I tried not to cry when I sat next to him on the couch and he scooted away. Eventually, he invited Robin to play with him but continued to ignore me. A couple hours later, the rain slowed to a trickle and Robin suggested we get fries. The fries from the place by her house were one of my all-time favorite foods, but I couldn't eat. Not with Greg chowing down, refusing to even make eye contact with me.

When we got back to Robin's, I grabbed Greg's hand and pleaded, "Talk to me." He wrenched away and I burst into tears. Before I could chase after him, Robin caught hold of my arm, asking, "What the hell is going on?"

"He wanted to have sex in your garage. I wouldn't and now . . ."

Robin's mouth puckered in disgust, which made me feel even worse, but then she said, "Thank you for not doing that. I'll try to talk to him. Wait here and try to eat those." She pointed to the greasy white bag that she hadn't let me throw away.

I couldn't eat my fries, though. I couldn't even sit down. Instead, I paced the short stretch of hallway between the edge of the kitchen and the bathroom, not daring to venture any farther for fear that Greg might spot me from the couch and I'd ruin any progress Robin might have made. Finally, she appeared with Greg trailing behind her, looking about as enthused as he had the day he got in-school suspension.

"Why don't you guys go in my room and talk?" Robin suggested. Then she tossed a warning look at Greg. "But just talk."

I nodded eagerly. Greg sighed but pushed Robin's bedroom door open. Before I could follow him inside, Robin stopped me, insisting, "Seriously, don't have sex in my room."

I didn't want to.

I didn't intend to.

But that was all Greg wanted and intended to do.

As soon as I shut the door, he shoved his tongue down my throat and guided me to Robin's bed. I went with the kiss because I needed it to soothe me; I was hungrier for it than those fries. But when he started to lean me back, I resisted, keeping myself upright, and pulled my lips from his to say, "We can't."

"Unbelievable," he growled, throwing his hands in the air. "This crap again? If you'd just been willing to sneak into her garage—"

"She saw us. She was in the window. And we can't now. Not in her bed."

Arms crossed over his chest. "You're rejecting me."

"No, I'm not. I love you." Reaching for him.

Scooting away. "If you loved me, you would show me."

"I *do* love you." Tears in my eyes.

Ice in his. "You just love the idea of being in love. I don't need that. I don't need more rejection, not after I gave up all of my friends for you."

"Are you breaking up with me?" Panic tightening around my lungs.

His words calm and even. "I don't want to, but it feels like you're breaking up with me."

"No, I love you!" Panic. Pain. Panic. Pain.

He shook his head slowly. "Then show me. Don't reject me. If you're going to reject me, we should break up."

"No!" I shook my head so vigorously I could have given myself whiplash.

Our conversation went in circles until I was on my back. It was the only way to prove that I loved him. To make his eyes melt. To get him to tell me that he still loved me.

Robin would have to understand. Or maybe she wouldn't find out. We'd be quiet, he said. And we'd do it on the floor, not on her bed.

The carpet chafed my ass. My necklace pounded into my collarbone as he thrust into me. But I was too scared to tell him to stop so I could adjust. He might take that as rejection. Also, I wanted it to be over as quickly as possible. Tears pooled in the corners of my eyes and a few escaped, trickling down my cheeks. If he had noticed and said something, I'd planned to tell him I was crying because I was so happy. But he didn't notice, or at least he didn't say anything about it. When it was over, he did give me that *I love you* I needed so desperately, and I clung to it like a life raft.

He floated out of the room, grinning triumphantly. I carried the used condom wadded up in a bunch of Kleenex that I hoped Robin would think were a product of all the tears I'd shed before we talked things out—I did have the puffy red face to show for it.

Of course, one look at Greg and she knew. She rolled her eyes at him. Boys will be boys, after all.

And girls will be girls. As Robin and I passed—me headed to the bathroom, her following Greg to the living room—she rammed her shoulder into mine and hissed, "Slut."

I hurried to the bathroom and sobbed silently. The bruise on my chest throbbed.

*Slut.*

*Slut.*

*Slut.*

I shook the condom into the toilet and flushed. Threw the Kleenex away and grabbed more to blow my nose. Splashed cold water on my face and told myself to deal with it. I deserved how I felt.

*It was all my fault. I let him down again . . .*

## VII.

"Look at that!" Greg's little sister, Lucy, exclaims as purple lightning flashes against the royal-blue sky. "It's not even raining."

"That's heat lightning," I tell her. It's ungodly humid for early June, but that's typical Chicago weather—shifting from frigid to sweltering in the blink of an eye.

"I don't like thunderstorms." Lucy presses her tiny body closer to mine. She's sitting on my lap on the front steps of her house.

Ignoring the heat, I squeeze her tight. I was terrified of storms at her age, so I want her to feel safe.

I want to feel safe, too. And what I wouldn't give to be her age again. Funny, considering all that I gave up to get here, sitting with her like a Band-Aid across my lap, healing me from what happened in the basement a couple of hours ago. ("Funny" in the Greg-sense of the word . . .)

"It's not gonna storm, not for a little while," I assure her. "Your parents will be home by then. Right now, it's just pretty. Like fireworks."

"It is pretty," she concurs, but then the sky rumbles, causing her to squeal and throw her arms around my neck.

"It's okay, Luce," I murmur, finger-combing her hair.

I want to joke like my mom used to when I was a kid, *Don't worry, Chicken Little, the sky's not falling*, but I don't want to keep lying to her. (Like I lie to myself . . .)

It's not okay, and the sky has been crumbling since that rainy afternoon in April. Big chunks of my world come crashing down every day. Like when Greg decided we should stop hanging out with Robin—she was jealous and getting weird, like she wanted to be his girlfriend, too, and I didn't want to share him, did I? He suggested that he would be open to that, but I put my foot down. I wouldn't play sister-wives with the girl who'd been my closest friend since eighth grade. I'd rather shut her out of my life. It was actually much easier than it had been with Acacia, since Robin had been taking her bad moods out on me even before Greg and I had started dating.

So I let that piece of the sky fall, and numbly climbed a tree and stitched the hole it had left back together. I was doing a lot of that lately. Practically every night when Greg called, crying because he missed the friends he'd given up for me, he missed being in a band. He missed it so much that he wanted to die. I managed to fix it, though. There was a girl in my gym class, Isabelle, who knew an eighth grader who loved Acetone. Isabelle and I played musician matchmaker, and now Greg and this kid, Jeremy, were practicing.

Jeremy wasn't able to practice today, though. That's why I had to do what I had to do in the basement. I'd learned back in April that there was only one surefire way to make Greg feel happy, loved, and not want to die. I had to do it, to hold the sky up over him even if it fell down on me.

I can barely feel it when the debris hits anymore, and I've gotten good at hiding the tears. I brought back that trick of touching my tongue to the roof of my mouth to keep from crying. When it gets really bad, I run my tongue back and forth between my front teeth and my upper lip. However, if I try to do that now, I'll squeal like Lucy just did because the insides of my lips are raw, torn up by my own teeth.

Another flash in the sky stops me from flashing back to the basement, to the short, stubby carpet digging into my knees (it's better than the drain grate in the bathroom floor at Ridgeland Commons . . .), to him demanding, "Faster! Faster!" and then yelping, "Hey, watch your teeth!"

Lucy is peeking out of the curtain formed by our hair. She whispers that the lightning is beautiful and then braces herself for the thunder, but before it hits, Greg emerges from the backyard and she relaxes. With him around, nothing is scary, because big brothers protect.

"Look at the heat lightning," she says as he sits down beside us. "Isn't it pretty? Like fireworks."

"It's pretty cool," he replies, handing her a bag of candy. Twizzlers Pull 'n' Peel, her new favorite thing. He must have gone inside for them after he finished his cigarette. He never smokes around her. Not because his smoking is secret—even if it was, she adores him, so she'd keep it, just like she won't tell their parents that I've been here while they were out. Greg doesn't smoke near Lucy because she doesn't like it and it makes her cough.

As she takes the Twizzlers, she wrinkles her nose at the cigarette smell that clings to his hair, and says, "You stink."

He and I both laugh, though I want to inhale all the smoke I can from his hair. I'd wanted a cigarette, too, but Lucy had wanted to come outside with us, and since I still felt guilty about how he'd sent her upstairs earlier (and sickened by the thought of what she could have seen if she disobeyed him . . .), I'd taken her out front instead of joining Greg.

"Have you had one of these before?" Lucy asks me, holding up the thick rope of red licorice made of spaghetti-sized strands. The end of it looks a bit like a honeycomb, which makes my skin crawl. Something about a bunch of small circles just bothers me. (Maybe it's like that bathroom drain . . .)

"No, I haven't, but I do like regular Twizzlers," I tell her.

She peels a strip of licorice and hands it to me.

"Hey, what about your big brother?" Greg objects.

Lucy laughs. "Just a minute. Ladies first." She peels off another and hands it to him.

He slurps it right up, like the Tramp from *Lady and the Tramp* does with his spaghetti. She'd wanted to watch that movie in the basement earlier, but he'd told her to take it upstairs instead, claiming that I wouldn't want to see it again after watching it with her last week.

Greg's Tramp-style Twizzler eating makes Lucy giggle, so I mimic him, which makes her giggle even more. She peels off pieces, saying, "One for you. One for you," as she distributes them to us. Like petals on a flower. He loves me. He loves me not.

She hands me the last one.

(Does that mean he loves me or not?)

"You should eat that one, Luce," I tell her.

"But there's plenty more," she says, holding up the bag.

So I eat all of the Twizzler strips in my hand. I don't even count them like I did those ten tortilla chips I had for lunch. For some reason I've been doing that with my food lately. I don't eat meals. I eat one yogurt or one granola bar, eight cherries, six potato chips. Tonight I told Greg to order the pizza with meat on it since I knew he wanted it that way. No need to get plain cheese for me even though Lucy said she'd eat it, too.

"I'll eat when I get home. I'm not that hungry anyway," I'd claimed. I was actually starving because I'd thrown my peanut butter sandwich away again at lunch.

We hadn't gone to Ridgeland Commons that day, but that was where the not-eating started. About a month ago, when he realized that the old bathrooms he remembered from Little League games were unlocked and there was no one around, so we could use them. When lunch became a "picnic" and then a trip to the bathroom. Every day, I silently prayed that the big brown doors would be bolted, but he could always open one of them. The floor was concrete, dirty and cold, too dirty and cold to lay on, so he'd put his coat on the ground, always making the same joke, "See, chivalry isn't dead!" as I pulled down my pants and got on my knees.

The first time I'd tried to get out of it, saying it wasn't romantic if I couldn't look at him, but he told me I should be open to new things, so I did it. What choice did I have? He'd taught me that there is no *no* after you've already said *yes*. There's only *I don't love you anymore—let's break up.*

Afterward, he grinned and said, "Wasn't that fun? Doggy style."

Doggy style. Great, I was a dog. A slut and a dog. But if he thought it was fun, I thought it was fun, and besides, I didn't have to worry about him noticing the tears in my eyes.

Eventually, there weren't tears in my eyes because I learned how to go other places while it was happening. I counted the ants on the floor, conjugated verbs in Spanish, mentally studied for my geometry test, examined the underside of the sink that my head kept ending up dangerously close to, and thought about how plumbing works until I heard the *plunk* of the condom landing in the toilet.

But I couldn't teach myself to ignore the smell: lemon air freshener and piss. Thinking about that smell made it impossible to eat my peanut butter sandwich at our "picnic." Thinking about that smell made peanut butter sandwiches seem disgusting even when we didn't go to Ridgeland Commons. So I started throwing them away. Food, and whether or not I consumed it, was the only aspect of my life or my body that I could control.

"That's enough, Luce," Greg says after she finishes her second Pull 'n' Peel.

She grumbles in protest, but dutifully hands the bag over to him. He sets it down and scoots closer, putting his arm around the two of us and his head on my shoulder. They watch the lightning, and I close my eyes, trying to put the sky back up.

Right here like this, things are perfect. This is like the little family we've talked about having someday.

Dread turns the Twizzler Pull 'n' Peels in my stomach into tentacles that tighten, tighten, tighten . . . *This is like the little family we could have sooner rather than later because of what I let him do today.*

Our supply of condoms ran out during our last visit to Ridgeland Commons a couple of days ago, giving me sweet reprieve, but this afternoon, while we were watching cartoons on the couch with Lucy, he decided he couldn't stand it anymore. He sent Lucy upstairs so we could make out.

"*Just* make out," I'd said, because I didn't want her walking in on us. And for a little while he was satisfied with kissing and touching under the blanket like we did when his parents were home.

But his parents *weren't* home and his sister *wasn't* going to come downstairs and he needed me. He pressed my hand to his crotch to show me how much.

I started to rub, hoping that would be enough, but he said that didn't do it for him.

*We can't. There are no condoms,* I reminded him. So he suggested I try using my mouth. No other girl had gotten him off that way, but maybe I could.

I failed. Couldn't go fast enough, and he swore he could still feel my teeth even though I covered them with my lips—probably because they were about to cut through.

He needed to fuck me. Had to or he'd explode. *I'll get a plastic bag or something to wrap it with,* he told me.

A plastic bag? That was . . . that wouldn't . . . a plastic bag! No.

But I couldn't say no to him. I could say no to the plastic bag, but not to him. *I'll pull out,* he said.

I racked my brain for statistics from health class. How effective was that? Fifty percent? Higher? Lower?

But I couldn't say no to him.

It hurt a lot. Way more than my first time. Even more than that day in April with the rug burn and the necklace bruising my chest. It tore me up inside. And I was scared the whole time, not just of getting pregnant, but of Lucy opening the basement door and seeing her brother with his jeans pulled partway down and me on my knees.

She hadn't, though. And now she's my Band-Aid. I hug her to me.

It starts to rain right as my mom pulls up. I hug Lucy and kiss Greg with my raw lips. When I get home, I tell my parents I've already eaten and head straight for the bathroom.

I turn the shower on hot as it will go, and when it scalds me, I open my mouth, trying to force out a sob, but I can't cry anymore. All I can do is punch myself repeatedly in the stomach, whispering, "No, no, no, no."

Today is the first time I admit to myself that I hate him, but only for a split second.

The next day in his bathroom when, after five months together that felt as intense as five years, he tells me that he wants to see other people, the sky falls and crushes my heart.

I'm so upset that I don't even remember how or why we've ended up in his bathroom (maybe because Jeremy is over for band practice?), but it's poetic. Bathrooms. Breaking me. Those two things go together like coffee and cream.

Greg says he thinks we'll end up together, but since it's summer, we should

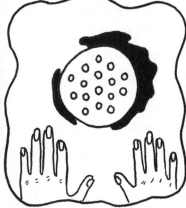

explore other options. I could see other people, too, he tells me. Just not Jeremy. That would fuck up their band.

He says that seeing other people doesn't mean that he and I can't still see each other.

He *means* that it doesn't mean we can't still fuck each other.

I tell him that for me it does.

He is disappointed.

I am heartbroken.

It dawns that maybe we are in the bathroom because he thought I would fuck him one more time, but there are still no condoms and I'm still in pain from yesterday.

I let him kiss me and try not to cry. I think about how if I'm pregnant from yesterday—because he didn't pull out, he decided at the last minute it was too gross—that I will swallow Drano. I imagine myself crashing through a glass table like in *Heathers* when Christian Slater tricks the bitchiest Heather into drinking it. I will say Greg's name instead of "Corn nuts."

No, that's pathetic. I will say nothing.

I run out of his house after he finishes kissing me. Out the back door because I'm afraid to see Lucy; I'll really lose it if I see her. And I didn't want Jeremy to see me either, because he'd probably think I was crazy. It's bad enough that when I get home, my brother is there. I'm pretty sure that he's thought I was crazy since junior high, but still. (I will never be able to be the protective older sister. I dropped the sky and I can't hide the damage . . .)

"Greg called" is all Dan says to me, though I can see concern in his thirteen-year-old eyes behind the thick lenses of his glasses. But before he can ask why I'm tearstained, out of breath, and home unexpectedly, the phone rings and I rush to answer it.

"I was really worried," Greg says. "The way you ran out of here . . . Are you okay?"

I don't know how to answer. I've never been more not-okay. "I . . . I love you" is all I can say.

He bursts into tears, says he loves me and he misses me and he will love me forever. I'm hopeful for a second, but it evaporates when he concludes that while he wants to come over to check on me, we need this time apart.

I snap then. Not at him. Never at him.

When we get off the phone, I head to the bathroom and take a shower even hotter than last night's. I emerge lobster red and put on one of the slips Greg banned me from wearing. A black one. I'd started humming Hole's version of "He Hit Me (And It Felt Like a Kiss)" while I was being scalded and decide I want to watch their performance.

Dan has one of his usual sitcoms on, but doesn't object when I kick him out, probably because I'm all glassy-eyed and our parents are out at a thing for my dad's work, so he has no one to report my Ophelia-like behavior to.

I put on the videotape of *Hole Unplugged* that I'd recorded when it aired on MTV and ask my brother, "Isn't Courtney's dress pretty?"

"Sure, I guess." He shrugs, grabs the book he's reading, and hurries out of the room.

I fast-forward to "He Hit Me (And It Felt Like a Kiss)" and watch it.

Then I rewind and watch it again, humming this time.

Then I rewind and watch it again.

Again and again, singing louder each time.

# PART 5

# Girls Will Be . . .

# JULIET

When I slept over at Juliet's house, she liked to play with my hair. In seventh grade, she usually braided it before we went to sleep. We'd sit, her on the bed, me on the floor framed by her knees, and I'd lean forward so she could pull the brush all the way through my hair, which reached the middle of my back.

It always started out nice. Jules ran the brush softly down the length of my hair and marveled at how it had gone wavy seemingly overnight.

"I can't believe you still have the curls I gave you months ago," she said, referring to the time we'd gotten bored and busted out my curling iron from the Liza/Brooke/Dani days. "It's like magic. Like I gave you a perm. You're so lucky."

I didn't point out that my mom's hair was wavy and apparently genetics (but why the fuck not puberty?) were finally kicking in. When I'd mentioned that before, Juliet's voice had gone flat. Maybe because I was being ungrateful, not thanking her for gifting me with curly hair the way she'd gifted me with the clothes she'd outgrown when we were in grade school. Or maybe because I dismissed the magic—*her* magic, and just months from being sent away to live with her aunt, she desperately needed to feel magical.

I also didn't tell her that she was the lucky one because her grandmother let her get perms and use Sun In, which was advertised as an easy way to achieve perfect, sun-kissed blond highlights. (It had actually turned Juliet's hair a brassy orange, which she hated.) Juliet had never liked being told that she was the lucky one, but especially not then. After Grandma's diagnosis, saying something like that would really set her off.

But sometimes, even if I mumbled something agreeable when she mentioned my magic waves, the brushing got violent. She hit a tangle and didn't even press her fingers to the roots to minimize the tugging the way my mom always did. The way Juliet used to do.

She ripped through another snarl. And another. I couldn't help it anymore. I squirmed.

Juliet pressed her knees into my shoulders, holding me still. "No pain, no gain, Stephie-Lou."

I took a deep breath through my nose.

"That's good," she said, probably thinking I was steeling myself against the pain—and I was, to a degree, but mainly I was trying to calm myself. I didn't need to panic yet. If she was still calling me "Stephie-Lou," things were okay.

Stephie-Lou dated back to the Liza/Brooke/Dani days. At one point Liza decided we should have "country" nicknames, meaning that everyone should tack "Lou" on the end of their name, which was to be shortened if necessary to make it sound right. So we became Stephie-Lou and Julie-Lou. I hated being called Stephie, and Juliet hated being Julie, but for some reason we loved these nicknames. We kept using them long after the novelty wore off for Liza/Brooke/Dani. Long after *our* novelty wore off for Liza/Brooke/Dani.

Juliet put down her brush and began to braid my hair. She pulled so hard that I struggled to keep my head still—and to keep from crying.

"No pain, no gain," she gnashed out as she wove the strands together.

When she finished, she gently dropped the braid over one of my shoulders and said, "There."

I turned around and she was smiling, pleased at her handiwork and expecting me to thank her graciously.

I always did, but sometimes it wasn't good enough. Sometimes when she came back from washing up for bed, she brought a pair of scissors and snipped at the air menacingly.

"You've got such beautiful hair, and I hate you for it. I'm gonna cut it off in your sleep tonight," she'd tell me, eyes gleaming. And then she'd laugh. A cruel laugh that reminded me of Liza. Sometimes she'd say she was just kidding and I'd laugh with her like we used to with Liza.

Whether or not she said she was kidding, I kept my hair wrapped around my hand all night and barely slept. On the worst nights, I told myself that this was it, I was never sleeping over again. But when we woke up, her laugh would be back to normal and when she said my hair was beautiful or my eyes were cool, there wasn't a trace of resentment. I was her Stephie-Lou again, for real, and holding on to that was all that mattered.

I forgave her her Dr. Jekyll and Mr. Hyde act. I forgave her for making fun of my favorite band. I forgave her when Robin said I shouldn't, and even when Acacia said I shouldn't. I always forgave her, for better or for worse, because her loyalty always outmatched her cruelty.

"Stephie-Lou!" she'd shout in greeting after we hadn't talked in a while, and I couldn't help but grin.

That's exactly how she responded when I paged her after Greg and I broke up. She was the first person I thought to turn to. Out of habit, comfort, and the fact that it wasn't abnormal for us to go months at a time without talking—she'd never known that the reason I hadn't been in touch was because Greg didn't like the metalhead guys she hung around. She called me as soon as my number flashed on her pager and invited me right over to her new apartment. She was living with her boyfriend and some friends because she'd had a falling-out with her mom. If she told me the details, I don't remember, but I don't think she did. Just like I didn't tell her the details about Greg.

She'd been let down by her family again. My first serious relationship had ended. We needed each other. That's all we needed to know. We laughed and reminisced. We watched *Star Trek* reruns. It felt safe and innocent, like we were young again—except with bong hits that got us mind-blowingly stoned.

As I was leaving we had the usual exchange about how we should hang out more often even though we both knew that our contact would continue to be sporadic. We led different lives, inhabited different worlds, even as we waved and smiled at each other across the grass at the same park.

This is how it turns out sometimes, how girls will be.

## BECKY

The one time that I landed in the principal's office was toward the end of seventh grade. It was my friend Becky's fault. I kept glaring over at her, but she had angled her chair so that her back was toward me. All I could see was her perfectly straight back and a curtain of brown hair—*stringy brown hair*, I thought meanly, *greasy*.

Her mom was on the other side of her, and my mom was on the other side of me. Maybe our dads were there, too. Mine was very busy at the time, going to grad school and running an AIDS organization that was actually housed in a building next to my school. The only man I remember in the room was the principal, though.

He was a stern Black man, older than my parents. His hair had gotten grayer over the course of that year because some kids kept calling in bomb threats. It wasn't as bad as what happened at Emerson, the other junior high, though. One day during passing period, one girl hit another girl in the head with the claw of a hammer. Rumor had it that the girl with the hammer in her head pulled it out, turned around, and started chasing the girl who hit her. My principal probably would have been better equipped to deal with that because it had witnesses, an obvious initiator, and cut-and-dried consequences. He had no idea how to wade through the murky waters of the nonviolent but emotionally explosive feud between Becky and me.

We were good girls, he said. Smart girls. He wasn't used to seeing girls like us in his office.

Indeed, Becky and I were honors students. We sometimes spent our lunch breaks studying together. We'd bonded over being proud nerds. We started having sleepovers. She might have become my Next Best Friend instead of Robin, but then she told another one of our other friends some of the secrets I'd told her in confidence. Things I'd said about what I was going through with Juliet and about a boy I liked. Fortunately, this other girl promised me she wouldn't say anything, but Becky's breach of trust had been a declaration of war.

At first, I fought mainly with silence—a tactic I'd picked up from Juliet—and by getting the rest of my friends to raise eyebrows, wrinkle noses, or whisper and laugh when Becky entered a room or passed us in the hall. Those were tricks of the mean-girl trade that I'd learned from Liza/Brooke/Dani, and I felt a twinge for using them, but I convinced myself that Becky deserved it for betraying me.

Then I told everyone that I was going to slap Becky. I didn't, but I said I did, and I described it so vividly that I actually felt the sting in my palm and saw the red mark that faded to pale white shock on her face. I built it up so well that I almost blocked out the gut twist of disappointment when I couldn't do it, that heaviness in my arm that kept it weighted down when I confronted her at her locker and told her I fucking hated her. I said I screamed those words, but in reality I was too afraid of a teacher hearing me, so I narrowed my eyes and whisper-growled it at her.

Becky struck back by telling her mom I was suicidal. Her mom then called our principal, and that was why we were in his office.

After rehashing that phone call and his own panicked phone call to my parents, the principal declared in an oddly joyful voice, "And as it turned out, Stephanie was at a slumber party, probably enjoying some fresh-baked blueberry muffins!"

He chuckled to himself, but no one else made a sound, probably all thinking, *Blueberry muffins? What the fuck?* like I was.

After his muffin remark crashed and burned, he went about awkwardly trying to sort through the wreckage of my friendship with Becky—a task that neither of us made easy. No one jumped up to swing hammers or even point fingers. He had to pull every word out of us.

He asked me the same question that my parents had: Why would Becky say such a thing? I'd told them that it was probably because of my mostly black wardrobe and because we were fighting and she was a lying bitch. I left off that last part in the principal's office, though I said it to Becky with my eyes—not that it did much good since she kept her head turned.

I can't remember what she said in her defense.

In the end, the principal seemed unable to determine if I was really suicidal like Becky claimed or if she was spreading vicious gossip to get back at me for ending our friendship and freezing her out of our group. Or maybe he knew that both things were true, but still had no idea how to handle what was beneath it all. The principal who'd had to deal with girls who fought with hammers instead of silence and gossip probably hadn't been able to work that out either. There is nothing more complicated than why girls try to tear one another apart.

He urged us to "work it out" and sentenced me to the guidance counselor, who had me decorate T-shirts with puffy paint.

"Do you think that maybe she told her mom that you were suicidal because she was honestly worried about you?" a friend asked me years later. Other friends and even the guidance counselor had suggested this back in the day, but I'd blown them off, desperate to repair my reputation—I was Straight-A Stephanie, not Sad Stephanie!

"Maybe," I said. "She knew I was cutting myself and I was a wreck about Juliet and about the boys who were tormenting me in gym class." Then I remembered, "She had her friends from Emerson chase me home every day after theater camp that summer, though. So if she was worried about me being bullied and then made it worse . . ." Trailing off, I wondered briefly what might have happened if they'd caught me. I didn't even know what I'd been so scared of at the time—that they would scream at me? Beat me up? My fear had been purely instinctual. But really, if I had stopped and turned on my skates to face them, what would Becky's friends have done? Called me a bitch? Spat at me? Would the main girl have lifted her hand as if she was going to slap me and then chickened out like I did? I wondered what she told Becky about the chasing and how Becky felt. Did she feel sick the way I had when I'd used mean-girl tactics against her?

I would never find out. In high school, Becky and I continued to stare right past each other in the hall, stony-faced, out of habit. She still looked the part of an honors student. I still was one, but I looked a lot more like the wreck I'd felt she'd made me out to be in the principal's office.

I wondered sometimes what she thought of me, not that I knew what I thought of her. We just were where we were because of how girls will be.

## LANA

After my falling-out with Becky, I started picking on my friend Lana.

I'd talk about sleepover plans in front of her, and then when she'd ask for the details, I'd say she couldn't come. Or I'd invite her but just to exclude and ignore her. She'd get less pizza. She'd have to sleep across the room from the rest of us because "there isn't enough space." She always had to do the worst dares. Eat something disgusting. Let ice cubes melt in her bra. And if she fell asleep first, we put her hand in a bowl of warm water, hoping to humiliate her by making her pee.

That summer I invited her to my thirteenth birthday at Kiddieland, and since there was an odd number of us, I colluded with the rest of my guests to make sure that we always paired up and Lana rode every ride alone.

Halfway through the day, when we got in line at the concession stand for lunch, my mother grabbed me by the arm and yanked me around the side of the building. Full of brand-new teenage sass, I huffed and rolled my eyes through her speech, which began with "What the hell is wrong with you? You don't treat people like that!" and ended in an ultimatum: "Stephanie Eunice, you sit next to that girl at lunch and on the rest of the rides or we are leaving."

I did as told, but I made sure that Lana knew that it was ruining my day to be stuck with her.

After the party, when she tearfully asked me what she did wrong, I said I still blamed her for the death of my guinea pig.

A month or two earlier, when my friends and I went down to the basement to play with Ashes, we found her on her side, warm but, my mom confirmed, definitely dead.

"Animals hide when they're sick, but she was right out in the open, so it must have happened very suddenly, and if she felt any pain, it was over instantly," Mom explained, trying to comfort me.

Juliet, who comforted with jokes, pointed out, "Lana was the first one down the stairs. Ashes probably had a heart attack when she saw her face."

Lana was already the butt of our jokes before Ashes died, and even though I insisted that it probably *was* Lana's loud voice, footsteps, or indeed, maybe her face that had scared my guinea pig to death, that was bullshit and I knew it.

Any reason, any excuse I had for tormenting Lana was stupid and most definitely a lie. The truth was that I was sad and angry and practically powerless. So I took what little power I had and used it to hurt Lana because she was the weak link, the one that my other friends had agreed was annoying or weird for reasons so petty that I can't even remember them. Reasons I feared that they might use to exclude me, so I focused all of the negative attention on her instead. I hated myself for this—I *liked* Lana, and what I was doing made me feel terrible, but I just blamed that on her, too.

"I do *not* understand why girls are so damn cruel," my mom would say of Liza/Brooke/Dani, of Juliet, and of Robin, and on my thirteenth birthday, with deepest disappointment, she would say it of me.

I couldn't answer her. This was just one of the ways that girls will be.

## ROBIN

Though she became my Next Best Friend in eighth grade, Robin and I first met on the playground of Washington Irving Elementary School in fifth grade. She was the new girl that year. She'd arrived at a good time, when Liza/Brooke/Dani was feeling more welcoming and inclusive . . . as long as you did what Liza wanted. And one sunny afternoon at recess, she wanted everyone to "chicken fight," which involved the bigger girls running around with the smaller girls on their shoulders. The goal, I think, was to run into one another and ~~try to knock one another off~~ remain upright—a typical Liza sort of ~~test~~ game. There wasn't much actual "fighting." Everyone swerved around one another, giggling, the bigger girls like Juliet trying not to collapse under the weight of the littler girls like me.

Medium-sized Robin wanted in, and when Juliet put me down, I volunteered to partner with her. I can't remember if I got all the way up on Robin's shoulders or if it happened as soon as I jumped on her back, but she tipped over and face-planted on the black asphalt. I screamed, and she screamed louder. There was blood on my knees and on her face. There were also bits of tooth. From Robin's front teeth. They cracked, right there on the playground. She had to go to the emergency room.

I'd never felt so guilty in my life. I apologized profusely when Robin came back to school with freshly capped teeth. She said it was okay—and she was okay—but I couldn't shake the feeling that it wasn't. That was probably why we'd never been close in grade school. That, and I had Juliet.

Whenever she really got mad at me, Robin brought up her teeth. She wanted me to know that it had really hurt when she fell and also that her dad really hadn't had the money to fix them. He'd accrued debt because of me. She'd never have perfect teeth because of me.

Sometimes I'd try to object: "It was Liza's stupid game . . . and you wanted me to jump on your back—you told me to do it. It wasn't my fault you weren't strong enough."

"You jumped too hard and I wasn't ready!"

"You just wanted to be like Juliet even back then."

"Fuck you!"

"No, fuck you!"

We fought a lot. Way more than Juliet and I did, though that might have just been because with Robin, I fought back.

We fought because she was jealous of Juliet, and later, Acacia, and even though I recognized her insecurity—perhaps because it felt so much like staring into a mirror—I often found myself stoking it.

Mainly, though, we were like two wounded animals. We'd bump into each other, igniting the pain of an old injury, and then spar instead of comforting each other.

For the longest time, we'd make up because we had to. We were alone and vulnerable otherwise, and that was worse than the harm we'd accidentally or intentionally inflicted.

"It wasn't really your fault," she'd admit. "My teeth. It wasn't really anybody's fault." Though I don't think she fully believed that. And while what happened to her teeth definitely wasn't my fault, I know I hurt her in a lot of other ways.

She hurt me, too. Most of all on April 11, 1995, when I walked out of her bedroom after Greg forced me to have sex with him and she called me a slut.

Our friendship limped along for a few years after that. She apologized, and I told her that it was okay, but I don't think I fully believed that. It wasn't really either of our faults, though. That much is true. It was just how girls will be.

## MARCY

During my relationship with Greg, rumors swirled about us:

*I was a slut.*

*I was pregnant.*

*I had HIV.*

*We both did heroin.*

*We wanted to be Kurt and Courtney—no, UPDATE: Sid and Nancy—and we'd taken it too far.*

While I was dating Greg, I laughed it off. I knew I'd only ever slept with Greg, and he and I weren't even smoking pot, let alone doing heroin. Also, a year ago, I'd been a total nobody. Suddenly, I was infamous? Like Courtney Love? That was funny. It was punk rock. It was . . .

But Greg didn't like it. Those rumors made us hated. They made *me* out to be dirty. They pitted us against the world, and in particular, they pitted us against his old friends/ex-bandmates, Acetone. In particular, Greg blamed Marcy. He insisted that the quiet girl with glasses and a thrift-store wardrobe was the source of every ugly story that had ever been spread about him and me. Before us, she'd talked shit about him and Acacia, he said. She was a jealous, lying bitch who trashed his girlfriends because she had a thing for him.

I believed him. So did Caci. Even after Greg destroyed Caci's duck. Even after he broke up with me.

(It's always easiest to blame the other girl.)

So, that summer post-Greg and into my junior year, Acacia and I screamed whenever Marcy came near us. At the top of our lungs, like we were alarms set off by her presence. We did this when we passed her in the halls at school or when we ran into her at the park. We drove past Scoville and even past her house blaring "Bruise Violet" by Babes in Toyland. "Yoooou fucking bitch, I hope your insides rot!"

My rage spilled into my zines. I published rants that pointed fingers at Acetone for making me feel as small as Liza/Brooke/Dani had. I spewed vitriol at the "fake feminist" with an eating disorder who had the nerve to put

"Rumor Queen"

I am the rumor queen,
Smeared eyeliner, such a junkie wannabe!
I fucked the devil on prom night,
Did it burn?
Wouldn't you like to know?
Gaping imposter, spurious storyteller:
We are the rumor queen and the suicide king,
Your implications, am I right?
We lived on the hill on the outskirts of Hell
In a hotel.
Screwing and shooting up underneath our tounges.
Please visit us, pick at us until you hit bone!
We have clear blood, after all, we are only a daydream.
Don't worry our outcast disease
Isn't contagious, it's self inflicted.
So what was your plan spineless queenie?
Did you think we'd marry on lover's leap
Or were you waiting for us to drown
In the violations you spit at us?
Such a petty game and you couldn't even conqueror it.
What's your next tale?
What runs in our veins?
What do we do in bed?
What's our baby like, I suppose,
In your head, she's long past born?
We keep her in the basement, you know,
Cleaning our needles.
The despondent blood child of
The rumor queen and her suicide king.
Please condemn us for what we've got
And you will not ever find.
We laugh at your senile shallowness.
Imagining we dine on and reek of bleach
When you are the one who will burn in gasoline.
Slit me open for the key
To shine the light on reality
Drowning in the stench of falsities.
The rumor king and his suicide queen
Still dance eloquently and
Live with their own fucking personalities!
                              -Stephanie Kuehnert

(⊙⊙) Albums + Books to check out

Pussy Whipped by Bikini Kill          the moon is Always Female + other
Love is Fersuckco by the Smears        by Marge Piercy       by both
Fontanelle by Babes in Toyland         The Bell Jar by Sylvia Plath  these womyn
(& the rest of BiT's Albums)           Rubyfruit Jungle by Rita Mae Brown
Daydream Nation by Sonic Youth         Braided Lives by Marge Piercy
Smackbunny baby by Brainiac            I know why the caged birdsings Maya Angelou

10

**A poem I wrote during my sophomore year while dating Greg**

anti-sexism stickers on her family's car even though she was the queen of slut-shaming.

Then one day I launched the America Online application, waited for the modem to finally connect, and found an angry email from Roger, the lead singer of Acetone, asking how I could possibly call *myself* a feminist when I was publicly airing Marcy's very private struggle with her body.

My (childish) response: She started it. She spread those rumors. You guys all acted like you were too cool for me.

"We didn't know you," Roger wrote back, explaining that even though he had *a lot* of problems with Greg, he'd never had a problem with me until I started saying nasty things about Marcy.

Then she started emailing me, too. Apparently, we all had parents who'd gotten the Internet for work and/or we'd talked them into AOL accounts. Marcy wrote that she had no clue that I hated her until Caci and I started screaming at her, and she didn't understand why until she read about herself in my zine.

Messages flew back and forth. (Well, not really. This was the era of agonizingly slow dial-up Internet. Listening to beeps and boops and dial tones was a special sort of torture when you were wondering if there would be a reply to your last missive.)

Roger said that Marcy was one of the kindest people he knew and he could attest that she'd never spread a rumor about me.

Marcy had a theory about why Greg said she did: She'd had feelings for him—that much, she was ashamed to say, was true—and before he dated Acacia, he'd toyed with those feelings. Using her as a scapegoat was another part of his twisted game.

Roger dropped a bombshell: Greg was the one who told *him* that I'd slept with Derek and Brandon, so I'd probably be . . . you know, easy.

But Marcy's bombshell was worse: She'd seen that we carried around the same dog-eared books about feminism and liked the same bands and had wanted to be friends. Even though we weren't, she'd been so excited about my zines. She'd liked the first couple issues, but then came the piece where I'd held up a mirror in front of her and reflected back all of her flaws and worst fears.

Hunched shoulders. Mousy brown hair. A body that she hated, that she damaged because she viewed it as worthless, undesirable, unloveable—by boys, by herself, by anyone. Friends she felt certain would leave because they always had. Boys who'd made her feel wanted for a minute and then told her she didn't know how to take a joke.

She saw what I saw when I looked in the mirror.

She was me. And that's why I hated her. That's why I hurt her.

As she would point out wisely many years later, I was, in essence, bullying myself.

I was not immune to the worst of it, the worst of what girls will be.

# PART 6

# How to Rebuild a Girl

How do you rebuild a girl who has been broken in the worst possible way?

You give her a summer with some wonderful new friends and the girl soulmate who her destroyer tried to take away. They will spend it stretching out in the sun at a new park. Crowding into diner booths. Piling into the den at her house to play that goofy video game about aliens who kept dropping their pants or getting nostalgic over *Degrassi* reruns.

You give her a driver's license, and she will take over the family's Honda Civic wagon, cram it full of her friends. They will sit on each other's laps and ride in the back, where there are no seat belts. They will drive aimlessly all over the near west suburbs. House to house. Park to park. The Denny's in Oak Park with the punk rock waitstaff to the Melrose Park Denny's where fewer people from school go because you need a car to get there. So many more diners are open to them now. Not to mention there are 7-Eleven parking lots. Cemeteries, forest preserves, and side streets. Doing donuts. Jumping train tracks. Teaching the unlicensed how to drive. Shouting, "PANTS," from open windows and laughing hysterically at this inside joke. Sitting out the car window to smoke. Sitting out the car window while it is in motion. Climbing from the hood of the car to the roof and into the branches of trees. Making the late-night playground circuit, where they will run to the swings and swing as high as they can until they see the lights of the cop cars, their cue to jump off and race to the next schoolyard.

You give her music. A record player stolen from her parents, which she will worship at like an altar, the speakers alive with angry girl voices. Kathleen Hanna of Bikini Kill calling for revolution girl-style now. Corin Tucker of Heavens to Betsy sharpening knives for the heart of one particular white boy. Punk rock blasting from her room and her car windows, following her everywhere she goes, announcing her, declaring war, declaring freedom, never, ever, ever surrendering.

You give her the incredible luck of landing front-row tickets to a daylong concert at the same place where she saw Janet Jackson six years ago with her mom. Now she will stay for band after band instead of leaving after four songs because after all the nights in small clubs and big ones, basements and bowling alleys, her ears are used to the loud. They are primed for it. They crave it. So now she will stand in the front row with her friends, arms wrapped around shoulders, hands gripping wrists, fingers intertwining as Courtney Love takes the stage. Courtney will howl. She will thrash, trash, smash. She will throw herself down. She will get back up. She is a mess, but she is still breathing, still screaming.

And that girl will watch as Courtney breaks and rebuilds over and over and over. And that girl will understand, deep inside, that this is how it will be for her, too, now. And as Courtney fixes her eyes on the darkening sky, that girl will lock hands with her girl soulmate and they will listen to Courtney chant:

"Live, live, live, live, LIIIIVE!"

**My front row Lollapalooza 1995 ticket stub**

# My Girls

*People are lonely because they build walls instead of bridges,*
read the caption on the bottom of a drawing I'd taped to the wall next to my
bed—a simple pencil sketch of a girl standing in the middle of a bridge, smiling
contentedly.

Isabelle, the petite, soft-spoken freshman from my gym class, had drawn it.
She doodled everywhere. Women with their arms wrapped around themselves
on the margins of the notes she wrote me. Tiny flowers on the sides of her Converse sneakers. She was the only new friend I made during my relationship with
Greg. She gave me the drawing a couple of weeks before my breakup.

During the sleepless nights that followed—as I tossed and turned in Greg's
pajamas, the soft sounds of my father typing in his office down the hall and Tori
Amos on my stereo singing about winter and silence and crucifixion and little
earthquakes—I often found myself staring at it in the light coming in through
the crack in my blinds.

I couldn't shake the feeling that Isabelle was trying to send me a message.
Like she'd known how isolated I was even before Greg and I broke up. I'd never
told her directly, but maybe it had been in my desperation to find a bandmate
for Greg. Or maybe she'd just seen into my soul, recognized that I was broken,
and drawn me a picture of how to fix myself.

I reached out through the darkness and ran my fingers back and forth over
the words at the bottom, soaking them in.

Pieces of a Girl

*Build bridges, not walls. If it's a message, answer it.*

The next day I called Isabelle and she invited me to hang out with her friends.

Her best friend, Elizabeth, who was about to be a senior, fast became the older sister I'd always wanted. Her hair nearly reached her waist, most of it dyed inky black, but her pale brown roots were always showing. She had a big smile that revealed a small gap between her two front teeth, features that made her look as kind as she was—and probably threw off anybody who wanted to put her in some sort of sullen, rebellious-kid box based on her hair and her paint-spattered, mostly black wardrobe. Elizabeth read as voraciously as I did—or as I had before my all-consuming relationship with Greg. I'd been wilting without books, like a plant without water and sunlight. Elizabeth arrived just in the nick of time to nourish me. To talk about Sylvia Plath, Anne Sexton, and Maya Angelou. To introduce me to a character named Weetzie Bat that reminded me a little bit of Elizabeth herself—bright and sunny, a touch spacey at times (especially when she fell for a boy), but always full of love.

We spent most of our afternoons at the park—well, not *the* park, a different one. Mills Park was in a quieter, more residential part of town. Instead of a statue on a hilltop that attracted skaters like flies, there was a historic mansion at the center that people rented out for weddings on the weekend. During the week, women pushed babies in strollers, dogs chased Frisbees, and we were the only teenagers. There were no burnt patches in the grass from too many cigarettes, no old sculptures to lazily scratch your initials into while passing a joint. It's not that I had a problem with those things—I still smoked both cigarettes and pot—but it was good to have a break from that. To be surrounded by books and journals and sketchpads and the occasional acoustic guitar. By girls who didn't just welcome me into their world, but helped me coax out the words that had run dry after my journal was no longer safe and "no" lost its meaning. I *needed* that break in order to find this girl, the one I'd buried deep inside of me.

But there was another girl I needed, too. A girl I couldn't be whole without. Even though we'd only been hanging out for a couple of months when Greg put an end to our friendship, it felt like he'd cleaved my soul in half. I'd never dared

**Me writing at Mills Park the summer after sophomore year.**

to cry about it the way Greg did the friends he'd "sacrificed" for me, but I'd never stopped aching for her.

Fortunately, the feeling was mutual.

I don't know who called who first after my breakup, but that didn't matter.

"You should come to Mills," I said, and she did.

When she arrived, lit cigarette in hand, wallet chains jangling, black-and-blond hair in her face, Isabelle and Elizabeth ran over, squealing an old nickname they had for her. Because of course they knew her—from junior high, from stage crew—everyone knew Acacia.

I didn't run to her. We said all we needed to with our eyes and a quick nod as she sat down, taking her place beside me. Where she belonged. Where she would stay.

There's a Bikini Kill song, the soft one at the end of *Pussy Whipped*, that speaks of wiping tears from each other's faces, of hiding nothing, holding tight, and never letting each other down. That, even more than "Rebel Girl," was my song for Acacia. Maybe it was supposed to be a love song, like the romantic kind, but it spoke to me of something different and deeper and more pure. The kind of love that would fix what the other kind had broken.

And Acacia didn't blame me for the breakage. There was no hidden anger, no sign that she would use what had happened against me later. That was the difference between her and the last two girls that I'd called best friends: she was never a bully, never passive-aggressive. When I finally worked up the courage to apologize for The Duck, she said, "I knew that was all him. You were just doing what you had to do."

We didn't talk about *why* I had to do what I had to do; I wasn't ready for that conversation yet.

At the end of the summer, I convinced my parents to let me stay home from the family vacation and let Caci (who basically lived with us anyway) move in for the week so we could take care of the dog and the cats. I swore we'd be responsible and well-behaved, and mostly we were . . .

Except for the concert in the living room. Except for the weed I invited everyone over to smoke in my bedroom with the windows open and incense burning. One night after getting high, we made a giant milkshake out of a whole carton of ice cream, put it in the biggest bowl in my house, and crowded around it, armed with straws, slurping and giggling. But my favorite night was the one when just the girls were over.

We got stoned, went outside, and turned on the sprinklers. Watering the garden was one of my responsibilities, but we decided to run through them, drenching our tank tops and cutoff jeans. As the sun set, we plopped down at the small glass patio table, smoked cigarettes and more weed, and let our clothes dry in the heat.

The idea arose somehow to become blood sisters. I remember it as a collective thought like most of the things we did together, but I know that Isabelle was hesitant. Acacia was as covered in cuts and scars as I was, and Elizabeth had some, too. Isabelle said that she understood why we did it, but she hated our need to hurt ourselves. Ultimately we decided that this was different. It wasn't about pain or numbness or blood. It was an oath, a declaration of sister love forever and always. So we all made thin cuts on our forearms and pressed them together one by one until everyone had each of her sisters' blood smeared across her skin and hopefully inside of her, too.

Then we went up to my room to resume work on the project that had become a mainstay of our sleepovers—our zines. We'd seen them before in book and record stores, sitting on window ledges in coffee shops. Xeroxed, mostly black-and-white, but sometimes in color. Sometimes all words, sometimes all images, mostly a mixture. The sizes, the designs, the content varied. Music, politics, poetry, rants, weird random thoughts. We realized you could do anything with them. We realized that people our age were making them. That *we* could make them. So we covered my bedroom in paper—in poems, rants, sketches, cut-up magazines—and turned it into an expression of our aching, truest hearts.

As we cut and pasted and wrote and drew together, I paused, just to look at them, to take it all in. This bridge we were building out of words and pictures. And these girls—it was hard to believe after so many years and so many attempts to fit in that these smart, passionate, well-read, gorgeous creatures were my best friends, *My Girls*.

# Sid the Punk-Rock Cat

For my sixteenth birthday, the only thing I really wanted was a kitten. My family had a cat, but I wanted one of my own that would hole up in my room with me at night like Caci's cat did. We decided that I would name it Sid after Sid Vicious. We were obsessed with *Sid and Nancy*. We watched it so much that we'd counted how many times Nancy screamed, "Siiiiiiid!" (eighty-eight, if I remember correctly), and we liked to scream, "Siiiiiid!" too. We did it at Kiddieland right before we went down the waterslide. At each other when we met up in a park or at Denny's. At cars on busy streets. Naming a cat Sid would provide even more opportunities.

Acacia was with me the afternoon I spotted the Kitten That Would Be Sid in a pet store at North Riverside Mall. It seemed fated—meeting the cat my mother would refer to as my familiar at the same place where I'd met my girl soulmate. He was black and white and had the cutest freckle on his nose, and giant ears and paws that he still needed to grow into. He stopped us in our tracks with a commanding meow.

We asked an employee to let us visit with him in one of their closet-sized rooms where most cats purr and rub up against their potential adoptive parents. He was so happy to be out of his cage that he ran around like a punk in a circle pit. That sight lifted the weight that had been sitting on my lungs for months. I laughed long and hard, something I hadn't been sure I knew how to do anymore.

"I think this is him, Steph," Acacia said.

"Yep. This is Sid."

**A collage of Sid's kittenhood, summer of 1995**

After convincing my parents that Sid should be my birthday present, the first place I went with my brand-new driver's license was to the mall with Caci to pick him up. The pet store put him in a cardboard carrier that looked like an oversized Happy Meal box. He immediately squirmed out when we got to the car, so Acacia said she would hold him.

Bad idea.

I was so distracted by the wriggling ball of fur in the passenger seat while we were waiting at the stoplight that I didn't keep enough pressure on the brake and rolled into the car in front of me. Fortunately, there was no damage, and the other driver looked from her bumper to the two blond-streaked girls with a kitten crawling all over them and decided that filing a report wasn't worth the hassle.

"You need to pay better attention," she scolded me with a shake of her head.

My cheeks burned as she walked off and I muttered, "Shit, my parents can never find out about that."

"It's okay. We'll never tell," Caci assured me, lifting Sid up to her face and narrowing her brown eyes at his big green ones. "Right, Sid?"

I laughed.

It was just one of our many secrets.

# And Out Come the Wolves

Acacia and I were both trying to outrun something vicious. That was the reason that we wore chains and combat boots and heavy eyeliner and carried razor blades in our wallets. That was why we screamed along to punk songs like the ones by Rancid about broken homes and broken bones, about journeying to the end, about escaping to destinations unknown despite the wolves snapping at your heels. The music, the clothes—it was all our armor.

Caci wore it better than I did. Everyone could see the chinks in mine, but they all thought her armor was her actual skin. Only I knew what was hidden underneath there. She and I knew everything about each other.

To most people, Acacia was just that Korean girl at Scoville who dated a senior when she was in seventh grade. Who put a cigarette out on her own arm without flinching. Who rarely went to school. Who once dropped acid every day for a month straight. (Actually, most people didn't notice she was high unless she told them; she was that good at appearing functional despite the mental chaos.)

Caci's closer friends knew a little more about the girl behind the legend. Like that she avoided going home whenever possible. A *very* select few had been to her house, had seen the holes that her little brother put in the walls, the reason she tried to stay away.

I was the only one that she talked to about it. The only one she stayed on the phone with while he tore around like a cyclone, screaming about shoes, money, all the wants that he thought were needs. He kicked, punched, and threw things while Acacia and her cat took shelter behind her locked bedroom door.

He never hurt her physically. Once when he was five and she was eight, he chased her around the house with a butcher knife, but he never went after her again after that. I asked if he'd become afraid of her, but she said, "No. I just don't have money or anything he wants, so there's no point."

He never hurt her physically, but her door would get smashed, her walls would rattle, her floors and all of her possessions would shake. Even though I heard it and saw the damage afterward, it was hard for me to imagine a little brother doing that, since the most that mine ever did was shout at the TV when his baseball team was losing.

He never hurt her physically, but when his fury lasted all night, she couldn't leave her room to do her laundry. She'd have to wait until he went to school the next day, and then she'd be late. Really late if she fell asleep while waiting for her clothes to dry. That happened a few times, and so did falling asleep and therefore falling *down* in the shower. People thought she was joking (or lying) when she said that's where her bruises came from—they had to be from a fight or mosh pit; they had to be hickeys or self-inflicted injuries. She let people believe what they wanted because it was more believable than having a little brother that raged like a terrible storm. It was easier to act like she didn't go to school because she didn't want to, not because she only got a good night's sleep at other people's houses. But I knew the truth.

I knew that even though he never hurt her physically, he broke her in unimaginable ways. "I think about my parents' funeral all the time," she told me. "I know he's going to kill them one day." She stated this like it was just an observation about the color of the sky. She didn't cry. She never did. But I knew that on the inside she was shattered when she pondered what she would do if she had to bury them before she graduated high school.

She was already basically on her own. At fourteen, she had no curfew, no rules. Her parents were too worn down by her brother to lecture her about the absences, the poor grades, the smoking. They didn't know about the acid or the cigarette burn scars or that seventeen-year-old she dated before she was even a teenager. She would be okay, they seemed to think. She could take care of herself.

My mom kept a chicken breast and a potato in the fridge for Caci, ready to heat up, at all times. She told me I never had to ask if Caci could sleep over, and she yelled at Caci's dad once when he called looking for her. "How do you not know where your child is for days on end?" she ranted. Another time Caci's mom called my mom to thank her, and my mom didn't know what to say.

"I wanted to ask, *Why did you fly across the world to adopt a child and then throw her away?* But I couldn't because she was crying," she told me.

"It's complicated, Mom," I said.

"I know," she replied through gritted teeth. But she didn't.

She knew some of it, but not all of it.

I was the only one who knew all of it.

How Acacia lived. That she was the tough girl because she had to be, because it made her feel a little less helpless. And that every once in a while, she couldn't deal.

I knew what that looked like, what it sounded like.

"I want to go to boarding school," she announced over the phone one summer night sometime between my sixteenth birthday and her fifteenth. "In Scotland."

We talked for a bit about how cool that would be. The castles. The Highlands. The sheep. The kilts. It would be like books we'd loved when we were little kids. This was how Acacia worked through her panic: she spun elaborate fantasies and kept spinning and spinning until she could make them real. And why couldn't she make them real? In her world, the very real bruises and broken doors and threats were denied and made unreal by police and social workers and parents, so why couldn't the opposite happen?

"This is fucked up, right? Nobody wants to be sent to boarding school. It's, like, a punishment. But I really want this, Steph. It doesn't even have to be Scotland. It could just be the East Coast, like Pennsylvania or something."

"I think you could make a convincing case," I told her. A part of me didn't want her to, not just two months into our renewed friendship. But a bigger part of me knew, just two months into our renewed friendship, that this was what she needed. "You can tell them that you aren't in the right educational environment here."

"Exactly! And that's why my grades suck!"

We both laughed.

"Yeah, and tell them if you stay you'll probably get kicked out anyway."

"That's not even a lie!"

"And you're running with a bad crowd. Those Scoville Park kids. I mean, they can just ask the school about them."

"Yeah, all my friends are on drugs."

"But not me. Don't tell them I'm on drugs," I said quickly.

"Of course. I'll keep you out of it. They love you anyway because they know you get straight As."

"Great, so tell them that *I* said this is what you need so you can get straight As, too." I managed to say this brightly, swallowing tears and the urge to make her promise to call me every day, not to forget me when she made cool boarding-school friends.

But she knew. She was feeling it, too. "You'll come visit, right?" she asked softly.

"Dude. Of course. Obviously I want to see Scotland."

We both laughed.

"It'll probably be Pennsylvania."

"Then I'll come to Pennsylvania."

But it wasn't even Pennsylvania. All Caci's parents could afford was Iowa. She tried to backpedal then, realizing what she'd done—that she'd given up me and the rest of our friends and the chance to see Rancid in concert that fall for cornfields. But it was too late. The arguments we'd come up with plus the card that she didn't play but her parents knew was on the table—that this would get her away from the holes in the walls and the yelling—it was all too convincing.

Acacia's parents sent her away, and it was worse than either of us thought it could be.

We spent hours on the phone every day in September. I heard Acacia cry for the first time during these conversations, but I knew it was really bad when she stopped crying and her voice deadened. She couldn't smoke, and they made her wear short sleeves after learning that she self-injured. Breaking these rules seemed like an obvious way to get kicked out, but Acacia was scared that she'd get sent somewhere worse. She admitted that her only form of release was banging her head against the shower wall.

"The back of it," she explained, "so they can't see any bruises through my hair. I was doing my arms first, but they noticed the bruises. I said I'd fallen in the shower, but I know they won't buy that again."

We'd been trying to get her out of a situation that led to her *accidentally* bruising herself in the shower, and now she was *intentionally* beating her own head against the wall, trying to pass out? When she told me that she liked it, how it made her vision go black, how she counted each hit, I got really scared. More scared than I was of her brother. I promised that when I visited, we would devise a plan to get her out.

My dad took me out to Iowa in early October and stayed overnight in a hotel not far from Acacia's school. I wished that it could have been my mom, but she couldn't get that weekend off, and Caci needed me immediately. When I arrived, she showed me around, introduced me to her peppy, blond, Southern-accented roommate, Carolann, and then we trudged down the long hill from her school. We found a forested area, swapped clothes, she smoked, we swapped back, and then we wandered around town, me smoking conspicuously the entire time because Acacia was certain there were spies from the school everywhere. Before we headed back, we returned to our spot, swapped clothes again, and she chain-smoked.

Darkness descended quickly as we hiked up the hill. Really quickly. And it was really dark. As a city girl, I hadn't known that it could get so dark.

"Dude, it's so dark out here that I can barely see you. We're probably going to walk right on by your school," I remarked.

Acacia swished an Altoid back and forth in her mouth, musing, "Well, if that happened, it wouldn't really be our fault."

"Yeah, totally. Not our fault. We didn't see it, so we kept walking." The wheels were turning; a new wild plan was in motion.

Our friends who'd tried to run away had gotten caught because of things like bus tickets and stolen cars. If we just *walked*, it would take a long time, but—

"Hey!" Carolann stumbled out of the cornfield. She had something shiny in her hand and she stunk like burning chemicals. She held up a baggie, casually offering us drugs like we were in a poorly written after-school special.

I saw Acacia's eyes widen, saw my best friend coveting her roommate's huge pupils and the oblivion that came with them. I nudged her forward, reminding her sternly that we were walking, and she ripped her gaze from Carolann's tin-foil pipe, muttering that we were headed back to school.

After we were out of earshot, Caci noted, "That was convenient. Now we have a witness. We *were* going back to school. Carolann can tell them."

"Carolann probably won't remember."

"Oh well." Caci shrugged and we went back to plotting our escape. We repeated the list of the things we had—bottle of water, pack of cigarettes, lighter, mints, sixty bucks, each other—making a song of it. "Walking Away": the nursery rhyme, the old campfire tune, the country ballad. The journey we took and the life we would build when we escaped across the Canadian border, *that* would be Laura Ingalls Wilder–worthy. Caci understood. She grew up on Laura, too. We were ready for our own real-life, modern-day Little House adventure.

Then we saw lights, the outline of an intimidating building. "Is that your school? It looks like a mental institution."

"Shit, yeah, it totally looks like a mental institution. We better keep walking. No one in their right mind would walk up to an ominous-looking potential mental institution."

"Yeah," I agreed, but after a few more minutes we saw the sign. There was no denying that it was her school.

We stopped. At a crossroads, literally and figuratively. The truth was Canada was far away and cold, and the sixty bucks that we had between us was not much money.

"I'm going to tell my dad that we were offered meth," I decided. "I'll say you were tempted to try it and I'm worried about you, so we have to get you out."

"I was tempted to try it, that's not even a lie." There was no levity to her voice this time, and neither of us laughed. "I'm not sure it will work, and if I'm stuck here and they try to make me rat on Carolann, things will be even worse." She stared toward the cornfields, in the direction we assumed was north but could have been south, east, or west.

"I'll make sure it works." Once again, I found myself wishing that my mom was there, but I figured that as a public health nurse, Dad would have to take this seriously.

Sure enough, with a trembling lip, tears that were not hard to conjure, and a worried statement that started with, "Daddy . . ." I had my father on board before we were down the hill from Acacia's school. My mom probably would have gone right back for her or called Caci's parents herself. Dad had me do it, promising that he'd get on the phone if they didn't listen to me.

That wasn't necessary. I was Straight-A Stephanie, and I was telling the truth.

Acacia was back in Oak Park just four hours after I was. Right in time for the Rancid concert. Right in time for me to start unraveling because I couldn't outrun the wolves anymore.

VT1817E G.A       GEN ADMIS A      10.00
10.00   NO BODYSURFING/STAGEDIVNG
  2.25          JAM/Q101 WELCOMES
CONVENIENCE CHARGE
G.A.                   R A N C I D
SECTION/AISLE
GJA    3X           NO BODYSURFING
G1 130          T H E   V I C
ROW/BOX    SEAT
31637  3145 N.SHEFFIELD/ALL AGES
A29SEP5  TUE OCT 17 1995 7:00 PM

PART 7

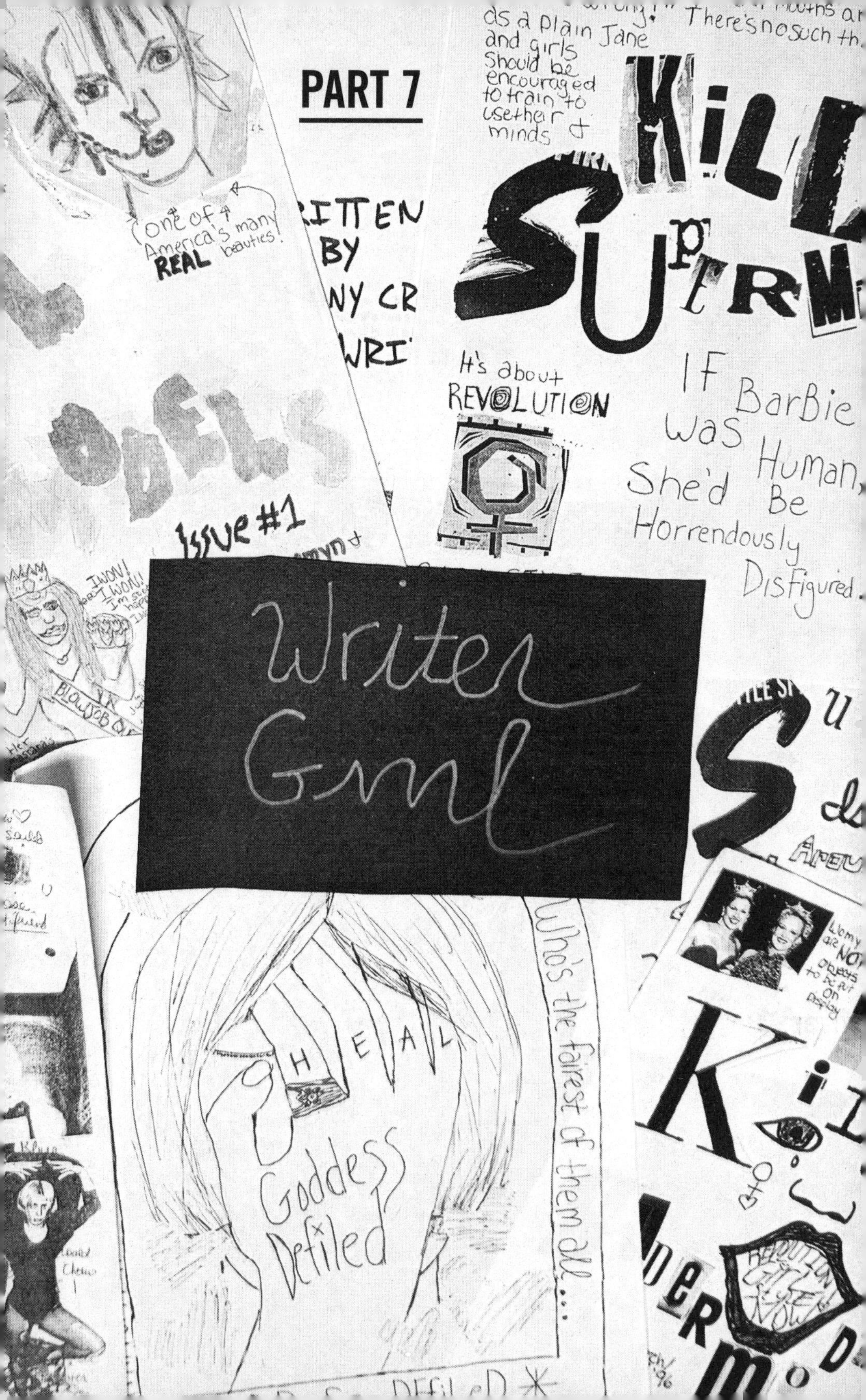

"one of America's many REAL beauties!"

ds a plain Jane
and girls
should be
encouraged
to train to
use their
minds &

There's no such th...

KiLL
SUpRM

WRITTEN
BY
NY CR
WRI

It's about
REVOLUTION

ODELS

Issue #1

IF BarBie
Was Human,
She'd Be
Horrendously
Disfigured.

Writer
Grrrl

HEAL
Goddess
Defiled

Who's the fairest of them all.....

KiLL

S

# Lady Lazarus

**Writer.** I've been one as long as I can remember. Since I could physically put pen to paper. It was something I loved. An escape. A thing I knew I was good at even when I was drowning in self-doubt.

Words: a life raft.

Words: a reason for living.

I processed everything through words. I read and screamed along to other people's words. I filled notebook after notebook with my own. Poetry. Memory. Imagined parallel universes. I wrote until I unearthed my deepest truths. I was not ashamed of my pain, my anger. No . . . wait, that's a lie. I was ashamed and sometimes I still am, but I found I could write my way through it. Especially with the chorus of women's voices that I kept in my head—Sylvia Plath and Maya Angelou; Zora Neale Hurston and Francesca Lia Block; Courtney Love and Corin Tucker. And then there were the girls—the *grrrls*—who gifted me with their words.

The grrrls who took my words and held them. Gently, when my words were fragile and new like the premature babies my mom cared for in the NICU. But I could also count on them to lift up my words. Hold them in clenched fists like a homemade poster at a protest march. Sharpie marker and Xerox ink staining their skin; Sharpie marker and Xerox ink staining mine.

Our words imprinted. Theirs on me and mine on them.

My words on me, bravely displayed, just like all those women and grrrls taught me.

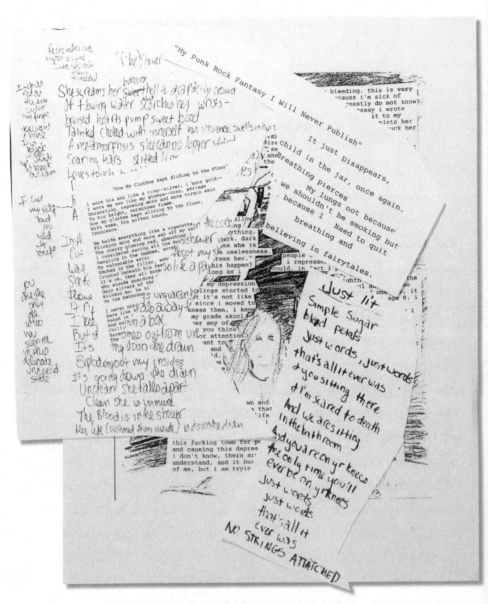

**A collage of my poetry from junior year**

# *Riot Grrrl*

I first read about Riot Grrrl right before eighth-grade graduation in an article in *Seventeen* magazine of all places. The grrrl in the picture had big black boots and RIOT GRRL written in marker across her knuckles. I was drawn to her immediately. I tore the pages out of the magazine and saved it, knowing I might need it someday.

(I already needed it then.)

(But two years later, I needed it way more.)

Right after sophomore year ended—right after Greg and I broke up—my mom decided we needed a girls' day: Vietnamese food on the north side of the city and a trip to Women & Children First bookstore. I picked up a book called *Girl Power*. It was filled with writing by teenage girls about their hopes, secrets, and fears. The chapters were broken down into the groups that the girls self-identified with: "Homegirls," "Surfers and Sk8ters," "Teen Queens." The second chapter in a section titled "Outlaws and Outcasts" was "Riot Grrrls." I stood there in the store, reading about grrrls. About the zines that gave them a voice. About the chapter meetings and conventions where they made plans to change the world.

My mom's gentle hand on my shoulder. "Do you want that?" She meant the book.

"Yes." I meant so much more. But the book was a good start.

I took it home and read like I used to read after a trip to the library when I was a kid. I took a break for dinner. I slept for a couple hours. Then I woke up and binged on these girls' words. All of them. I even saw myself reflected in places where I didn't expect to—in the stories of girls who did 4-H, who joined sororities, who rapped, who played sports. We were all looking for the same thing:

Girl Power.

But after reading the section on Riot Grrrls three times, I knew I was looking for something more specific:

## GRRRL POWER

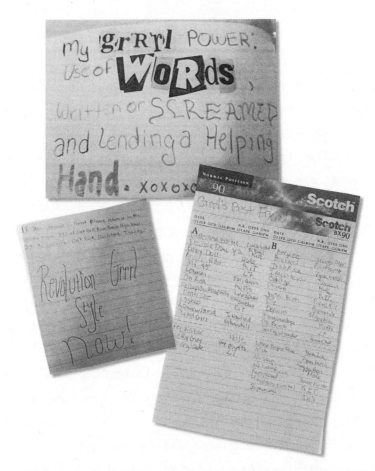

**GRRRL Power infusing my mix tapes and school projects during junior and senior year**

I found Riot Grrrl in a place that would soon become the go-to for anyone seeking community, but in 1995 was still largely unexplored territory—a vast new playground for those who could afford a computer, a modem, and the monthly subscription fee.

My brother and I had convinced my parents to sign up for Internet service from America Online (AOL) around the time Greg and I started dating. After the breakup, it became my lifeline. AOL had chat rooms, but I usually avoided those because the "conversations" seemed to revolve around requests for nude pictures that were either coming from pedophiles or horny twelve-year-olds. Instead, I spent my time cruising the music forums to read about my favorite bands. In one of them, someone asked if anyone hung out in the Riot Grrrl forum.

*There was a Riot Grrrl forum?!?!!*

Ever since I'd read *Girl Power*, I'd been wondering if there was a Chicago chapter of Riot Grrrl. And how I could find it. And if I'd be able to work up the nerve to go to a meeting.

*But there was a Riot Grrrl forum on AOL!!!!*

A few clicks of the mouse and there it was, the clubhouse for misfit girls (grrrls) that I'd been searching for my entire life.

There were threads about all of the record labels and bands. Threads about zine-making and for arranging zine trades. And then there were the threads that went deeper, more personal.

To protect our private thoughts and pain from Internet trolls, we eventually took those conversations to a listserv, forming the Riot Grrrl Online chapter. This also made the community a little more accessible as it didn't require an AOL subscription to access, just an email address, something that was becoming a little more available in 1995 and 1996. Our chapter spanned the US and Canada. Someone was always awake when you were. Through email, we were always there for each other, always listening. No fear, no judgment, no shame. We kept one another's secrets and provided a safe space to work through memories of assault, struggles with depression, coming out to homophobic families.

Anything that one of us was facing, we faced together.

We were a sisterhood.

We were:

**My Riot Grrrl zine collection and uniform**

I met a lot of grrrls through Riot Grrrl Online. Emails flew back and forth constantly. We became pen pals, exchanging letters and zines. There were road trips to and visits from the long-distance grrrls; punk shows and sleepovers with the local ones. But in the end, the most important grrrl in my life was Mia.

We met through the listserv. Her screen name paid homage to the furies from Greek mythology, so I knew immediately that we shared the same passion for literature (I prized my dog-eared childhood copy of *D'Aulaires' Book of Greek Myths* as highly as my copy of *The Bell Jar*) and that we were both angry. Powerfully so. An epic, mythical, force-of-nature wrath was somehow contained (and sometimes not) in our teenage girl bodies.

Our emails to each other got longer and longer as we discovered more and more that we had in common: We were both "gifted" academically, but never fit in socially—in fact, partway through high school, Mia had switched to a homeschooling program. We both struggled with depression and had skin covered in cuts and scars. We both had been abused by boys we loved, though hers had been a family member, and when we met, I didn't yet have the words for what had happened to me. And there was something else, too: Mia lived in a Chicago suburb forty-five minutes from mine.

At first we were hesitant about meeting IRL—our group was a haven for shy girls better at writing than talking, and when someone knows your heart so well, it can be terrifying to let them see your face. But in April of my junior year, Sleater-Kinney, a band born of the ashes of Heavens to Betsy and Excuse 17—two Olympia greats that had broken up before I'd discovered them—played a show nearby, and we both decided to go.

We made tentative *maybe I'll see you there* plans. I still wasn't sure if I was actually going to look for her, and she would admit to me later that it took all of her courage to clear her throat and say, "Hey, are you Stephanie?" when she realized she was standing in line behind me. She'd recognized me by the sticker-covered Hello Kitty lunch box and the army jacket that I'd described to her, with RIOT and GRRRL sharpied on the cuffs and various band names written everywhere else.

She was wearing corduroys and boots; I remember because that's where I looked first—her feet. I turned when she spoke my name, but it took a minute before I could meet her bright blue eyes, take in her reddish-brown pixie cut (a color and a length I'd dreamed of trying but was afraid I couldn't pull off) and her fuzzy black coat (the kind I was constantly looking for at the thrift store but had yet to find). She was pale and red-cheeked, maybe from the spring night chill, maybe from embarrassment. She laughed nervously, a sound that would quickly become one of my favorites on the planet—the non-nervous version, I mean. Our first hug was awkward, and our conversation was stilted, too, but it got better within the fifteen minutes it took for the doors to open. Halfway through Sleater-Kinney's performance, we were bouncing up and down together, holding hands, looking at each other with tear-sheened eyes because this was the best, most important music we'd ever heard and we were discovering it with someone who really, truly understood.

That was and would continue to be the core of our friendship:

## GRRRL LOVE

**Grrrl Love images from my zines**

As much as I loved my online chapter, my pen pals, and the grrrls I traded zines with, I couldn't stop thinking about the Riot Grrrl convention that *Girl Power* described. I imagined myself there, surrounded by a hundred other girls, the same way I used to imagine myself as Laura on the prairie or as an officer on the starship *Enterprise*. But this was a fantasy I could make real if I could get help from someone more experienced, who knew what they were doing.

Eventually, through my online friends and the zine-trading network I'd become a part of, I met a group of older grrrls who had been involved in the scene when it started in Washington, DC, and Olympia, Washington. I was late to Riot Grrrl by about three years. The real scene, the *original* scene, had already fallen apart. These older/ex-grrrls lived in a couple of different apartments in the Logan Square neighborhood of Chicago, which at the time was predominantly Latinx. The punks that lived there in the few blocks around the Fireside Bowl—a decrepit bowling alley–turned–concert venue that was the heart of Chicago's punk scene from the midnineties through the early aughts—were the only sign of impending gentrification. My mother was very nervous about me going to Logan Square because she had a friend who'd been shot on her front porch there. However, since I had my driver's license, she knew she couldn't stop me from going to shows at the Fireside, and eventually sleepovers at my older friends' apartments. She drove the route to the Fireside with me once, told me to listen to my instincts and always walk with a friend at night, and then gave me her reluctant blessing. With that, I entered a new, secret world.

It was like a Scoville Park that I'd followed a trail of bread crumbs to get to—a trail I hadn't even been looking for, but one that seemed designed expressly for me. Riot Grrrl repurposed some of my most significant childhood symbols, like Ramona Quimby, my kindred spirit and fellow little brown-haired girl who was smart but perhaps also a nuisance. In the original illustration by Louis Darling, Ramona is fists-clenched, limbs-locked, eyes-closed, mouth-as-wide-as-it-goes *screaming*. The Riot Grrrl version simply inserts a microphone into one of her hands. I purchased multiple stickers and patches of that image—screaming, miked-up Ramona decorating my backpack and the metal box I carried as a purse. Another grrrl had lifted the image from my beloved childhood poster that depicted Smurfette walking into an office marked PRESIDENT that touted GIRLS CAN DO ANYTHING! She emblazoned Smurfette's briefcase with RIOT GRRRL and surrounded her with the words REVOLUTION GRRRL STYLE NOW and screenprinted it onto a T-shirt that, of course, I had to buy.

The original Smurfette poster, while inspiring when I was a child, seemed laughable and impossible by high school. Society was not built for girls to do anything—quite the opposite, in fact. It left us, like Ramona, to scream in frustration, but Riot Grrrl was an attempt to push forward. "Revolution Grrrl Style Now!" was about creating the world where girls (and queer kids and boys who did not embrace traditional masculinity) could do anything. Riot Grrrl was there to put a mic in the hand of any frustrated girl who wanted it.

In Riot Grrrl, I found the immediate acceptance I'd sought but failed to find at Scoville. While plenty of the grrrls I met online and in person were shy and socially awkward like me, there was no cool-and-aloof front to break through. Our commonalities were often quite literally worn on our sleeves, as mine were on that jacket that I'd bought along with my combat boots at the army surplus store. On the pocket of it, right over my heart, I'd scrawled the lyrics from a Babes in Toyland song: "You don't try to rape a goddess!" Friends like Mia and I bonded so quickly because we clearly signaled to each other that we were "safe."

There were other reasons that I was able to walk so easily into this world, though. Reasons I did not want to see at first even when the older/ex-grrrls spoke about them the first time we hung out at their apartment in the city.

White privilege. Classism. Punk-rock elitism. Those were the things, they told me, that had torn apart the Riot Grrrl scene I'd read about. And they ran so deep that they were not sure it could be fixed. That Riot Grrrl could be redeemed, transformed, or saved.

I believed them, but I also didn't want to hear this at the time. I was a middle-class white girl who still had a lot to learn about my own privilege. And, above all, while I *thought* I understood the ugly problems they were talking about, I didn't want to give up on Riot Grrrl, because I believed in it. I needed it. And I knew that so many others did, too.

When I told them this earnestly in my pitch for their help with some kind of Riot Grrrl Chicago convention, they nodded. They understood. They wanted what I wanted: a safe space for girls to talk, to learn from one another. And we all agreed that that safe space needed to be inclusive. So instead of what I initially proposed, we began to plan the Midwest Girl Fest.

It seemed like a slight difference, "girl" instead of "grrrl," "fest" instead of "convention," but these were words that felt more open, welcoming, and that was important. Words are very important. That was something I'd always believed and Riot Grrrl reaffirmed.

We met every week to work on the fest, which meant a lot of trips to the city for me. And while my friends from high school came to Logan Square with me to see shows at the Fireside, this was something I did on my own, and I loved it. I spent the night in my new friends' basement apartment, staying up until the wee hours to talk or read their huge zine collection. We went on adventures, too, like sneaking into long-abandoned subway tunnels. But that taste of freedom, of Real Adult Life, was nothing compared to what I got from the event itself.

The Midwest Girl Fest spanned a weekend in May of my junior year. More than fifty girls ranging from places like Omaha, Nebraska, to upstate New York crammed into an anarchist community space in Chicago to listen to presentations on self-defense, herbal healing, and reproductive health, and to share their own experiences as working-class women, assault survivors, young mothers. And I was one of the organizers as well as one of the participants.

I was a part of it. The crying, the hugging, the laughing, the speaking out. The Revolution Girl-Style Now!

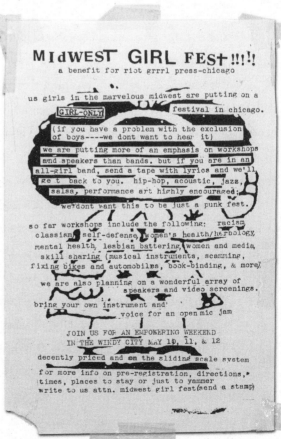

# These Words
## Are All I Have

Here's the thing that's hardest to admit. It was the hardest thing to admit back in high school, and it's still the hardest thing to admit now:

I loved Greg.

Not just during our relationship—I still loved him after. For months. For almost an entire year.

Because there was a side of him that I thought only I knew. Greg told me secrets that he said he'd never told anyone before. Awful, dark secrets I still haven't told. Secrets I still believe even though he lied about so many other things. Secrets that I used to explain and justify his actions.

He got moody and distrustful, and lashed out because he'd been hurt. I understood that. Juliet and Robin had both acted that way. I had, too. And I thought I loved Greg even more than I loved them; I definitely loved him *way* more than I loved myself. So I gave up people and things and forgave his cruelty because of what I saw underneath. Because he cried openly in front of me. That was real. A realness I didn't even have with my own father.

We talked about everything, including our parents. Greg told me how his were always angry and disappointed. I told him how my dad was so busy that it felt like I hadn't seen him since fifth grade even though we lived in the same house.

I trusted Greg with all my vulnerabilities and insecurities. How I'd struggled to make friends since I moved to Oak Park. How much my own depression scared me. How the boy-beast in junior high made fun of my hair and lack of tits on a daily basis and I'd tried to pretend that it didn't bother me, but it made me think I'd be alone and unloved forever.

He told me that he understood. He felt the same way. Boys aren't supposed to think they're fat and ugly, but he did. When I'd begged for a photo of him to put on my nightstand so I could look at it while we talked on the phone, I got one of Greg the grinning infant with a telephone propped up next to his face. He noted that his cheeks were chubby then, too, but it was okay because he was a baby. He couldn't stand any pictures of himself from after kindergarten. He said that he had stomach problems because he couldn't stop eating crap even though he wanted to. He'd tried throwing up. He'd considered doing heroin, not because he wanted to be Kurt Cobain like his ex-friends teased, he just wanted to be skinny like Kurt was.

These were the kinds of conversations that kept us on the phone past midnight. Sometimes his mom would scream at him to go to bed and he'd call me back from under the covers, playing the copy of the first Sunny Day Real Estate album I'd made for him just loud enough to mask his voice but not so loud as to incur her wrath. ("Oh, I dream to heal your wounds, but I bleed myself.") I crawled under my blankets and turned my lights off, too. Every night we whispered like kids at a slumber party, telling secrets and making oaths in the dark.

"I love you. I think you're perfect," we always said.

"You won't ever be alone again. You have me now," we promised each other.

"You're not just my girlfriend. You're my best friend," he told me night after night.

He *was* my best friend. That was the hardest part about all of it even after we broke up. Especially after we broke up.

That summer I still saw him fairly often. I looked forward to hugging him, to feeling his arms wrapped around me and pressing my face to his chest, taking in the scent of him. We still talked on the phone, practically every day at first, and I was still telling him I loved him, finding ways to hint or even say straight out that I was a mess without him, in the hopes that he would take me back. Eventually, he said, in his gentle voice, the one he used with his little sister Lucy, that I was too dependent on him and we needed to move on, so we should probably put some distance between us. After that we only talked when he needed to. When he was depressed or thinking about running away.

I got a few of those phone calls in late June, shortly after I had moved on . . . with the one person he'd asked me not to.

It just happened, Jeremy and me. We'd been hanging out a lot at Mills Park. My Girls and I called Jeremy and his friends "The Little Boys" because they'd just graduated from eighth grade. Jeremy was only a month older than my little brother, but he was really cute. Tall, skinny, with wavy brown hair, and long-lashed brown eyes. Most of the time he moved like a colt—kind of skittish, like he was still figuring out how to operate his long limbs—but at the battle of the bands, he strode offstage full of rock-god swagger and kissed me right on the lips in front of everyone. Including Greg. Then he got all shy again after the kiss. Taking my hand and playing with my fingers, he asked, "So, uh, Stephanie, will you go out with me?" I laughed and said yes.

For the next three weeks, we held hands everywhere we went. We hung out in his basement, and he played guitar for me or put on his favorite records. He made me a mixtape and I showed him my poetry. We never did more than kiss. It felt like he was my first boyfriend. He should have been my first boyfriend—could have been if I'd never gone to Scoville, never dated Derek or (sort of) Brandon or Greg, just kept waiting and crushing and daydreaming until I met Isabelle in gym class and she introduced us. I thought about that for years afterward. How different my life might have been. How normal.

But it was too late to rewrite who I was, to trade the drama I'd thought I wanted for cozy moments that I'd look back fondly upon.

I wasn't the kind of girl who got happily-ever-afters with nice boys like Jeremy. I'd chosen not to be. I'd chosen Scoville and all of those other guys, especially Greg.

It wasn't entirely Greg's fault that Jeremy and I broke up. There were other factors that led to Jeremy's stammering speech, which started out about birds and ended with "I think we'd be better off as friends." For one, he was right, we would be better off as friends—we were close and had a lot of fun together, but the chemistry wasn't there. However, I knew that Jeremy had been getting those phone calls from Greg, too. The ones that kept me up all night, sick with guilt and worry that Greg would do something and it would be our fault. Because of course—and Jeremy knew this, even mentioned it during his speech—I still loved Greg.

I still loved Greg during Jeremy and after Jeremy and even after that midsummer night when he cut Jeremy's hair off in jagged chunks on my front porch.

This happened while my parents were out of town. I'd invited their band to play a show in my living room. It was the first time I'd seen Greg in a few weeks. He'd cut his own hair short and spiky and lost weight. We didn't talk much— even though Jeremy and I had broken up, Greg said it was weird to be around the two of us at the same time. He was quiet at first, sitting in my living room, playing with Sid. I wondered if he was remembering all of the time he'd spent at my house. Because I was.

Then out of nowhere, his mood snapped like a rubber band. He started goading Jeremy about his long hair, saying it wasn't punk enough. Some people agreed. Others, like Jeremy's best friend, said Jeremy could have long hair if he wanted. I loved Jeremy's hair as it was, but didn't dare take sides.

Jeremy gave in. Greg's eyes gleamed as he brandished the scissors, smiling the victorious smile I knew so well. Jeremy swallowed hard, Adam's apple bobbing up and down in his throat; I knew the look in his big, fawn-like eyes even better. It was too soon for me to connect it to how I'd felt when Greg had gotten me to do something I didn't want at Robin's, but it reminded me of Juliet with the scissors.

(Except she'd never used them . . .)

I collected Jeremy's hair afterward and put it in an envelope for him. He said he didn't want it, but I couldn't bear to throw it away. That envelope sat in my dresser drawer for years, along with the pages I'd ripped out of my journal.

Even though I saw that night that something was wrong with Greg, I still loved him and I didn't blame him for the things that were wrong with me. For my continued inability to eat much of anything or make even the smallest decision on my own, like picking out what I was going to wear or what route I was going to walk. I told myself that I'd always been fucked up.

Greg had always been quick to point this out. Whenever I got upset, he used the ~~condescending~~ sweet, talking-to-Lucy voice to say there was something wrong with me—I was depressed, crazy, in need of professional help—even though when he was upset there was something wrong with the world and I had to fix it or it would kill him.

By the middle of my junior year, I was beginning to piece it together. What was wrong with me. What was wrong with Greg. How it all connected. There was a part of me that had known it all along. Before Greg cut off Jeremy's hair. Even before Greg broke up with me.

That part of me made zines—and not just so My Girls and I had a place to showcase our creativity and speak out against sexism.

That part of me sought out Riot Grrrl—and not just because I loved the music. Not even because I'd been seeking a community of girls for all of my life.

That part of me started volunteering at a domestic violence agency—and not just because I needed an activity to look good on college applications; I could have volunteered at my dad's AIDS organization for that.

That part of me knew that I needed help. That I'd never make it unless I found it.

I was an office volunteer for the first few months, but then I was invited to attend a forty-hour training so I could work more closely with survivors and their children. I would be the first high school student to do it, since it was mainly for hotline volunteers who had to be at least eighteen.

Honored, I agreed immediately, and that's how I ended up in the basement of a church with a fat blue binder in my lap open to the Power and Control Wheel where I saw in black and white What Greg Did.

Memories from my own relationship became the slideshow that accompanied the descriptions of the different spokes on the wheel—the way Greg had slowly picked off all of our friends, The Duck, the fishnets, all of the *it's just a joke* and *you're too sensitive* remarks, his insistence on reading my journal, the suicide threats, the threats to break up with me if I didn't . . .

**Duluth model Power and Control Wheel**
**DOMESTIC ABUSE INTERVENTION PROGRAMS**
**202 East Superior Street**
**Duluth, Minnesota 55802**
**218-722-2781**
**www.theduluthmodel.org**

I felt faint. I could barely take notes, barely think, barely breathe.

At the end of the session, I rushed out to my car, hoping everyone would think that I had to get home to do my homework.

It was one of those early spring nights where the temperature hovered right around freezing, but I drove home with the windows rolled down, needing to be numb so I could go through the motions when I got there. I don't remember exactly what those motions were. My mom was out of town—if she had been there to ask how training went, I probably couldn't have just smiled and nodded. I know that my path to the computer was clear, so there was probably a basketball game on—that was the only thing that would keep my dad away from the desk. He and my brother both would have been in the living room, completely distracted, so I could have given a quick wave and run upstairs to log on to AOL. And that is the only thing aside from the cold night air—so cold that I couldn't stop shaking—that I remember for sure.

I opened up my email and addressed a new message to my Riot Grrrl list-serv. With unsteady hands, I typed the line, "I think my ex-boyfriend Greg abused me." Then I deleted it. Typed. Deleted. Typed. Deleted. Finally typed it again, but followed it with another sentence: "Maybe, I don't know."

I shared the memories that had come back while we were going through the Power and Control Wheel. Peppered throughout were more *maybes* and *I don't knows*. My self-doubt. My continued denial because I still loved him. I didn't want to believe anything ugly about what we'd had.

But the replies that I got all said there was no doubt about it. What I described was abuse.

Definitely.

Yes.

They helped me face the memories. They helped me use the right words to describe them: Emotional abuse. Sexual abuse. They didn't judge me for what happened or even for my desire to deny it. They just kept listening and urged me to keep talking.

That spring, almost a year after we broke up, I wrote Greg a letter. Not a love letter like the one I'd sent right after we broke up or the ones I'd continued to write in my journal. This was different.

I typed it up. I emailed it to my listserv. I read it aloud at the Midwest Girl Fest, where Mia held my hand and hugged me. I showed it to Acacia, who volunteered to be the one to give it to him. As right as that would have been, we figured that if it came from her, he would immediately throw it away, so I asked Jeremy to deliver it instead.

I tried to tell myself that it didn't matter if Greg read it or if he responded, but that was a lie. I wanted him to read it, and I wanted a very particular response from him, one that would repair the schism I'd created in my head over a year ago to separate The Greg I Loved from the one who'd destroyed Acacia's duck, who'd destroyed me.

Though I told everyone, even myself, that I wrote that letter to call Greg out on what he'd done, I secretly hoped that if I told The Greg I Loved about this other ugly, hurtful Greg, he would have an epiphany, he would apologize, and we could work through it together. I didn't want to our relationship back—I'd moved on from that—but I wanted The Greg I Loved to heal, to live. I still cared about that above all else.

But The Greg I Loved hadn't read the letter. I knew this as soon as I answered his call—which interrupted a conversation with Acacia just like old times. "So what's the deal with this letter?" spat The Greg Who Destroyed Me. "What do you mean I was psychologically abusive? Did I, like, get inside your head and tell you when you could go to the bathroom?"

I tried not to hyperventilate, glad we were on the phone and Acacia was waiting on the other line, which felt like she was standing behind me, arms crossed. Drawing strength from that, I managed to rehash it all without crying.

He sighed like he had that day Robin insisted that he and I "just talk" in her bedroom. "What do you want me to do about it? I don't have a time machine, and I'm not thinking of inventing one soon."

"I want you to think about it, your actions, how they affect people. To stop the cycle." The phrases I'd learned while volunteering at the domestic violence agency empowered me. I was strong. I helped others. I could help me. I could maybe even help Greg . . .

Or not.

"I thought," he replied immediately, in a voice that was biting but childish, like he was singsonging *nah-nah-nah-nahnah* on the playground with his tongue sticking out.

"Really, you thought? About everything I just said? Already?"

"Yeah. I'm done," he snarled. "Tell your friends, tell your family, put it in your little Riot Grrrl newsletter, but I don't want to hear it anymore."

So I did. Especially that last part.

Once I confronted The Greg Who Destroyed Me and he shrugged off

Maybe you can make me cry, you can make me scared you can make me angry you can make me hate myself you can make me hate the world you can make me scream

But you can never stop me from dancing. (& this is a sign that I'll get it all back)

**Forbidden fishnets zine page from my zine *Hospital Gown***

everything he'd done, the anger took over. It grew and it grew like a white-hot fire, consuming The Greg I Loved and everything we shared.

The moments that used to be the brightest, shining in the sun like polished gemstones, got tarnished like metal—like his grandmother's ring, which I held to a lighter until it turned black before leaving it covered in my blood in front of the bathroom door at Ridgeland Commons.

Then there was the doll he'd given me for Valentine's Day. A boy doll about four inches tall, formed out of hard plastic. It was hollow, and Greg had colored it with a black Sharpie. While we were dating, it sat on my nightstand next to the porcelain figurine of a doe-eyed blond girl clutching flowers that my aunt had given me for being her junior bridesmaid when I was eleven. The pairing was my romantic vision of our future. After we broke up, I put the boy doll in a box in my closet. Then one day, in a fit of rage, I stomped him repeatedly with my bare foot. For a while, I saved the plastic shards.

It was harder to let go of the notes Greg wrote me. My favorite ended like this:

*I love you, a bushel and a peck!*

*A bushel and a peck, and a hug around the neck!*

*A hug around the neck, and a barrel and a heap*

*A barrel and a heap, and I'm talkin' in my sleep about YOU!*

He scrawled these words in his big, almost girlish print.

Beneath it, he added: *My mom used to sing that to me and someday I'll sing it to you!*

I still have that part memorized because I kept that one the longest. I even let mingle with the other notes I'd saved from high school, like it was just a normal part of my life. But eventually I burned it. Made the ashes part of a protection spell, my way of begging the universe not to have to see him again. I burned his baby picture then, too.

I had some of his clothes, including the Nirvana T-shirt that he was wearing the night I lost my virginity to him and the pajamas he'd worn under his jeans during the concert in his basement that brought us together. I don't remember how I ended up with the shirt, but he gave me those pajamas after spending a week at my house.

He'd gotten into a fight with his parents, run off, and then been told not to come back until he was ready to follow the rules. I convinced my mom to let him stay with us.

"He's fifteen," I heard her tell my dad. "Who does that to a fifteen-year-old?"

But the thing that got my dad on board, which I did not overhear, was my mom telling him that she was terrified that if they didn't take Greg in, I would run away with him. "You being on the streets scared me, but you being out there alone with him scared me even more," she admitted to me later, after I told her What Greg Did.

So he stayed for a few nights, sleeping in the guest bedroom on my old, soft *E.T.* sheets in those pajamas. We hoped that it would last forever—kissing good night, being able to talk through the one wall that separated us—but then his mom decided she wanted him back home, so she blackmailed us with notes she'd found in his closet. Notes from me. Notes about sex. Notes she threatened to give to my parents if Greg wouldn't come home. He didn't want me to get into trouble, so he gave in to her demands. We both cried, and he decided to leave his pajamas with me. That way, he said, we'd always be close when I wore them.

I slept in those pajamas for years. They became a security blanket. Then one day I got angry at myself—*A security blanket from* him? *How sick are you?*—and I tore them up and used them to clean the toilet.

I still have the Nirvana T-shirt. Because they were my favorite band, too.

That's the only thing of his that I have left. And this is the last untainted memory:

We ditched school one day in March. My mom dropped us off like usual, but by the time we got to Robin's locker, our usual hangout spot before the bell rang, Greg and I decided that it was too beautiful outside to stay cooped up. Robin was pissed, begged us to wait until the next day because she had a test she couldn't skip. But it needed to be that day. The next day might be rainy or cold. And this was a spontaneous idea. We had to roll with it. So we left her behind and hurried out the doors.

The bell rang as soon as we stepped outside. We looked at each other, laughed, grabbed hands, and ran. Across the street. Down the block. Down the alley. We stepped behind a church and kissed, kissed, kissed. It was like a scene straight out of a movie. The rest of it is like a montage: Us at the music shop, where he played with the guitars. Us at the grocery store, where we flipped through *Spin* and *Rolling Stone* and then worked up the nerve to buy condoms. Us at Chrissy's '50s diner, where we sat on the same side of a glittery red vinyl booth, ate pancakes, and played "Leader of the Pack" on the tabletop jukebox. Then we walked to his house and hid in the park across the street until his mom left for work. We took a bath together. He wrapped me in a towel and carried me to his bedroom, where we put the condoms to use. We lay naked in his bed talking. Telling secrets. Secrets I still keep.

If I could burn this memory from my brain, if I could smash it or tear it into shreds and douse it in bleach, if I could trade it so that last of my scars would vanish, I would.

Maybe.

It is all I have left.

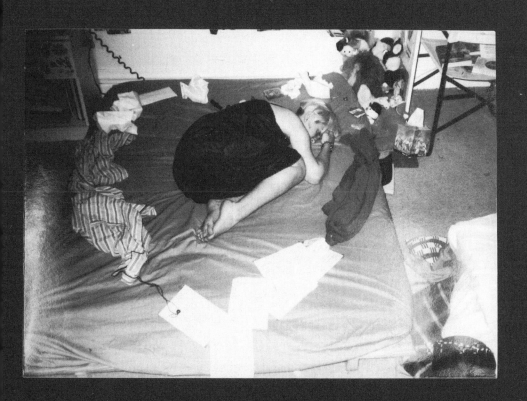

Heart of Greg's stuff, a photo taken for *Hospital Gown*

# Bloody Ice Cream

"The Sylvia Plath story is told to girls who write . . ."
-BIKINI KILL

I cut myself for the first time in seventh grade at stage crew.
It was an accident. I was lost in a fog of upsetting thoughts—about Juliet and whatever insults the beasts at school had hurled at me that day and who knows what else—and I snagged my arm on a nail that stuck out of the wall in the tool room. I almost screamed, but I gritted my teeth, stopping myself. Then I realized that I felt strangely calm. I hurt so much inside that hurting myself on the outside was like opening up a pressure valve. Instead of telling one of the supervisors, who would make a big deal out of it, I hid the little cut beneath a long-sleeved shirt. Later that week when I was feeling crappy again, I went back to the nail and accidentally-on-purpose ran my arm across it.

I had a bunch of little round scars on my stomach from when I got chicken pox in second grade and scratched too hard. I hated those scars so much that I spent the summer between fifth and sixth grade laying out in the sun to try to tan over them to no avail.

But I wanted the cut from the nail to scar. In fact, I really didn't want it to

heal at all, but I knew I couldn't keep going back to that nail without getting caught so I picked at the scab. I watched the skin go from angry red to pink to white. I was pleased. It would be part of me forever.

(Actually, I can't identify it anymore. It's lost among all the other scars.)

I cut partially for that pressure-release feeling and partially for the scar. The reminder that something had hurt and I had survived.

I cut because sometimes I felt so bad that I went numb and I needed to know that I could feel.

I cut because sometimes I felt so sad that I saw the world in black and white, and the sight of my own red blood could shock everything back into color.

Those were a few of my reasons for cutting, anyway. There would be more. They shifted with the circumstances. That's part of what makes self-injury so hard to explain. To others. To yourself.

I was careful to hide the cutting from my parents, especially after the incidents in junior high where I got sent to the guidance counselor, first because Becky claimed I was suicidal and then because I handed in this poem to my eighth-grade English teacher:

Stephanie
Kucher
pg 5
5/5/93

Incense & Music

~~Can I?~~ Would I? Should I?

Incense burning, Music blasting
Is this all that keeps me alive?
I lie there thinking, wondering
How would it be if I were gone?
Would they cry? would they care?
I glance over at the scissors
They stare back at me, gleaming, shining
I think no Go away, I can't
Can I? No I can't
I start crying, bawling
No longer do I care
Why should I no one else does
I listen to the song about a girl
In an insane asylum
I don't want to be that girl
~~I pick up the phone to call my best friend~~
I get up & dry my eyes

I argued that the girl in the poem had chosen not to kill herself, so if it really was about me (it was), obviously I was fine in the end (I wasn't).

I should have known better than to turn that poem in. I might have thought my English teacher was cool, might have thought she would understand because she'd introduced me to the work of Sylvia Plath, but there was a reason that the line "I pick up the phone to call my best friend" got crossed out, replaced by "I get up and dry my eyes."

(At least I'd been smart enough to leave one step out of the poem: I pick up the scissors and drag them across my forearm, but not because I am trying to kill myself, I just need that release so that I *can* dry my fucking eyes.)

Pens and sharp things. They were reliable. Nonjudgmental. They kept your secrets (except when you stupidly gave them away). People betrayed you, like Becky. Or they misinterpreted your poetry as "a cry for help," rather than just portrait of teenage girl life. (Maybe it was both, but I would never admit it.) Clearly, I needed to study Sylvia more closely, figure out how I could be confessional without leading everyone to believe I was on the verge of suicide.

I cut because I was depressed, but not because I wanted to die. That feels important to name. I mean, I did want to die sometimes—a lot of the time, depending on how bad the year—but that was separate from the cutting. If I were going to kill myself, it would have been with pills. Maybe jumping from a high place, but even that seemed painful. If you were exiting life because it hurt too much, why make it worse on the way out?

I didn't know why I was depressed. Maybe, I overheard my parents whisper, it was something caused by hormones or something that I'd inherited from my father's father—a man who'd fallen into such a dark place that his wife left him, a man who chose electroshock over talking about his feelings. Maybe, I told myself, it was because I was creative, and being creative, particularly when you were a girl, meant you had to self-destruct.

Whatever it was, though, the nail, the scissors, the other objects that drew blood and were supposedly hurting me? I thought they did a lot less damage than people.

The night that Greg and I broke up, I threw a glass bottle against the wall of my closet. Again and again.

In the background, Courtney Love howled all the questions I could not answer:

"Is she pretty on the inside? Is she ugly, ugly, ugly, ugly, ugleeeee?"

and

"Was she asking for it?"

I hurled that bottle harder and harder. I wanted it to shatter like I was shattered.

(Like he'd shattered me.)

Most of all, I wanted the glass. I wanted sharp things. I wanted to see myself bleed.

But the bottle didn't break. It put a hole in the plaster.

I cried until I couldn't breathe.

The next morning I got up and went to school.

I don't remember telling my parents about the breakup, but I must have.

I don't remember taking finals, but somehow I still wound up with straight As.

I don't remember the first cut I made or what sharp thing I used.

It just started happening again.

I got a new box of razor blades, and SLUT appeared on my upper arm; the letter G on my thigh.

I accidentally-on-purpose shattered my hand mirror (Seven years of bad luck? Pfft. My whole life had been bad luck.) and used the shards to scratch LOST GIRL into my stomach before meeting Jeremy at Denny's.

I don't remember if this was during our brief relationship or after. It doesn't really matter. We hugged outside of the restaurant, and I winced. Jeremy's brow wrinkled, and he started to ask, *What's wrong?* but only got the "what" out. His eyes widened, and I followed them to the center of my tank top. I cut much deeper After Greg. Sometimes it was hard to stop the bleeding, and occasionally my cuts reopened inconveniently, like the *L* in LOST had, leaving a rusty imprint on my shirt.

Traffic zoomed by on the busy street, stirring up a hot breeze as we stood there in painful, shameful silence. Jeremy's "What—" still hung between us, and I waited for it to become an accusation, turn into *What did you do?* or *What the fuck is wrong with you?* That was how Greg would have reacted. Cutting meant I was compulsive, weak, damaged, secretive. Bad. Bad. Bad.

Instead, Jeremy whispered, "Please talk to me," and when I looked up from the bloodstain, I saw a tear slide down his tanned cheek.

I wanted to. I wanted to let kindness from this sweet boy fix it, but I cut because I wasn't worthy of him. He was an innocent kid who cried at the sight of my blood, and I was damaged, a LOST GIRL, a SLUT.

Not that I could explain any of that. I cut, as I always had, when I couldn't have conversations or even write poetry about how I was feeling. When there were no words other than those short, sharp ones, and I never planned them, they just seemed to flow from the tip of the blade.

So I shook my head, told him I was fine, and told myself that I needed to do a better job hiding the fact that I wasn't, especially from the non-cutters in my life like him.

**Acacia's Mr. Peanut drawing**

Acacia drew a picture of a smiling, waving, top-hat-wearing peanut on the back of her Denny's place mat. *This is a peanut,* read her caption, *to make you feel better when you feel like a walnut.* She carefully tore free the corner with the drawing, folded it in half, and handed it to me.

"Keep it in your wallet," she instructed, because she knew what else I kept in there—the razor blade I turned to when the increasingly angry/ugly/sad feelings boiled up beneath my skin. It was getting worse. So bad that sometimes it hurt to be around anyone, even The Little Boys and My Girls. I told myself I didn't deserve them. I ran off from them at lunch, at diners, at parks. Occasionally, I even bolted out of class.

"Maybe, you know, swap it for that," Acacia suggested. "Maybe we both can, you know . . ."

"Maybe," I said. But these pacts I tried to make with her or Mia or the other grrrls from my listserv to quit, they were the only promises to each other that we couldn't seem to keep.

It was an addiction. Like cigarettes. It had felt good when I started, and it still calmed me every time, so even though I knew it was unhealthy I kept doing it. I made excuses. I told my friends, told *myself*, that I loved my scars. That they were real. They spoke the truth that I couldn't. But the *real* truth was that I hated looking at them.

(Especially that stupid *G*. I sliced through that scar again and again because I wanted it gone. At least part of me did. If all of me had, it would have been.)

And the *really real* truth was, like with any addiction, I'd lost all control.

I got blackout depressed like other people got blackout drunk. I fell into it like a trance, and I'd awaken with something sharp in my hand and blood on my arm, my leg, and/or my stomach. I'd feel relief at first, but it was always quickly followed by shame.

Sometimes I'd get scared, too, like when I found myself in a construction site with my dress hiked up, blood gushing from a wound in my thigh that was much deeper than usual, and a rusty piece of metal in my hand.

*Jesus Christ,* I thought, *what if I've given myself tetanus or something?*

I started crying then, and not just because I was scared and ashamed. I finally saw what I was doing.

That particular cut was so close to the place where my legs met. The place only Greg had been. Only he had touched. I was trying to let the dirty out, but I couldn't. The only way I knew how to do it just made me feel dirtier.

I wanted help, more help than my friends who were stuck in the same cycle could give, but I still didn't want to tell my parents. I'd managed to keep it from them for four years, hiding my wounds beneath flannels and jackets even during the summertime. I still felt like my messy feelings, my problems, were flaws that I didn't want my parents to see any more than I wanted to get a B on my report card. My problems were also problems that my parents couldn't solve, and since I knew they couldn't fix them—couldn't fix *me*—I didn't want to risk them finding out and taking away my only method of coping.

Then came the car accident. It wasn't really a big deal. I made a left turn, miscalculating how fast the guy coming up the street was going, and he clipped the back corner of the Honda, ripping the bumper off. No one got hurt—a lucky break since one of my friends was sitting on the floor of the hatchback. He scrambled over into the backseat before anyone saw him there.

My parents didn't even raise their voices at me, but I had never been angrier at myself. The rage and self-loathing festered as I waited in the living room while they finished inspecting the car. I couldn't contain it anymore. I felt like a madwoman. Like Ophelia. Like Sylvia. Like Susanna Kaysen or one of the other girls she wrote about in another book that had recently become my bible, *Girl, Interrupted*.

I could hear my heart pounding. Blood pulsing in my ears. It matched the same frantic pace of one of my favorite new Sleater-Kinney songs. I could hear Corin Tucker screaming, "Call the doctor! Call the doctor! Call the doctor!" like my headphones were on and the song was at top volume.

I was a madwoman.

I was Ophelia/Sylvia/Susanna.

I might as well own it.

When my parents came inside, I threw my army jacket on the floor and displayed my arms, crisscrossed with bright red cuts, fading pink scabs, and tons of little white scars.

"I cannot handle any of this anymore. I am fucking crazy. You need to check me into the mental institution right now!" I declared.

This was it. That cry for help that everyone had been anxiously waiting for.

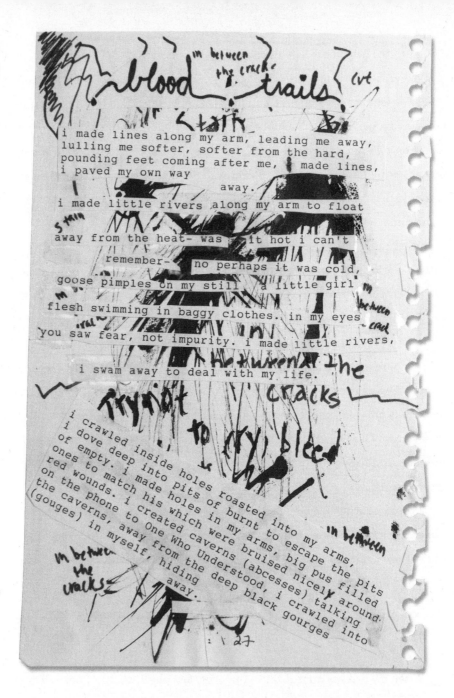

The beginning of my *Bell Jar* chapter. We all knew it would come eventually. *Girl, Interrupted*? Me. *I Never Promised You a Rose Garden*? Let's go. *One Flew Over the Cuckoo's Nest*? I was well versed and fucking ready for it.

Even though I knew mental institutions were sad and frightening places, I

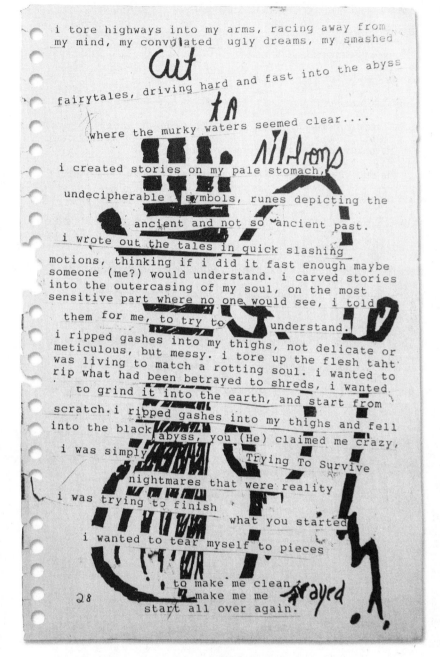

i tore highways into my arms, racing away from
my mind, my convoluted ugly dreams, my smashed

Cut

fairytales, driving hard and fast into the abyss

ta

where the murky waters seemed clear....

ribbons

i created stories on my pale stomach,

undecipherable symbols, runes depicting the

ancient and not so ancient past.

i wrote out the tales in quick slashing
motions, thinking if i did it fast enough maybe
someone (me?) would understand. i carved stories
into the outercasing of my soul, on the most
sensitive part where no one would see, i told
them for me, to try to understand.
i ripped gashes into my thighs, not delicate or
meticulous, but messy. i tore up the flesh taht
was living to match a rotting soul. i wanted to
rip what had been betrayed to shreds, i wanted
to grind it into the earth, and start from
scratch. i ripped gashes into my thighs and fell
into the black abyss, you (He) claimed me crazy,
i was simply

Trying To Survive

nightmares that were reality

i was trying to finish

what you started

i wanted to tear myself to pieces

to make me clean frayed
make me me
start all over again.

28

"Blood Trails," from my *do not go quietly unto yr grave* zine

imagined that a padded white room would be like a safe cocoon compared with
the outside world. A nice little break. I'd either come out feeling better, with a
story to tell, or I'd turn out to be so crazy that I'd stay forever. A small part of me
wanted that, so I wouldn't have to deal with real life anymore.

It didn't work out.

"No one is going to the mental institution" was the first thing that one of my parents said. Dad, I think.

I don't remember much of our conversation. I know they were both shocked. I assume that my mother cried. No one yelled, except for me as I continued begging them to commit me so my problems would go away.

In the end, it was decided that I would see a therapist instead. And my mother insisted that I stay home from school the next day as if I had the flu. Just rest. Read. Sleep. "A mental health day," she called it. She stayed close by and made me soup. We played card games and watched soap operas. Whenever I needed to do this, I could, she told me. I could even call her from school and say I was coming home. No questions asked. She'd call in my absence so I wouldn't get in trouble.

The car came back from the repair shop in a week, looking good as new. It would take me much, much longer. I would never be unblemished. I would need frequent tune-ups. But I wasn't totaled. My mom made sure of that.

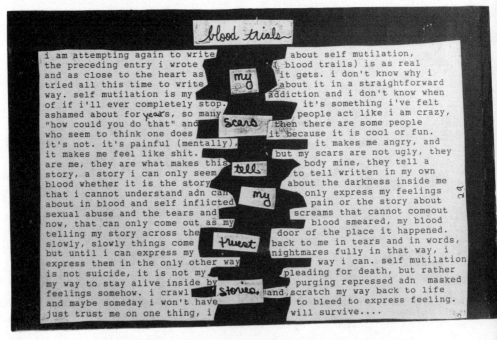

"Blood Trials," a follow-up piece in *do not go quietly unto yr grave*

# Zine Queen

**Zines and Riot Grrrl were inextricable to me.** I knew that zines had been in existence before the Riot Grrrl scene, a ubiquitous part of punk rock. Probably, as with most things punk, I'd heard Kurt Cobain mention them first, calling them by their full name, "fanzines," which led me to believe at first that they were just about music. Album and concert reviews. Interviews with underground bands. Like *Punk Planet*, which came into existence during my freshman year of high school and became a guide to the punk scene for me and every other burgeoning punk rocker in the Chicago area that I met in the nineties. But I thought of *Punk Planet* as a magazine. I bought it at independent record shops and bookstores. I was able to subscribe to it. Sure, it was on newsprint rather than glossy like *Rolling Stone* or *Spin*, but it was bound rather than folded or stapled, xeroxed, and assembled by hand. It was not something that, as a kid in high school, I could make. But the zines that I discovered through Riot Grrrl—that were discussed briefly in that *Seventeen* magazine article and more in depth in the chapter on Riot Grrrl in *Girl Power*—they were within my reach, especially with My Girls' help.

Elizabeth and I both loved to write. Isabelle loved to draw. Caci wasn't as passionate about either of those things as the rest of us, but she had just as much (if not more) that she needed to express. Her contributions were more compact. Small doodles. Little poems under a masculine pen name. Anonymous, incisive paragraphs that laid bare the hurt of being female. That female pain—the specific, awful things both big and small that happen to teenage girls—was at the center of what we created together. We didn't go into zine-making with a ton of direction. There were no YouTube tutorials or wikis, just a Zines subforum within the Riot Grrrl forum on AOL. Other zinesters would answer newbie questions there or offer one another tips on affordable mailing or photocopying, but there wasn't a post or a thread with straight-up instructions. The beauty of zines, after all, was that they were DIY—do-it-yourself. Your own way. Let your content, your personal aesthetic, your creativity guide you. The main thing that the Zines subforum gave me was access to more zines. People there offered zine trades or sales—just enough to cover postage and copying, because no one was trying to turn a profit. I sent out a lot of envelopes with a buck or two and a couple of stamps to individual zinesters, but my big discovery on AOL was that there were zine distributors—"distros"—catalogs full of zines that you could order from one place. I was able to collect the zines I'd read about in *Girl Power*: Like *Bikini Kill*, the zine/manifesto authored by members of the band. And *Girl Germs*, *Sourpuss*, *Fantastic Fanzine*, *i'm so fucking beautiful*, and *Supergirl*, the zines created by grrrls who had become minor celebrities/heroines/crushes for me after reading and rereading the snapshots of their lives presented in that thirty-four-page chapter.

It was a long wait for the zines to arrive, though. I had to send my payment and stamps and then await photocopying and return shipping. I was eager to create before I got these examples, and so were my friends. We had two projects in mind. One was a poetry zine called *Crust*. You see, our school's lit magazine was called *Crest*, and Elizabeth and I as well as a few other friends had had our work rejected from there. We were convinced it was one of those situations where the student editors only published their friends, and in my perception anyway, those students were all clean-cut, overachieving, preppy kids. *Crust* would be for us crusty Scoville Park kids—the punks and the rebels who weren't going to censor swear words or real-life fuckin' experiences out of our writing to get a stupid credential for our stupid college apps. (Yes, the idea for *Crust* very much came out of my bitterness. *Crest* was my first rejection—the first time my writing hadn't been lauded in a school setting, and since it happened During

Greg, it was like being kicked while I was already down.)

The goal of our other zine was to bring Riot Grrrl feminism to Oak Park. We

called it *Kill Supermodels*.

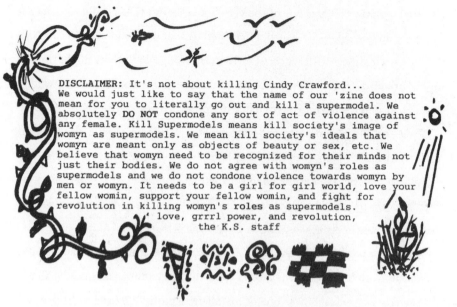

DISCLAIMER: It's not about killing Cindy Crawford...
We would just like to say that the name of our 'zine does not
mean for you to literally go out and kill a supermodel. We
absolutely **DO NOT** condone any sort of act of violence against
any female. Kill Supermodels means kill society's image of
womyn as supermodels. We mean kill society's ideals that
womyn are meant only as objects of beauty or sex, etc. We
believe that womyn need to be recognized for their minds not
just their bodies. We do not agree with womyn's roles as
supermodels and we do not condone violence towards womyn by
men or womyn. It needs to be a girl for girl world, love your
fellow womin, support your fellow womin, and fight for
revolution in killing womyn's roles as supermodels.
    love, grrrl power, and revolution,
      the K.S. staff

*Kill Supermodels* **disclaimer**

We decided we would use *Kill Supermodels* to solicit submissions for *Crust*,

so we focused on it first, determined to have it ready to hand out at the begin-

ning of the school year. We discussed what we wanted to write while at the

park—sometimes starting pieces in our notebooks then and there. We left

some things handwritten, either because they looked just right or because we

didn't have time to type them. As middle-class kids, we all had computers at

home, and at least two of us had printers. Elizabeth's printer was older than

mine—my dad had needed something for work/grad school—so even without

our names attached, you could tell which of us wrote something. We used dif-

ferent fonts and her ink was always lighter than mine. But we didn't care. We

all brought what we had to my bedroom to cut, paste, illustrate, and arrange.

I considered myself a writer rather than an artist. I'd tried to learn to draw

and paint. I had an easel in my room (covered in a collage of detention slips that

I told my parents were "computer errors"), but it had been years since I'd sat at it because I could not excel at art. Collaging I could do, though. Collaging was free-ing. It had no rules. I could jaggedly cut out pictures and letters and slap them down, or I could work with precision, slicing things out with an X-Acto blade and carefully laying them out. I could flow with my mood and/or the emotions I wanted to convey. It was one of the very few activities that I could actually get lost in. Somehow when I collaged, I managed to shut off my inner critic and fol-low my own instincts without constantly questioning what others might think. I could work until I was satisfied with what I'd made, and I would *just know* when I was. It was a high without the comedown—pure pleasure, no regrets.

Zine-making would be a next-level version of this because it also brought in my writing—my deepest pride. Greg had turned up my inner critic as loud as it could go. I didn't even know I *had* gut instincts anymore. But I started to get them back thanks to zines, Riot Grrrl, and the love of my girls, who praised my writing and saw no limits in what we could create together.

The cover page of each issue of *Kill Supermodels* featured a title spelled out ransom-note style. Finding the letters from the stack of magazines we'd all un-earthed from our closets was one of my favorite parts. We used mostly maga-zines that were aimed at us, that we'd read back in junior high: *Seventeen*, *Teen*, *YM*. It was fun to rip them apart—those glossy pages that we felt had projected an unachievable "all-American" teenage girlhood that was only accessible if you were tall, thin, and white with the perfect long, straight, and preferably sun-kissed blond hair. A world where periods were embarrassing and zits were a nightmare and goal number one was finding and keeping a boyfriend. We liter-ally tore all of that to pieces, plundering not just lettering but photos and ads that we wrote commentary about. However, we always paid homage to the one magazine we'd admired—the cool, skateboarding, and indie-band-discovering big sister *Sassy*—by incorporating that paintbrush swoop of an *S* from its page into ours.

While there was a lot of pain, rage, and anguish in the pages of our zines, especially from me, and increasingly as I processed What Greg Did, there were also gushing tributes. We made lists of albums we were listening to and books we were reading—a feature we saw in a lot of the zines we read—but I also wrote a two-page ode to *Degrassi*, particularly my favorite character, Spike, and Elizabeth wrote short essays or poems about some of her heroines, like Nellie Bly, an early investigative journalist, and Amelia Earhart.

Almost all of the zines I created were on standard eight-and-a-half-by-eleven paper, with content photocopied onto each side and stapled in the top left corner. When I started mailing them out to people, I would fold them in half and staple them closed. Half-standard zines—letter-sized paper folded in half so they opened like a book or magazine—were much more common. There were even people who did mini-zines—quarter- and eighth-sized—but while I liked how those looked and worried sometimes that my big zines were amateurish, I wouldn't make a typical, half-standard zine until my very last one. I think part of this came from urgency. I was in a rush to get what we'd made out to the world, and then I wanted to keep a schedule—to have something coming out every other month. I didn't have time or interest in the slightly more compli-cated layout that a folded zine required. Full page just meant keeping to an odd number of pages so that the back would be blank.

It also allowed me to cram in more content. Every full-page zine I made was covered in doodles and notes to the very edges of the page to the point that sometimes I would have to hand-correct pages after photocopying because the copier cut me off. It was a compulsion of mine to fill those pages. I thought it looked cool. Messy, sure, but that was punk rock. I realize now that this was me taking up as much space as I could in the one place that I felt was fully mine. Whether I realized it or not, I was so desperate to have a voice again after being silenced by Greg.

After years of journaling and filling notebooks with poetry, this was the first time I put my writing out in the world for people beyond my very closest friends and my teachers (who got a carefully curated version of my creativity to avoid any further trips to school counselors). We handed out *Kill Supermodels* at our high school to our friends and anyone else who seemed remotely inter-ested. I'd talked my dad into photocopying it at his work, so it wasn't costing us anything to produce—not until reprint runs were necessary, and by that point, we'd found people were happy to contribute a buck or two for copying. I was approached in the halls and at my desk by girls I'd known only vaguely from my honors classes or who I'd been closer with in junior high before I'd traded in my role as conscientious smart girl for rebellious Scoville Park punk rocker who happened to skate by in her honors classes. They wanted to talk about feminism with me. They wanted to submit their writing. They wanted to sign the petitions that *Kill Supermodels* would spearhead to get a women's history class added to the curriculum (that one worked) and to get rid of the ridiculous tradition that forced girls to wear white dresses to graduation (that one did not, but the cause was picked up again and won a couple years after I graduated).

We also advocated for more information about date rape, dating violence, and self-defense. I didn't think about those resources being for me—I wasn't ready to fully admit what Greg had done yet, and even when I was, I quietly thought myself too damaged to be worth helping. Instead, I spoke up for the girls who left notes in what would become the *Kill Supermodels* locker—an unassigned locker that we discovered and put a lock on, directing our readers to put any messages through the slats. Some of the notes were signed, some of them anonymous. Some of them thanked us, some shared resources, and a heartbreaking few shared their own stories of assault and abuse. Every once in a while we got hate mail—the "feminazi" comments we expected—or more often teenage boys mansplaining bands or artists or things they disagreed were problematic. But none of that mattered like those personal notes did. Those personal notes gave me purpose. They helped me to believe in myself, in my writing, what My Girls and I were doing together. I might have thought myself damaged beyond repair, but my blood, my pain, my sharp edges—they were still useful and even provided comfort to other girls who were in desperate need.

In addition to handing out zines at school, I worked to get them listed in zine catalogs and distributed across the country. This meant that total strangers started reading my work and even writing me about it through the email address I provided in the zines, and eventually through the PO box I decided to lease. The fifty bucks I put into two years of PO box rental was the most money I'd spend on zine-making, but as a link to a wider and wider community of readers, writers, and common souls, it was so worth it.

*Kill Supermodels* collage

By the fourth, and what would be final, issue of *Kill Supermodels*, it was basically my zine. The cover was entirely my design. The handwriting was mine, even the simple sketch of a girl's face, lips open wide to showcase the words, *Revolution Girl Style Now!*

The first issue had a picture of a girl I'd drawn, too, but it had been an old drawing. Something I'd carefully sketched in seventh or eighth grade, copying a picture that fascinated me from a random photo book about counterculture that my parents had. The girl had purple and yellow liberty-spiked hair and a chain of safety pins that connected her nose ring and her ear piercings—the epitome, I thought, of cool and tough. She was the girl I'd hoped Riot Grrrl would transform me into—sharp, beautiful, and, above all, someone that everyone was afraid to fuck with. That was who I thought I needed to be. But instead, the more zines I read, the more grrrls I talked to online and in person, the more I was reassured that I could just be who I was. Honest. Raw. Vulnerable, even. This made me brave enough to print not only my words, but my own, often rudimentary pen-and-ink sketches in my zines. It made me brave enough to read at open mics and to introduce myself to and befriend people who were older or younger than me and from different parts of the Chicago area, and in fact, the entire country.

By the end of my junior year, I was more connected to the world I'd found outside of high school that centered feminism and zines. My Girls had other things going on. They all had boyfriends. Elizabeth was deep in the world of college applications and decisions. Acacia was just trying to survive her family, and zine-making was not her way of coping. It was mine.

So much was bubbling up within me—stuff that had been there for years, like my struggle with depression, and the new stuff, the Greg stuff. I poured all of this into my zines. Unwilling to go on with *Kill Supermodels* without my collaborators, I started making one-off personal zines.

My penultimate project was the zine that Greg dared me to write about our relationship, which I named *Hospital Gown*. I went a step further than simply incorporating found images into this one. I used my mother's hospital bracelet from when I was born and pages from my journal. I bought some black-and-white film and asked Mia to help me do a photo shoot one night when she slept over. I wrote HOSPITAL GOWN across my thighs and lifted my skirt for one photo. I posed in a leotard and the fishnets that Greg had forbidden me to wear in several others. In big, black, inky letters I carefully printed SURVIVOR down my scarred arm. I held a lighter just below his love notes to me, though this was just for show as I could not bring myself to actually burn them. Instead, I balled them up and used them, along with every other thing he'd given me—photos, CDs, pajamas, a sweater—to create the outline of a heart, which I curled inside in the fetal position.

Of all my zines, this was my most cathartic. It was a full-body, mixed-media expression of my deepest vulnerability, rage, and pain. My emotions ran so deep and, especially when it came to Greg, were so tangled and confusing that they needed a physical outlet. Too often that meant cutting, burning, or bruising my own body, but zine-making gave me another way. I cut paper, sometimes in big jagged slashes and other times carefully to create a jigsaw puzzle out of my images and words. I wrote in big, angry, swooping, dark letters or in careful, tiny print. I stayed up into the wee hours assembling pages for xeroxing or darkening the lines, stapling and addressing photocopies. I did this with others and alone and felt content either way. I felt productive and accomplished—even more than I ever had when acing tests and papers at school. I felt seen and heard—my zines traveled the country, and I got letters, emails, and even an invitation to be featured in a book called *Zine Scene* that was being put together by two of my favorite writers, Hillary Carlip, who introduced me to zines in *Girl Power*, and Francesca Lia Block, whose work I'd been introduced to by Elizabeth. But even the thrill of seeing my name in print (slightly misspelled, "Kuhnert" instead of Kuehnert) couldn't match what zine-making gave me:

As broken and aching as I might have felt inside while I wrote and cut and pasted and photocopied and assembled, the sliver of a belief surfaced that I had the power to make myself whole again.

A collage of pages from my personal zines

# PART 8

# Dig Me Out

And you will never know how it feel to light up the sky

Penway
Com...

Name _____
School _____
Grade _____

9¾ in. x 7½ in. 100 Leaves

ITEM 863951

Distributed by: Walgreen Co.,
Deerfield, IL 60015

0 70972 83030 1

11/25/96

KUEHNERT, STEPHANIE

OAK PARK, IL 60304
GUARDIAN- ▬▬▬▬▬
HOME PHN- ▬▬▬▬▬

OAK PARK - RIVER FOREST HIGH SCHOOL
STUDENT SCHEDULE TERMS 3 - 4
1996-1997

DSTR-350  BOWMAN

DEAN-GALLUZZO

OSS.581

ID- 83150
YIS-    12
SEX-    F

LKR-200-21

CRS   SEC WT PER  SUBJECT       ROOM   TEACHER       DAYS TERM
***                NO SCHEDULE            IN TERMS SELC ***

Can
call to
verify
graduation!

Sleater-Kinney live at O'Cayz Corral in 1997, photo taken by me

## MAY 4, 1997

*Sleater-Kinney is onstage. Mia and I are dancing, screaming, holding hands. In some ways, it's a lot like that first time we saw them, but actually everything is different.*

*What a difference a year makes.*

*For one, this is not the Fireside Bowl. In fact, we are not even in Illinois.*

*For two, it is a school night, and we don't care because we are not in school. Tomorrow we will go to our jobs. They kind of suck (Mia: gas station attendant. Me: grocery store cashier.), but whatever because tonight we will go home to our apartment. Ours. And we will recount this night. How we met Carrie and Janet from the band and gave them our zines. How our hands shook and we sort of cried a little bit and they smiled and thanked us earnestly. And we will also talk about the boy, the pretty goth boy—wait, can you still say "boy" when they are in their twenties? And when they are completely otherworldly and different?—the one I spent last night with, all night, kissing.*

Oh my god, yeah, what a difference a year makes.

*Sleater-Kinney has a new album,* Dig Me Out, *and they close with the title track, with Corin Tucker wailing about digging out, out of messes, of her own head, her own body, her own skin. And I think,* Yes, this is what I'm doing. What I did.

*So I guess I better back up and talk about all of that digging.*

# *Firefly*

I wasn't hanging out with Isabelle, Elizabeth, and The Little Boys as much by the end of my junior year. I knew this was the way of things. That friendships shifted. There was still love, still letters and presents and drawings and mixtapes exchanged, but there were also growing pains. I felt like it was my fault. That I was losing them, pushing them away, and to a certain extent I was. Because of the inner turmoil that came along with facing What Greg Did.

It didn't help that I couldn't seem to avoid Greg. He lurked around the people I hung out with like a hungry shark. The Little Girls, freshmen who said they looked up to me, said they loved my zines, all ended up dating Greg, one by one, despite my loud warnings. Words, no matter how true, no matter how loud and angry, weren't a real weapon against a dangerous creature like him. That's probably why he'd dared me to go ahead and use them.

(I thought I had a voice, a strong one. I thought people were listening. Why weren't they listening?)

It all came to a head on a warm night in one of The Little Boys' basements. Acetone was there, too, and everyone was swapping instruments and coming up with new incarnations of bands. Then Greg showed up. Someone, I don't remember who, invited him onstage, encouraged an Acetone reunion.

People who knew What He Did were clapping. *For him.*

(*I thought they were listening. Why aren't they listening?*)

The members of Acetone who had hated him even before What He Did just let him take his place behind the drums.

I ran from the basement, sick to my stomach.

(If Greg's drumming skills outweighed everything in my zines, why had I even written them?)

Outside, one of The Little Girls was crying. Over Greg. Because he was ignoring her and she was in love with him. I'd been there. I got it. I wanted to help her. Helping her would distract me. So we got into my car, and I drove while she talked. I stopped the car when she explained how she and a friend had slept in the same bed as Greg, and the next morning, her friend told her that she'd woken up with Greg's hands all over her.

"She said she didn't want him. She was crying these crocodile tears, but she's just trying to ruin what I have with Greg. She's such a slut."

The urge to puke got even stronger. "Is that what you think or what Greg said?"

She shook her head like it didn't matter, rambling about how her friend was a compulsive liar and liked to play the victim.

Finally, I managed to say, "*Greg* is a compulsive liar. *Greg* abused me. I've told you these things. You've read my zines. Why do you believe him over her? Over me?"

I don't remember her excuses. I don't remember if she told me that Greg said I was crazy before or after I told her to get out of the car because I wanted to drive it into a brick wall as fast as possible.

I didn't do that. Instead, I went to Ridgeland Commons, needing to be in the place where the worst of it had happened—or maybe where I made it up? I didn't know.

Greg was making me crazy. Oak Park was making me crazy.

(And crazy girls' words don't matter.)

Eventually, the crazy got so bad that I wanted to numb it, and thanks to Brandon, I knew how to do that.

Earlier that year, during the spring, I'd found him stumbling around a party like a zombie. I'd heard that people were doing heroin—that *he* was doing heroin—but I hadn't wanted to believe it. There was no denying how fucked up he was that night, though, and Brandon had never been one to lie.

He came into consciousness just long enough to catch me up on his life. Yeah, he was using. Yeah, he would try anything at least once to see if it was good. And H was pretty damn good. He thought I would like it. Did I want to try it?

I declined. That night I was okay. I was with friends, having a good time, not thinking about Greg too much. But I paid close attention to everything that Brandon shared about heroin:

Who was doing it. ("Not Greg." He laughed. "I know," I said with a sneer. "Sorry, that's not . . ." He didn't finish his sentence, maybe because he'd briefly nodded off, but there was also a look that passed between us. He Knew. He'd heard or sensed it. I wanted to tell him something like, *Yeah, I would have been better off sticking around and being "used" by you*, but that wasn't really true either. Then he continued, "Everyone. Okay, not everyone, but a lot of people at Scoville. More people than you'd think.")

How they were doing it. (Snorting it and smoking it mainly. Brandon hadn't shot it. He gave an exaggerated shudder—a gesture that seemed bigger and more energetic than he should have been capable of. But some people, the people who were more into it, they shot it.)

Where to get it. (At Scoville. Easy. Well, most of the time. Sometimes you have to go into the city. Drive up Division into Austin. It's really easy there. Even for dumbass white kids. *Especially* for dumbass white kids. But yeah. You could get it at Scoville from certain dealers.)

I tucked that information away in my brain. Told myself I'd never use it, but knew somehow that I would. That one night it would all feel like too much and I'd go to Scoville looking for Brandon. Usually, when I wanted to see him, he magically appeared, but maybe I was too damaged to tap into that magic. Or maybe I needed it to happen anonymously like it did.

Afterward, I lied to my friends about it. Not an *I didn't do it* lie. I was honest about that, but I made up a prettier story. One that was more romantic than me walking up to a guy I sort of recognized and saying that I knew Brandon and Brandon said . . . then getting high with this virtual stranger in the bathroom of Scoville Park.

(Fitting. Dirty park bathrooms are where I belong. At least Scoville's bathroom is cleaner than Ridgeland Commons'. And getting fucked up is better than getting fucked.)

There was one thing I told my friends about the experience that was true, though: I loved it. I'd never felt so numb. This was what I'd been searching for since I'd scratched my arm on that nail at stage crew in seventh grade—pure and absolute relief. The next morning when I awoke, sober, my body and my mind aching because I could feel too much, I wanted more than anything to do it again, and that terrified me.

*This will kill me,* I thought. *This will take me on a ride that I can't get off.* So I stopped doing drugs, stopped drinking, stopped smoking. All of it.

It sounds more dramatic than it was. Up until that point the only drug I'd done was pot, which like alcohol I only partook in casually. Cigarettes were the hardest thing to quit. I wavered on that a few times, but I drew on that same willpower that had gotten me straight As since freshman year. I was very good at depriving myself of things—be it sleep or nicotine—to prove something to myself, *especially* when what I was proving related to getting out of Oak Park.

Of course, this self-control just meant everything spilled out in other ways.

I couldn't stop freaking out. Breaking down. Killing the mood on happy summer nights. Making everyone uncomfortable with my crazy/angry/sad and the ugly reasons behind it.

No one ever knew what to do but Caci. She could always tell when to listen, when to hug, when not to touch, when to leave the fuck alone, and when to follow me into the plastic tunnel on the playground where I was communing with an unmoving firefly.

Acacia crawled in beside me. We were both short, so we fit. It was snug, but snug was good. Snug was safe. Especially with Caci.

"I've been watching it, waiting for it to light up and fly off, but it won't. I don't think it can," I told her.

*Translation: I've been working so hard, but the pain and the anger won't stop. I'm pretty sure I'm never going to get through this.*

"I think it's just resting."

*Translation: You will work through this. I'm here. Take your time.*

"No, I should probably just crush it."

*Translation: I want to die.*

"I think if we just sit with it, it will be okay."

*Translation: Please. Ride this moment out. I'm here.*

We hunched awkwardly over the firefly.

"And you will never know how it feels to light up the sky," I whisper-sang the Heavens to Betsy song, "Firefly," to the firefly. I couldn't sing, but it was okay since it was just me and Acacia and a bug I thought was dead.

"It's definitely dead."

"It's not." Acacia nudged a finger under it. "See, it's moving."

"No, you're moving it."

But then it flashed. She lifted it triumphantly. Then she pressed her finger to mine, transferring the firefly to me. It crawled around, and I shifted my hand so it wouldn't fall. Sitting in my palm, it lit up again.

Its tiny feet tickled my palm, and it flashed once more and flew off.

"See. It was fine. It was just resting," Caci said.

*Translation: You will be fine. I will be here. I will pick you up. I will let you go even if it means you leaving me behind. Years later, I will tell you to get a firefly tattooed along the inside of your scarred arm. We will also get matching tattoos: a pair of big, black boots intertwined by lyrics from the Rancid album we listened to whenever we wanted to run away: "To the end, to the end, I'll journey to the end."*

I started crying.

*Translation: I'm sorry. I still have a long way to go.*

# Are You There, Dad? It's Me, Stephanie

dear daddy, I miss you.

pain eats away at my heart, my words and this
is the one thing i keep running from, running
from and i run like a child because i never
grew up in our relationship you weren't there
to let me, but you talk to me like i am on yr
level and i'm not and i never will be, i can't
live in yr reality, stiff upper lip and handle
this with a business like accord, with your
voice at a normal speaking inside level, don't
let that feeling infiltrate no no no, be a
good girl, quiet girl we can talk this out,
fine then i have nothing to say to you, calm,
cool amd collected has nothing to do with my feelings and anything other than what you call
acting out. i don't think my outburst fits into
yr schedule anyway, i can't always keep my
rants down to 30 minutes so take a long lunch

Excerpt from a piece in *do not go quietly unto yr grave*

Dear Daddy,

The first thing, the last thing, and the worst thing that Oak Park took from me was you.

You've been letting me down since the day we moved. Do you remember that?

We stopped for lunch and when we got back to the minivan, we didn't see our little gray tabby sunbathing on top of the TV in the back where we'd left her. After a cursory appraisal of the situation, you said, "We'll just get a new cat. Snuggle wasn't very nice anyway."

I was seven. Dan was five. Our screams could have set off car alarms. Both of us were adamant: we would not go anywhere without Snuggle. It was true that she hadn't been as cuddly as we expected when we named her for the Snuggle fabric softener bear, but we still adored her.

Fortunately, Mom, the only one who Snuggle was snuggly with, was not going to give up her beloved cat for lost and listen to her children cry about it the rest of the way to our new home. Convinced that Snuggle had been scared by people in the parking lot and hidden somewhere in the jam-packed van, she pulled things out until she could see underneath the backseat. Sure enough, there was a pair of glowing green eyes.

We arrived in Oak Park with our family intact, but it wasn't long before you started to fade away.

First it was your Sunday meetings, your discussion groups about workers' rights and Marxist theory. I had no clue what that meant—all I knew was that whenever you left, Peachy, our newly adopted, poorly behaved collie mix, seemed to sense the lack of authority and broke out of the yard. Mom, Dan, and I would spend the day chasing him around the neighborhood. We always caught him, but not without a lot of tears and the occasional sprained ankle. I was freaked out and hurting and you weren't there—the beginning of what would become a familiar refrain in my life. To make matters worse, you didn't give up the meetings, we gave up Peachy.

Then the meetings I didn't understand were replaced with ones I did—work I knew was so important. "My dad cofounded an organization to help people living with AIDS," I would tell everyone. I was so proud of that. Proud of you. Even if it meant you missed seeing me do front walkovers on the balance beam or showing up late (which you know I hate because it makes me anxious as hell) to see me in the school play. I tried to stay close to you by reading your books, listening to your music, watching Bulls games. And do you remember when you worked right next to my junior high? I'd drag Juliet or Robin by to visit. We'd always giggle at the dishes of condoms that were there for the taking, wrapped up like chocolate coins, and occasionally, because we were kleptos, we swiped them.

I can't remember when your business moved, whether it was before or after I finished eighth grade, but either way, once we were no longer school/

work neighbors, our relationship completely disintegrated. Maybe it wasn't just that. Maybe it was because I stopped listening to your music and you never even tried to listen to mine—it gave you a headache; you couldn't tell Nirvana from Pearl Jam. Maybe it was because of the dark cloud that had descended on me; maybe I scared you, reminded you of your father.

Either way, by the time I started high school, you were nothing but a ghost in our house, and the only place you haunted was your home office.

Are you there, Dad? It's me, Stephanie?

I hear you typing. It's after midnight. We're the only ones awake. It's been like this for years, you know . . .

No, you probably don't.

You haven't poked your head in to see if I'm awake in a long, long time.

Almost as long ago as popcorn for dinner on the weekends when Mom worked. When was that? Third? Fourth grade?

You'd bring out the old, blackened iron pot. You taught me the amount of oil and kernels to add and how to run the pot back and forth over the flame. We both loved our popcorn extra salty.

I mean, we still do. It's not like we're dead. Even if it feels like our relationship is—killed by your work and all the new things I want to do that you don't even ask about before declaring, "Absolutely Not." Even if I wish I were . . . Yeah. Dead. Yeah, I just told you that. No, never mind. It's a good thing you can't hear my thoughts over your typing.

Anyway, you made popcorn for Greg and me once, do you remember that? When we all watched the basketball game? I'd long since stopped pretending to care about basketball just to spend time with you, but that night, the two of you in the living room, bonding by yelling at the TV, I told myself it was perfect. I told myself I had everything. I told myself I was so happy.

Lies.

I told myself so many lies.

Could you see me lying with every smile?

Probably not. You barely see me at all.

*The soundtrack to my sleepless nights is still the combination of Tori Amos's* Little Earthquakes *and you typing away just two doors down the hall from me.*

*Just two doors. Less than ten footsteps. And yet . . . a world between us.*

*A long, long winter between us.*

*"Winter," the fifth track on* Little Earthquakes, *is our song. Yours and mine. Even though you don't know it. As soon as Tori starts singing about her little girl hands in her father's warm gloves, my thoughts always turn to you. I picture your beard and thinning brown hair, both neatly trimmed instead of wavy and wild like when I was little; your hazel eyes, tinged with blue, lighter than mine; and your wire-rimmed glasses, reflecting the words on the computer screen that absorb all of your attention.*

*But we don't have the fairy-tale relationship that Tori sings about, full of that gentle fatherly acknowledgment that things are going to change, that I should learn to stand up and love myself like you love me. (Do you love me? Isn't that the whole problem, that I'm loving myself like I think you love me, i.e., Not Enough? And now I'll do anything to feel the love I wanted. Anything. No matter how much it hurts.) Our winter isn't one of frolicking in the snow, warming by the fire, and looking toward spring and new growth. Our winter is subzero windchills, blinding snowstorms, and patches of black ice that make navigating the road between us impossible.*

*The only respite from the cold comes when you take me to your new downtown Chicago office to photocopy my zines. I relish those quiet Sunday mornings. Our Sundays. Years ago, you disappeared to do your activist work, and now you're bringing me along. We're both doing slightly different things, but we're doing them side by side.*

*Then one day you take me out to coffee and we almost have an incredible conversation—you tell me about getting arrested as a teenager for picketing in support of migrant workers, and I tell you that the new zine I'm working on is about Greg . . . who abused me. I open up to you like I never have before. I want you to get angry. I want you as outraged and protective as Mom, who* visibly shook and wished Greg dead when I told her. I want you to take a little time away from saving the world to save me.

Maybe you are upset, but I can't see it—you always keep your emotions on a tight leash. And the only thing that you say that sticks with me is: "You can't print his name. He could sue you."

I won't ask for your help with copying that zine.

When I want to get a tattoo on my seventeenth birthday, you are actually cooler about the idea than Mom. You take me in to sign the forms and confirm that the shop has all of its licenses in order and will be using a new, disposable needle on my skin.

I get a ring of female signs that goes halfway around my right bicep. I want a full armband, but the tattoo artist refuses, saying the underside is too sensitive. "I seen marines cry," he tells me. "I ain't going to try it on no seventeen-year-old girl."

I don't argue with him, even though nothing about the tattoo process hurts as much as you leaving as soon as you give your permission. You have a meeting. Even though it's Saturday. Even though it's my birthday. Even though I don't want to be alone, no matter how tough I act.

"I'm so sorry, honey. I would have gone if I'd known," Mom says when I tell her what happened. "I thought he was going to stay."

So did I.

You were always leaving. Always had one foot out of the door, so it shouldn't have come as a surprise when you announced that you were moving out.

The zine photocopying, the coffee date, probably even the permission to get a tattoo, were just a ploy to soften the blow, or keep me from reacting the way I do, which is to blame you. Mom is not prepared for this; I can tell from her shell-shocked expression. I later learn that you guys went to a few counseling sessions, but you apparently had your mind made up. I'm furious.

*You tried about as hard to save our family as you did to look for Snuggle all those years ago. We have never been worth your time.*

You pack up and leave while Mom's at work and Dan and I are at school. For weeks we keep discovering things you took and things you left behind. Hot angry tears spill down my face when I find the popcorn pot missing, but I laugh when Mom notices that Snuggle peed all over the Marxist books you left in the basement.

You move into an apartment building right next to Scoville Park. You park your car in the same spots that I do when I go there after school. Of course, your car is never there when I am. You're still at work. Or traveling. Or something. I wonder if you ever look over your shoulder at the statue where my friends skateboard. I wonder if you look for me. I wonder if you even fucking know that I hang out there.

Those questions burn as I pace around your apartment the one time I go over. I have to print out my college essay. You took the printer and the new computer, leaving us the shitty one that is forever crashing and corrupting my files. "I'm trying to graduate fucking high school!" I screamed at you repeatedly over the phone.

"Just come over," you said, and I ranted about how I was stretched too thin already. Between school and babysitting and my grocery store job and homework and therapy, I didn't have an extra hour—especially one that would fit conveniently around your schedule. (Like father, like daughter.) I hoped you would acquiesce and bring the printer to me, but you needed it for Your Business, which is more important than my senior year, so I had to go to you.

I let you struggle with my files, all of the technical difficulties I've been facing without you, and go into your kitchen, squinting through the window, through the trees at Scoville.

Do you know what I've done there? *I want to ask.* Do you know what some of my friends are doing over there now? Heroin. And I did it once, too. But don't worry, I don't even smoke now. It was hard to quit smoking both pot and cigarettes because I'm so stressed, so angry and sad, over Greg. Over you . . .

*"Are you sure that you aren't going to apply to Sarah Lawrence?" you ask, sounding like my fucking high school adviser. "Or maybe to Mills? I'm sure you can get into any of them. Why not apply to all of them and see what kind of scholarships you get?"*

Is that what it will take to impress you? No, I can't. I fucking won't. Because I know this game. I bend over backward. I break myself down. And you don't bat an eye. Besides, the college I chose—that I'm applying early decision to—was supposed to impress you. Maybe it would have if you'd gone to visit it with Mom and me last spring, but even though you keep pushing me toward these East Coast and West Coast schools, you didn't have two days to check out the one in Ohio. To see the graffiti-covered dance space where one of my favorite bands first formed and played in the eighties. To hear about how it's the most radical of all the radical schools, where the students overthrew the administration in the sixties and created community government. Isn't that like the utopia you and your friends talked about building at your Sunday mystery meetings? It's *my* utopia, Dad—or rather, my "boot camp for the revolution," like it says on the T-shirt I bought when I visited, when *I* decided that this school is my destiny. And even though Elizabeth found it for me, *not you,* and Mom visited, *not you,* I chose it because of you, *for you.*

*"Mills and Sarah Lawrence both have great creative writing programs," you needle.*

Right. Because your secret dream was to be a writer. You told me, and I've seen the password-protected files on the computer. The poetry you won't share with me. Why should I share mine? Why should I live out your dream for you?

*Even though I want to shrug or shake my head, I have to remind you, "I'm going to be a social worker. I want to work at a domestic violence agency and make a difference."*

Like you.

BUT I WON"T BE LIKE YOU DADDY cause
politics start at home daddy, politics start
inside you, politics are personal daddy,
politics are people and feelings, are you
blind to that now? politics are me and my
brother and my mama who you abandoned in
october whether you want to see it that way
or not. politics come from the heart and you
run from yrs

"*Your writing can make a difference, too.*"

I want it to. More than anything, but so far it hasn't. Not to you. Not to Greg. And when Mia and I went to that Riot Grrrl convention out East in August, we saw all the problems I'd heard about. White middle-class girls leading workshops on race and class. Working-class girls and girls of color silenced. This movement that gave me my voice is stifling others. And I don't know what to do. What to say or write. I feel betrayed and disappointed by everything—by punk rock, by Riot Grrrl, by you. So Mia, Acacia, and I have started listening to Nick Cave, Joy Division, and the Cure instead of our punk favorites. We dress in black and bloodred velvet. I smear my eyes in kohl and put on black lipstick. Have you noticed? You must have noticed, but you haven't said a word.

"*My writing is for me,*" *I tell you, ending the discussion without showing a sliver of emotion. (Like father, like daughter.) Without telling you about Scoville or heroin. About the utopia I want but fear will fail me just like punk, like Riot Grrrl, like you. About the words that I write to keep myself going, to stay alive, and how terrified I am that they will fail me, too.*

*I know I won't get the reaction I want from you. Just like I didn't when I told you about Greg. Or that time we went to the office supply store and I had a sobbing-on-my-knees meltdown in the pen aisle.*

"*Stand up,*" *you hissed. "You're acting like a child. You're making a scene.*"

"*I am* a child!" *I screeched. "And I know I'm making a scene. React! Fucking react!*"

*You shook your head and walked out the door. Stoic. Always so fucking* stoic. Even when you showed me around your apartment, pointed to the second bedroom, and said it was for me or Dan to stay whenever we wanted, and I laughed in your face.

It doesn't matter if I'm sad or angry, agonizing or antagonizing, you don't cry, you don't yell, and your face—beard and mustache shaved, which I tell you spitefully makes you look old—doesn't betray any signs that you're straining not to.

But then, after the papers are printed, when I'm on my way to the door and I notice the pictures—the old ones of my brother and me—scattered around the apartment.

"You stole these," I accuse. "When you were moving out. You didn't take your stupid communist books, but you went through our photo albums and stole *these!*"

"I . . . I just wanted them," you sputter. And your cheeks are a little red and maybe, maybe . . .

I wait for tears to spill, but they don't. So I shake my head. Aside from my senior picture, which won't look like me anymore after I dye my hair black in a couple of weeks, none of the photos show me over the age of eleven. "It doesn't matter. Those aren't really me anyway," I tell you. And then I leave.

The cold air outside feels warmer than your apartment, than our endless winter.

# The Final Frontier

"I don't know how to tell you this, so I'm just going to tell you," Acacia said somberly. She turned her head away and blew cigarette smoke into the crisp fall air.

"What?" It was moments like these that I wished I still smoked. I leaned forward, trying to inhale the scent of her cigarette. I was a senior, but graduation couldn't seem to come fast enough. It seemed like bad shit kept happening. Some kids from Scoville had gotten caught breaking into a vet's office to steal ketamine. More and more people were doing heroin. There'd been drug overdoses. No one I'd known well yet, but that's what I was bracing for. Someone we loved was arrested or hospitalized or maybe even dead.

"Juliet's pregnant."

I felt my jaw drop.

"That's just what I heard," Caci added quickly, probably because I'd gone ashen or red or green.

It might not be true, she reassured me. In fact it probably wasn't if Juliet hadn't told me herself.

I knew it was, though. I felt it.

Sure enough, before I could decide if I should reach out to Juliet, I got a rambling phone call from her that began, "I know you probably already heard even though we were trying to fucking keep it to ourselves for a little while and I wanted to be the one to tell you. I was going to tell you before I told other people and I should have because you actually know how to keep a fucking secret, but now that all of fucking Oak Park knows . . ."

She took a deep breath and so did I.

"I'm pregnant, Stephie-Lou."

She went on to say that she was going to keep the baby and marry her boyfriend, even though the last time we'd talked she'd told me that she wanted to break up with him.

"Are you sure this is what you want?" I asked her.

"My mom kept me" was her nonanswer.

Before we got off the phone, she pleaded, "Can you tell your mom? I was going to come over and tell both of you, but I can't face her."

"She's not going to judge you, Jules."

"I know, but I can't." Her voice was small. Like a child's. Because even though she'd been living on her own for over a year, even though she was having a baby, she still was a child.

So I told my mom. I was actually glad Juliet asked me to because I needed to tell her. She was the only one who would ache like I did for the bright fifth grader who had waltzed into our house eager to work on science experiments. Who thought it was so cool that my parents were nurses because she wanted to be a nurse or a doctor or some kind of scientist someday.

"This was one of my worst fears," my mom said. I could tell by the way her jaw moved that she was fighting tears. "After her grandmother died, there was no one there for that girl. She was a throwaway kid. Everyone let her down." She swallowed, adding softly, "Including me," and then excused herself from the room.

A few months later, outside of the strip mall bookstore where she worked, my round-bellied childhood best friend asked me to be one of her bridesmaids. "I know it's kind of last minute, and you're probably really busy, so . . ."

"Yeah, I am really busy. You know, finals and papers and packing . . ."

"You're really getting out of here, huh? Graduating early. Getting the fuck out of Oak Park for real. You go, girl."

"Yeah. I'm almost out."

We spoke like I was getting paroled. That's kind of how it felt. Oak Park was a prison that my friends and I had been talking about busting out of forever. Sophomore year, Brandon and I plotted to go to the middle of nowhere Colorado to write; then Greg and I planned to run away to Minneapolis because he heard it had a good music scene and there were colleges I was interested in nearby. I fantasized with My Girls and The Little Boys about finding a house in Minneapolis (still my dream) or San Francisco (Elizabeth's, which I was happy to adopt) and living like a big, artsy, teenage runaway family. Acacia and I had *almost* walked away from her boarding school in Iowa and we'd never stopped talking about doing it for real—walking to Minneapolis, to Canada, wherever. The destination didn't matter, we just wanted to disappear.

But something was holding me back:

School.

Even when I was ditching class and getting stoned at lunch, I still did all of my homework, and counter to what I told people when I was trying to play cool, I wasn't just maintaining those straight As because they would distract my parents from the unusually high number of absences on my report card. I'd wanted to go to college for as long as I could remember, and I couldn't let go of that. Not even to escape Oak Park.

Then a surprising solution presented itself. I had gym class with my old smoking buddy, Jo, during junior year. We sat out a lot, claiming to be sick. (Gym was the only class I regularly got Cs and Ds in because it didn't affect your GPA.) One day, she mentioned that she was graduating in June, a whole year early. I asked how she'd swung it, and she revealed one of the universe's best-kept secrets:

"Practically everyone graduates high school with way more credits than they need."

Unfortunately, since I hadn't learned this as early as Jo had, I couldn't graduate with her, but my adviser begrudgingly confirmed that I could cut my senior year in half. He tried to talk me out of it, saying I wouldn't be able to get any AP credit, but I didn't care. I just wanted out ASAP with my high school diploma.

"You're so fucking lucky," Juliet said, rubbing her belly. Then she cleared her throat and spit on the ground. "No," she corrected herself. "You're smart. That's what you are. You've always been the smart one."

"You are just as smart as me," I insisted, my hazel eyes drilling into hers.

She rolled her eyes and shook her head. "I am gonna graduate, too, though. Early even. Just not from OPRF." She was finishing high school through some sort of alternative program. She'd told me this before, had wanted me to be sure to pass it along to my mom. "Ain't getting out of here, though."

"Someday," I said.

Juliet shrugged. "Anyhoo. So you're probably too busy for the wedding, right? It's gonna be at a church anyway, and I know that's not really our thing." She laughed her throaty laugh, which had gotten even throatier from smoking. The habit we'd both picked up even though we knew it had killed her grandmother and that death had changed our friendship forever. The habit she still couldn't completely quit even though I told her that my mom would freak if she saw her pregnant with a cigarette in her hand.

"Yeah, churches . . ." I muttered. Like churches and finals were a valid excuse for not being there on her wedding day.

She looked away, flicked her cigarette butt into the parking lot. "You don't want to see me anyway. Hell, I don't want to see me." Her voice cracked, but she laughed again to cover it. "I'm gonna be so fucking fat."

I stared at the profile of her face, the same profile that had always been there on the couch beside me, playing Nintendo, watching TV. "You're going to be beautiful," I told her.

She blinked a couple times before turning to meet my eyes. "Thanks, Stephie-Lou. I love you."

"Love you, too, Jules."

We hugged and she repeated the date and time just in case I could make it. She said she would call to remind me, but she didn't. I remembered, but I didn't go. Even though I knew I was letting her down like so many other people had, and there was no excuse, not even my real one: that this wasn't what I wanted for her and maybe if I didn't go, I could pretend it wasn't happening. I could hold on to the Julie-Lou and Stephie-Lou, who'd been Weirdos and signed notes *Love You Like a Sister* and had the whole world in front of them.

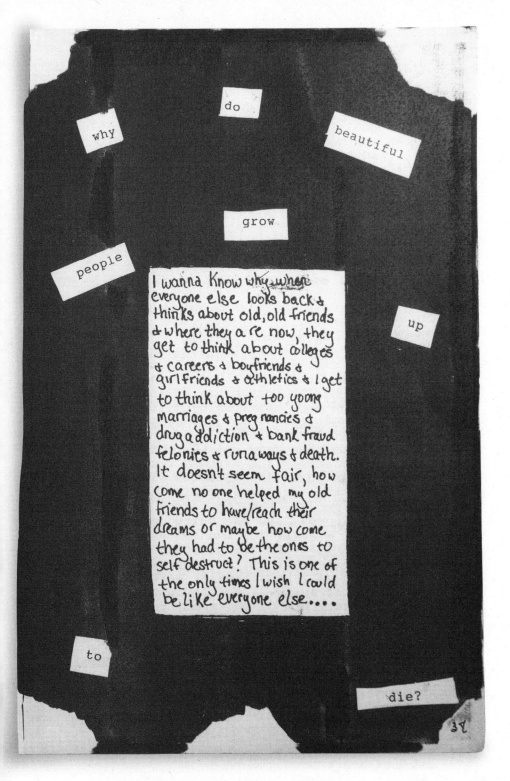

why do beautiful

grow

people

up

I wanna know why, where everyone else looks back & thinks about old, old friends & where they are now, they get to think about colleges & careers & boyfriends & girlfriends & athletics & I get to think about too young marriages & pregnancies & drug addiction & bank fraud felonies & runaways & death. It doesn't seem fair, how come no one helped my old friends to have/reach their dreams or maybe how come they had to be the ones to self destruct? This is one of the only times I wish I could be like everyone else....

to

die?

Piece from *do not go quietly unto yr grave*

# Journey to the End

The bottom shelf of the bookcase in our dining room held all of the
family photo albums, along with a "memory book" my mother made of pictures of
St. Louis before we moved away. My brother liked to look at that a lot. I suppose
that was his way of escaping from Oak Park; no one was surprised when he chose
to return to St. Louis for college. I was drawn to a different book, though, stuffed
with random papers, newspaper clippings, photos, little-kid art. It had a white
cover embossed with gold lettering that read: OUR BABY'S FIRST SEVEN YEARS. Dan
had one, too, but his was not as diligently filled out, since he was the second child.

That white book was like my first diary—the one my parents, mostly my
mom, had kept for me since I couldn't yet. Taped onto one page was an exten-
sive list of words, more than fifty of them written in both of my parents' handwriting. *Book* appeared at the top and was actually listed more than once. My
mom wrote beside this impressive list, *@15mos.*

According to this book, I talked early and a lot. I also walked early, read
early, and of course one of my mom's favorite stories to tell about me was that
I'd potty-trained early, of my own volition, because I wanted to go to preschool
that badly. I was always looking ahead, toward the horizon, toward what and
who I'd be next. One note from when I was five states: *Admires older children a
lot.* Then, at age six: *Very independent. Wants to do all things for herself and behave
in a grown-up manner.*

This is why it didn't come as a surprise to my mother at all when I announced that I wanted to graduate high school and leave Oak Park before I turned eighteen. She'd braced herself for this, the destiny I'd been gunning for for as long as either of us could remember, the prophecy foretold in her handwriting by that white book.

"Ever since you were a little girl, all you wanted to be was grown-up," she said with a sigh.

For once, my dad didn't try to fight what I wanted either. It turned out that he knew the secret that Jo told me. His high school administration had encouraged him to graduate early after he'd spent the first half of his senior year wearing black armbands and organizing antiwar protests. Since he'd hated high school (like father, like daughter), he'd jumped at the offer and went on the road with an activist youth group that spring. I just wanted to move out of Illinois, and my parents said I could as long as I came up with a reasonable plan and the money to execute it.

Caci helped me brainstorm my escape over numerous phone calls and cups of diner coffee, but we had to face one hard truth right away:

She couldn't come with me.

Even though walking away was *our* thing, even though it was supposed to be the two of us *always always always*, when I graduated, she would only be sixteen. She probably could have talked her parents into it—hell, she probably could have gotten a judge to emancipate her—but like I could never drop out of high school just to escape Oak Park, she could never abandon her parents just to escape her brother.

I respected that, and she told me to go anyway. That's how our friendship had always been: a mutual understanding, ensuring that the other person did what was best for them even if it hurt like hell.

"You have to get out. For both of us," Acacia reminded me practically every night from her side of the cracked vinyl booth at Ambrosia Café, the twenty-four-hour diner we always headed to after everyone else went home.

Punk Rock Denny's, Melrose Park Denny's, Bakers Square, Jedi's

Garden—we shared those places with the rest of our friends. But Ambrosia (or Ambrosia's, as we called it because every other diner's name took the possessive form), with its elderly waitresses who took our orders with cigarettes dangling from their lips and the guy who always stood by the kitchen door with his thick arms crossed, feeding our theory that the near-empty restaurant was a mob front, it was Acacia's and mine.

"I know," I said, picking at my lemon meringue pie before I repeated for the thousandth time, "I wish you could go with me."

"I know."

She never said, *I wish I could, too.* I'm not sure why. Maybe because she knew it would start a loop, we'd just go back and forth wishing for something that couldn't happen until someone, probably me, cried, and she didn't want that. Or maybe because she *didn't* wish she could go; she knew this was my path, not hers.

"Why don't you just ask me to go with you?" Mia said one night.

I was crying to her about how hard I was working to get out—I'd taken a job bagging groceries on top of babysitting and arranged my senior semester schedule so I could get out at noon to work and I was saving all my money to move away because it would kill me if I had to stay—but while my parents were fine with me graduating early, I wasn't allowed to move out unless I found a roommate.

I couldn't believe I hadn't thought of asking her. It made perfect sense on every level.

Practically speaking, Mia was turning eighteen in the fall and finishing up a homeschooling program around the same time I was graduating, plus she had a bunch of money saved from working at a health food store.

And emotionally speaking, well, as a fellow abuse survivor, she understood me better than anyone. She'd accompanied me to Greg's house three times as I attempted to retrieve my poetry notebook from him. On our last visit, when he told me to "check the landfill," Mia squeezed my hand tight and only let go of me when we got back to the car, so I could punch the steering wheel and she could turn up the part in the Heavens to Betsy song about the knife that was sharpened for the heart of a particular white boy.

Our friendship had also quite literally kept me from starving. I was still having trouble eating a year After Greg. The idea of food sickened me; I felt disconnected from my own body, used and dehumanized, like I didn't deserve nourishment. When I shared this with Mia, she understood immediately, explaining that she'd gone vegan because she empathized with the cows on factory farms. It helped her to eat in a way that felt respectful of all life. She was teaching me to cook and helping me go vegan—something that would be even easier if we lived together.

I laughed and asked, "Do you want to go with me?"

"God, yes," she said. "Where are we going?"

The original plan was Minneapolis just because I'd been fixated on it for so long, but I'd never been there, and neither had she. We drove up there one weekend—it took seven and a half long hours—and even though it was summer, the city was cold and gray. I couldn't imagine what it would be like in February, when we planned to move, and I confessed, while we were sitting in the hot tub at our hotel, much as I hated it, I was scared of being that far from home. I fought tears, so close to admitting defeat, but Mia convinced me that we should stop in Wisconsin on the way back. She'd been to a city there that she thought might be the right place for us.

It was sunny when we arrived, and I felt a lot more comfortable only two hours from Chicago. We walked around, stopped into a feminist bookstore, and had lunch at a restaurant serving dal soup.

"This is the best soup I've ever had," Mia marveled.

"I know!" I agreed as I sucked down the last spoonful of smooth, perfectly seasoned lentils.

It tasted cozy, we decided. Like home. And with that, we had our plan. We would live in the city with that soup and let it nourish us, rebuild our strength, make us ready for college and the future.

"where are you going my little girl, my pretty little girl?" he chants softly, a smile revealing the red of my bloodstains on his teeth his eyes beckon, trying to instill fear in mine where there was once hope, but not this time....

"i am going to a place where my blood is not yr wine and my body isn't yr meat. i am going where i will not be scared into fucking you, where i will not live in fear of you or any thing; where my teardrops will not form icicles because of the necessary numbness i must summon to suurvive; where i can dance to my soul's delight, where my heart will learn to dream again, where if tears fall they will not become weaknesses to be sprung upon and violated, whre i can learn learn learn and not be forcefed yr teachings and lies about why iam crazy and worthless; where i will find solace after waking up from nightmares instead of a continuation of my fears; where i will be able to scream about pain you've caused without fearing yr threats or yr dick shoved into my mouth. i am going where i will never have to be silent again; i am going where i will learn to trust and dream again; i am going where i can feel safe, iam going to live; i am going to be free!"

and the strength in my eyes shatters him, glass on the concrete i sweep him into the trash, allthe power he had nothing but tiny see thru pieces never to touch me again.
*WE ARE STRONGER THAN YOU EVER WERE*

★ FREEDOM ★
to live our dreams

this is for my awesome roommate and sid our kitty, a dedication to our little vegan girl power (sorry sid) haven away from the abusive hell of our past.
here's to starting over and living yr dreams.

Piece from *do not go quietly unto yr grave*

I fell twice during my last month in Oak Park. First on New Year's Eve when I was running around with my friends. Totally sober, I slipped on a patch of ice and sprained my ankle.

It was almost healed, and then a couple days before the big move, I went with my mom to close the bank account she'd helped me open when I'd started saving my babysitting money in sixth grade.

Once again I wiped out on the ice, re-injuring my bad ankle. My mom helped me up and to the car, talking about ice packs and elevation and ibuprofen while I fought a losing battle against my angry tears. Why today of all days? Why did I fall when I walked out of that bank with the two grand I'd worked so hard to save—my ticket to adulthood? What did that mean? Was it foreshadowing that I was going to fall on my ass?

Then, when I insisted on driving—because it was only a few blocks and I'd hurt my left foot, not my right—Mom said she wasn't sure I should.

"I have to drive two whole hours on Friday, and I have to move all my stuff. Heavy stuff." My voice arced toward hysteria. The tears had won, and I was so afraid, so suddenly and completely afraid of everything.

"I know. I'm a little worried about that," she admitted.

My hands clenched into fists. "You don't want me to go. *YOU* don't think I can do this and you don't want me to go. You never have! You want to keep me here!"

"Honey, I meant your foot—"

"You don't want me to leave! But I'll die if I stay here. I'll *DIE*."

"Honey, honey!"

She hugged me and I tried to push her away. Then I yelped that my ankle hurt and she hugged me again and I let her. She told me softly the same thing she had since I was a little girl: That she wanted what I wanted. That she believed in me. That I could do this. That I would be okay.

It was what one half of me wanted to hear. The other half wanted what she was probably stopping herself from saying: *Please stay with me. It won't kill you. Not if you become my little girl again and stay that way forever.*

Eventually, I let her help me into the car. I let her drive. I took the ibuprofen.

I sat on the couch with my foot iced and elevated for twenty minutes. Then I returned to packing.

The day of the move, Caci rode in my car along with Sid (who was in the back in a cat carrier because we'd learned that lesson). Mia drove her car, and my mom followed us in a U-Haul that contained our meager amount of furniture and much larger book and music collections. We unloaded all of that stuff in the snowy parking lot of our new apartment building and carried it up to our one-bedroom on the second floor. I was slow and somewhat unhelpful, but did not fall again, and we managed even the big furniture on our own.

"Now that's girl power!" my mom declared when we finished, and even though it was cheesy, we all smiled. It was true. I looked at them, the woman and two girls who'd always listened, who'd lent me their strength even when I felt crippled. Everyone and everything else had failed me, but they hadn't let *me* fail. I was here. I was out.

The only problem was that now I had to say goodbye to two of them.

My mom saw my face faltering and remembered, "Your phone. You know where you packed it, right?"

I did. Per her advice, I'd put it in the box that contained everything I would need for my first night, so I wouldn't have to paw, exhausted, through all the stuff I'd just hauled. She found it, got the phone out, and plugged it into the wall.

"There. When I get home, I'll call and . . . oh." She frowned after putting the receiver to her ear. "No dial tone."

We tried the two other phone jacks and it yielded the same result. I'd called the phone company to activate our service, but apparently it hadn't worked.

"We'll get it fixed tomorrow," Mia assured me. "We can call from a pay phone or go to the phone company or something—"

"I can call," my mom volunteered. "And I really should get you a cell phone—"

"No, we can handle it," I said, swallowing hard and pressing my tongue to the roof of my mouth. *Stiff upper lip.*

My mom must have been able to tell what I was doing, because when she hugged me, she asked, "Do you want my handkerchief?"

She laughed lightly at the reference to my tearful preschool days, but I told her, "No," almost angrily. I resisted asking if she wanted me to fail and triggering another argument like we'd had at the bank—or more accurately, like I'd had with myself. Instead, I said I would be okay and that I loved her. I knew the last part was true at least.

I managed to wait until she and Caci left to burst into tears just like I had on my first day of preschool . . . and kindergarten . . . and first grade, where on a paper tucked into that white baby book, I'd written about feeling "ex[c]ited and sad." I hated that about myself—that I could never just be brave like I thought truly independent people should be.

"I'm just tired," I told Mia.

She knew I was lying, but she also knew that I needed her to go along with it. So she did, the first night and the second night, too. She let me have that time to miss Oak Park and everything I'd left behind, the good and the bad. She hugged me, and we curled into each other like cats on the futon she'd brought to serve as our couch while Sid, the actual cat, prowled among the boxes and scaled the kitchen cabinets, fearless and happy to be free from his cage—the way I would finally feel after I got all of the tears out.

## ~Ruby Red Slippers~

this is about freedom,
                    this is about dreams come true
this is about moving on....

Last friday i clicked my heels together 3 times...
Last friday i moved out of my mom's house...
i graduated high skool early so i could go live
on my own, i started planning this when i was 15
and Last Friday i actully did it....

*Click yer heels together 3 times girl and let
those ruby red slippers fly you home*

what the fuck is home?  what the fuck is home?
home is where the heart is.
      *home is where the ♡ is.*

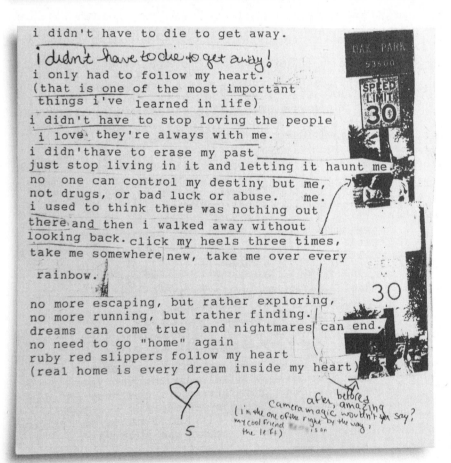

i didn't have to die to get away.
*i didn't have to die to get away!*
i only had to follow my heart.
(that is one of the most important
 things i've learned in life)
i didn't have to stop loving the people
i love they're always with me.
i didn't have to erase my past
just stop living in it and letting it haunt me.
no  one can control my destiny but me,
not drugs, or bad luck or abuse.   me.
i used to think there was nothing out
there and then i walked away without
looking back. click my heels three times,
take me somewhere new, take me over every

rainbow.

no more escaping, but rather exploring,
no more running, but rather finding.
dreams can come true  and nightmares can end.
no need to go "home" again
ruby red slippers follow my heart
(real home is every dream inside my heart)

♡
5

before
after
camera magic, amazing
(i'm the one of us right by the way?
my cool friend   is on
the left)

**Excerpt from *do not go quietly unto yr grave***

# A Sorta Fairytale

During the first couple of months in Wisconsin, I relished the small but significant moments of my newfound independence with Mia:

- Walking to work (I was hoping for something cooler than another grocery store job, but at least I made fifty cents more per hour than I had in high school.)

- Paying the bills (Rent, electric, and phone—we couldn't afford Internet or cable, so we wrote a lot of letters and rented a lot of movies.)

- Going to the laundromat and the giant twenty-four-hour grocery store (We usually did those two things at midnight because why not? We could!)

- Cooking (We made so many feasts—vegan pancakes, hand-cut French fries, lemon tofu "chicken," stir-fries, huge batches of potato soup, and something we called "tofuttibeast" even though it was really seitan wrapped in phyllo dough.)

- Exploring our new city (We found an all-ages punk club, two co-ops, and a vegan coffee shop that made blueberry scones so amazing that even Sid wanted them.)

We performed adulthood with childlike wonder.

We sneaked into hotel pools by pretending to be guests and nearly froze to death when we realized that since we did not have a room to change out of our wet suits and dry our hair, we would have to run out to the snowy parking lot with our clothes thrown on over our damp bodies.

We laughed until we cried when Mia called about a want ad for "spa attendants," and her end of the conversation went like this:

"Yes, I'm eighteen, but my friend isn't. She's a high school graduate, though . . . You'll have to talk to your lawyers? But . . . Oh my god, this is *not* a job handing out towels, is it?"

When we heard a hardcore band playing during one of our late-night walks around our new neighborhood and were invited in by a couple of spiky-haired guys drinking forties on the nearly collapsed front porch, we said sure. We moshed, just the two of us, and then hung out, ears ringing, until the wee hours with the small group of kids slightly older than us who were either renting from a slumlord or squatting in a building that would soon be condemned. We walked home arm in arm, delighted to have met "new neighbors."

We did not like the guy who lived below us in our apartment building, though. We never saw him, but we heard him, belligerent and abusive, screaming at someone night after night. We thought about calling the cops on him, but instead turned our music up. Nick Cave's *Murder Ballads* and the German industrial band Einstürzende Neubauten, so he would know not to fuck with us. We also talked about releasing spiders under his door.

Once we had jobs, we went out to dinner together or we filled up one of our gas tanks and cruised around the countryside, taking random county highways, and stopping in random small towns. We marveled that Main Street was an actual thing in most of them, and it usually looked the same: a grocery store, some sort of fishing/hunting/cowboy boot outfitter, and a bar. No one batted an eye when we walked into those bars—except for the creeps who were eager to buy us drinks. Though I'd started smoking again—mainly because those dark country nights seemed to call for it—we turned them down. We were giddy enough that we didn't need to be drunk. We had dance parties in our apartment, jumped on Mia's bed in our underwear, and drank Kool-Aid, giggling like it was spiked.

Though it involved bills and annoying coworkers and cars that sometimes wouldn't start, the world we'd created for ourselves felt like one long slumber party—like everything I'd been seeking in high school but without parental supervision or all the teenage drama and baggage.

Caci called regularly, though we could never talk for as long as we used to. Because long-distance calls cost more. Because I was working and she was working. Because I was here and she was there, mostly at her boyfriend's house or another friend's since her brother was still her brother, prone to his fits and rages. She kept me updated on that, assuring me that she was still safe, and provided dispatches on everything else that was going on in Oak Park. Sometimes when the updates were light, we laughed a lot and I almost got homesick:

*The lead singer of Acetone was campaigning to be crowned king at the King of Hearts Dance, ironically of course.*

*Maybe she'd go to prom with her boyfriend this year, but it wouldn't be as fun as last year, when we all got dressed up and had dinner at Jedi's Garden and danced to ska blaring from a boom box by the statue at Scoville Park until the cops came.*

Others reminded me why I left:

*Another kid from Scoville, one of the metalheads she used to hang out with in sixth grade, had overdosed on heroin.*

*No one had seen Greg lately. Maybe he had finally really run away. Or he was dead. Either way, good riddance and nobody cared. He'd burned everyone in Oak Park and some of the Berwyn punks, too.*

*Juliet looked really pregnant now. Was she happy? Well, she was smiling . . .*

*Brandon was probably going to jail. No, not drugs. He and Derek and someone else found a checkbook. They didn't steal it, but they used it. Fraud, and you know he's got other stuff on his record . . . Steph, are you okay?*

When the phone rang really early one morning in mid-April, I shot up out of bed. I was afraid it was going to be Caci telling me that something had happened to Brandon, or my deepest fear, that it would be Caci's boyfriend telling me that something really bad had happened, like with her brother . . .

"She's here!" Juliet declared when I answered. She spoke her daughter's name, "Ava," breathlessly and kept repeating, "She's so beautiful," and, "I love you, Stephie-Lou," all in a tone more soft and gentle than I'd ever heard from her.

I hung up feeling hopeful. I thought maybe, *maybe* it would actually be okay. This baby would transform her like Wisconsin was transforming me. Maybe we were growing into functional, productive, healthy adults.

I'd finally put out another zine. I hadn't made one in nearly nine months, and though Juliet might have begged to differ, it was like its own birthing process—or maybe more of a rebirth. I wrote first drafts in my journal, curled up in bed with Sid or on the couch with him and Mia. Then I'd type them up on the typewriter I'd asked for as a graduation gift (even though the refurbished computer my dad offered to look into getting for me would have been more practical) and let Mia read what I'd written. She'd do the same with stuff for her zine, and we'd end up talking and crying our hearts out until we fell asleep on the couch.

I cut and pasted, found a copy shop with Mia, and employed the trick we'd learned in our Riot Grrrl days that involved strategic tinkering with a paper clip so the counter wouldn't log your copies until you wanted it to. (You had to pay for *something*, otherwise you'd get caught.)

The zine looked different—stark, lots of black, pen-and-ink drawings. It read different—still confessional, more confessional even, but I experimented with new forms. I thought it marked the end of one thing and the beginning of another. I didn't know it would be my last zine—I had two more planned!—but I knew I was stepping into something new.

Sometimes I wonder what would have happened if I'd held on a little longer to that world that Mia and I built. The fairy-tale version of Real Adult Life where I briefly found my footing, my voice, myself.

I don't actually know when I crossed out of it. When the curtain lifted. When rehearsal ended and the playacting became real. When what I'd thought was a costume was just . . . me. And there I was, living out the role I'd always dreamed of.

I named that last zine perfectly, though, after a song by the band Morphine: *do not go quietly unto yr grave.*

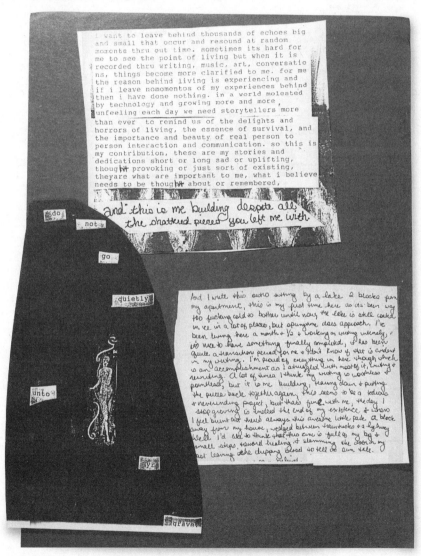

i want to leave behind thousands of echoes big and small that occur and resound at random moments thru out time. sometimes its hard for me to see the point of living but when it is recorded thru writing, music, art, conversations, things become more clarified to me. for me the reason behind living is experiencing and if i leave nomomentos of my experiences behind then i have done nothing. in a world molested by technology and growing more and more, unfeeling each day we need storytellers more than ever to remind us of the delights and horrors of living, the essence of survival, and the importance and beauty of real person to person interaction and communication. so this is my contribution, these are my stories and dedications short or long sad or uplifting, though provoking or just sort of existing, theyare what are important to me, what i believe needs to be thought about or remembered,

and this is me building despite all the shattered pieces you left me with

**Excerpts from *do not go quietly unto yr grave***

# PART 9

Some

Girls

Wander

by

Mistake

# Child of the Night

I started wearing black lipstick just a few months before I moved to Wisconsin. Manic Panic brand. I bought it at a store called Medusa's Circle on Belmont in Chicago. The lipstick went on smooth and smelled a little bit like modeling clay. I put it on with a Cure shirt and one of the velvet jackets I'd started collecting—I had one in black, one in wine red, and one in moss green—and I went like that to a queercore show at the Fireside Bowl.

One of my punk friends laughed and asked, "What the fuck, Stephanie, are you goth now?"

I blushed a little and glared at her. "I'm just . . . me." It was too loud, too crowded to offer up all of the defenses that I wanted to share:

*Winona Ryder in* Beetlejuice *was one of my first idols: "My life is a dark room. One. Big. Dark. Room."*

*I read everything Anne Rice wrote during the summer before eighth grade.*

*I saw* The Crow *in the theater three times.*

*I've had this T-shirt since the beginning of high school. The Cure was actually the first band poster I put on my wall.*

The Fireside had been my smoky, noisy home-away-from-home for about a year. I'd started going to shows there when I was already deeply entrenched in punk, so until that night, it had never been somewhere I'd felt self-conscious. Like I'd walked in naked, or more accurately, I felt like a snake caught shedding its skin. My other transitions had been either been more subtle or more gradual. Grunge to punk had meant I lost the flannel, kept the ripped jeans, and added more chains.

I realized right then that I didn't belong to or in the punk scene anymore. Suddenly, I was an outsider. I didn't fit in. Again.

Thank god I was leaving soon. And thank god Mia was coming to that show.

Mia, my fellow shapeshifter, was more graceful at it than me. Her black lipstick had a tinge of purple, like a bruise, and paired well with her naturally pale skin. When her hair went from deep red to black it was less dramatic than when I changed to jet-black from white-blond. But as long as I had her—my partner in darkness—I was all right.

She even found a Chi-Goth listserv for us. Before we left for Wisconsin, we met up with some people from there for coffee. It was a little weird because they were all twice our age. They talked about nightclubs we couldn't get into, but they didn't treat us like baby goths. They were happy to point us to the record store with the big Skinny Puppy symbol in the window near the Abbott Hotel, recommending obscure artists who broke up when we were still in diapers and newer ones we might like, too.

*Get this compilation from Cleopatra Records. You'll love Switchblade Symphony if you like Siouxsie Sioux!*

When we told them where we were moving, they were excited for us.

*Great scene! Fly away, little blackbirds! May you find your every dark delight!*

# The Goth God

I first spotted him on Valentine's Day weekend when Mia and I decided
to check out the goth/industrial night that was held every Saturday in the student
union of the university. The flyers said it was for students, but no one asked us for
ID. It gave me a little rush to pass for a college kid. I didn't know how to feel about
the event itself, though. It had a few cool touches—in the center of every table there
were gummy worms sitting atop red paper hearts that read *Fuck Valentine's Day!*—
but despite the fancy strobe lights, it was clearly an all-purpose room at a school,
not a nightclub. In fact, it reminded me a little bit of the "morp" I'd gone to in high
school. At least the music was good, so Mia and I stayed to dance and eat candy.

Then he arrived.

But even though we joked about him, I couldn't keep my eyes off him. *He fascinated me to an extent, but he also seemed super pretentious,* I wrote in my journal the next day, before going on to describe him from boots to sunglasses. I concluded that I didn't want to judge anyone, but I wondered if we'd meet people who would talk to us.

Because I wanted to talk to him. He was exactly the sort of dark star I wanted to orbit. He was in a completely different solar system than the one I'd left behind in Oak Park, and if it was the one that I belonged to, maybe it would make up for all those years of feeling like an alien.

But I reminded myself that I was only going to be in Wisconsin for six months. I had college to discover new solar systems.

# From the Edge of the Deep Green Sea

**It would have been the perfect summer fling.** It should have been. The Goth God and me.

I had three months left in Wisconsin when we crossed paths again at goth night.

His name was Simon, and he was wasted, but this time we actually interacted. After the dancing was over, Simon, a friend, and their jug of wine came back to our apartment. The night ended with Simon sprawled out on our hallway floor. His friend tried to rouse him, but he insisted he had to rest.

His friend said she had to go, assuring Mia and me, "He's harmless, I swear. He'll just let himself out when he sobers up."

I don't know why we trusted a girl we'd only met that night—most likely our desire to befriend these older goth kids outweighed common sense—but we went along with this. I stepped over Simon to get the door for her, stepped over him again to get to the bathroom to wash up, and stepped over him a third time to get to my bedroom.

I usually shut the door, but while I was in the bathroom, Simon had moved closer to my bedroom. I had a feeling he wanted to be invited in. I wasn't sure I was ready for that, so I just said, "Good night," turned out my light, and left the door open.

I lay awake as over the course of the next hour, he moved even closer to my room . . . and then into my room . . . and then right next to my bed, which, being a futon, was right on the floor.

"Stephanie," he eventually murmured. I was shocked that he'd somehow retained my name, and I loved how it sounded in his quiet, wispy voice.

"Yeah?" I finally managed to say.

"Can I hold you?" he asked.

*No!* my mind screamed. *It was idiotic to let a strange boy into your home; you definitely don't let him into your bed.*

He put a pale hand on my mattress. "I'm not going to try anything."

*No, c'mon, don't be stupid.*

*But he's gorgeous, and he seems like he wouldn't hurt a fly.*

"I just want to hold and be held." His voice was so soft, like a little kid's.

And I just wanted to hold and be held, too. I had for a long time.

"Okay."

He crawled into bed beside me and wrapped his long, bony arms around me. True to his word, he tried nothing, just held tight and fell fast asleep.

I stayed awake all night. At first I might have been a little scared, but that quickly turned to excitement—especially when he ran his fingernails up and down my arm, which stirred memories of old thrills and that fireworks show in my stomach that I'd never thought I'd feel again—and I knew this was another big, life-altering moment that I needed to preserve in my mind. The real beginning of my Real Adult Life.

# Inferno

Simon was mesmerizing, larger than life. Larger than the nearly six and a half feet he stood with those heeled boots and his crazy hair. And he ruled the local goth scene—or at least he acted like it.

"Just tell them you're friends of mine," he said when he invited Mia and me to meet him at a new goth club and we'd pointed out that we were underage.

It worked. We arrived at nine thirty, just half an hour after the club opened. Only a handful of people were there, most of them staff, and only one guy was on the dance floor, doing what looked like tai chi. Mia and I exchanged an uncomfortable look: *We're too early. Naive. Imposters.*

We nursed a shared vodka cranberry. A lot of thought was put into ordering that drink. Mia had never been much of a drinker and I'd been sober for almost a year. But, we rationalized, we were in a nightclub—an actual twenty-one-plus nightclub! This was a rite of passage that had to be marked. *And there's an ocean of difference between having a drink and doing heroin,* I told myself. We chose vodka cranberry because it sounded classy—gothy even, since it would be blood red—and we hoped the taste of the juice would overpower the booze. We only ordered one because we didn't have much money and we didn't know how it would affect us—one of us had to drive, after all. The drink-sharing earned us quizzical looks from the bartender and some of the other patrons, though. This embarrassed me, so I told Mia we'd have to get our own drinks the next time, even if we didn't finish them.

As it turned out, the vodka cranberry tasted pretty good and made me feel less self-conscious among the older club-goers, whose makeup and outfits were much more elaborate than our black thrift-store dresses and smudged kohl eyeliner. As Simon had promised, the club was way cooler than the university goth night, but I worried that maybe it was too cool. It felt a little like my first time at Scoville Park—except with black walls, red velvet couches, and a dance floor with a strobe light and a fog machine.

I could tell Mia was as uncomfortable as I was—we spent a lot of time sitting on one of the couches with our shoulders pressed together, nervously crossing and uncrossing limbs as we sipped from our drink—but she was more game than Robin had been at the park. We braved the dance floor after it started to fill and we befriended the DJ's underage girlfriend, who took us down to the basement and showed us the storage room where we were to hide if the cops came. We started smiling then. It was like we were flapper girls at a speakeasy. And we'd been initiated. We were in.

However, the night crept on and there was still no Simon. Mia yawned and reminded me that she had to work at six a.m. I pleaded like a little kid. *Just five more minutes. Just a little longer.* I knew Simon worked until ten, but he'd said he was going to be there after he got off. (I didn't know yet that his getting-ready ritual took at least an hour.)

He finally glided into the club just before midnight and right as Mia's patience had worn out. We talked only briefly, but we hugged for what felt like a blissful eternity. He smelled like clove cigarettes and Aussie Instant Freeze hairspray, and he wore a red velvet jacket that was soft as a well-loved stuffed animal. He bent down, putting his lips right next to my ear so I could hear his lilting whisper over the throbbing beat of a spooky electro song. He reminded me about the upcoming party Saturday night at his house—the address he'd already written down in spindly handwriting before he'd left my apartment the other day. Aside from that, I don't remember a single thing he said to me, just the feeling of his breath on my neck and his lips grazing the side of my cheek as he pulled away. A song had come on that he just had to dance to.

I watched him as we walked out—lithe and perfect on the dance floor, reaching his big, pale hands up toward the flashing lights—and I thought, as I would again and again, *How could someone that beautiful be interested in me?*

# Lost Souls

We didn't know how old Simon was until we got to the party, which turned out to be a birthday celebration for him that his roommate had planned. He hadn't told me that because he didn't like to acknowledge his birthdays. He idolized the vampires in *The Lost Boys* and wanted to stay young and party forever—but no mullets, he joked, and no getting staked in the end. His roommate outed him, announcing that he was about to turn twenty-four. Simon sighed heavily and hung his head in shame. This didn't faze me, even though I was still a couple months shy of eighteen.

The party was a relaxed affair in Simon's living room. There were maybe ten or fifteen people who came and went throughout the night. Mia eventually decided to go, too, but Simon asked me to stay, saying he'd drive me home in the morning. I told myself and Mia that it would be okay since his roommate was female—even an elementary school teacher by day.

When Mia left, Simon and I retreated to his room, where we spent most of the night kissing. Things got hot and heavy fast, but when they moved toward sex, I froze. Simon noticed and asked if I was okay.

"Yeah . . . no . . . I had this boyfriend . . ." And the story of Greg came tumbling out. More of it than I'd really wanted to share—not that I'd wanted to share any of it. I'd hoped that my body would just function like it was supposed to. This was embarrassing, and surely, I thought, he'd want me to leave. He was too drunk to drive, so I'd have to call Mia . . .

But he stroked my hair, told me how sorry he was that it had happened. "You are so beautiful. You are so strong, and I'm happy just to hold you," he said. We fell asleep, curled in each other's arms on his bed, a nest made of blankets and a thin futon mattress on the floor.

I still thought it would be over in the morning after he drove me home. Why would a gorgeous older guy who could have any girl at the club want a seventeen-year-old who froze up and cried at the possibility of sex?

But he kept showing up. Sometimes he invited me and Mia to hang out with him and his friends at an abandoned house or one of their favorite cemeteries. My favorite was the one about half an hour's drive into the countryside that sat on the edge of a small lake and had a playground beside it. We swung on the swings and went skinny-dipping in the dark water and held moonlit picnics on gravestones, smoking clove cigarettes and drinking red wine, which I quickly developed a taste for.

A few times a week, we'd go to the club where Simon and I danced around each other, swaying slowly, lifting our arms to the sky or wrapping them behind our backs, staring seductively at each other through the flashing lights. I drank vodka cranberries—two or three of them, not shared with Mia—and he drank gin and tonics, which I started to enjoy as well.

On the other nights after he got off of work, he came to my apartment and we retreated to my bedroom or he called and I went to his and we kissed and talked and drank wine—bottles when he had money, boxes of Franzia Chillable Red when he didn't. After a month or so of making out, I told him I was ready. For sex. He asked if I was sure, told me that he would stop if anything felt wrong, but it didn't. Because he made me feel beautiful, he made me feel safe, it felt right. It felt good. And I'd been fairly certain sex would never feel that way again.

We spent long hours just talking in the dark, sharing our dreams—the nighttime kind which seemed so much more relevant than the future hopes I was becoming so much less certain of—and our writing. He wrote dark, cryptic poetry, and soon mine shifted in tone to match. He read my zines and said they were powerful, but he really loved the snippets of short stories I'd started writing. "Stark," he called those. "Bleak" and "haunting." "Beautiful," "masterful," and "one of a kind." He thought they could make me famous.

"Why aren't you going to school for writing?" he asked, and since it was coming from him instead of my dad, I started to wonder about it, too.

# She's in Parties

I brought Simon and Mia home to Oak Park with me for my birthday in July. I'd only been back once, right after I moved, for my grandfather's
funeral. My mom had wanted me to come home in June to take part in graduation, but having already firmly slammed the door shut on high school, I refused.
I didn't want to miss work to wear a stupid white dress on the football field, I
told her, not when she could just pick up my diploma for me. (Her response to
my refusal was to leave "S. Diploma @ OPRF" permanently undone on her list
of tasks. I actually hadn't known she was upset about it until we were at my
brother's graduation three years later and I realized that I still didn't have my
own diploma. "Should've come back to get it yourself, I guess," she'd said with
a wry smile.)

I'd been away for five months, which both seemed like forever and not long
enough, and we were only there for forty-eight hours, which I'd thought might
feel too short, but I would end up wishing I hadn't gone at all.

On the first night, Simon complained because we'd arrived after the liquor
stores closed, he hadn't brought any wine, and my underage friends didn't have
any. The next night he, Mia, and I got drunk. Acacia and her boyfriend were
straight-edge at the time (aside from Acacia's smoking), so as we got louder,
they got quieter. I drank more because it was my birthday and I hated the tension in the air that hung thicker than the humidity.

Before I headed back to Wisconsin, Acacia's boyfriend handed me a scathing letter about how fake and clownish he thought we all were. He hated Simon and questioned what a few short months away had done to Mia and me. We weren't as cool and mature as we thought, he said.

I didn't care about his opinion, but what bothered me was Acacia, who barely spoke a word the whole time. Who stood in his shadow, when Acacia didn't belong in anyone's shadow.

I could tell that she wanted an explanation, maybe a promise that the Stephanie she'd set free was still out there and would still come back to her someday. I didn't know what to say that wouldn't be a lie.

# *Disintegration*

During our last month in Wisconsin, my relationship with Mia started to unravel. She was dating one of Simon's friends, but she didn't let herself get as caught up in her older-boy romance as I did. Sometimes I stayed at Simon's for days at a time until she called, frustrated, reminding me that she'd been feeding Sid, but he missed me and I needed to scoop the litter box. I was so lost in Simon that I forgot everything else.

I didn't see that, though, and I didn't understand why Mia was so mad. This thing with Simon was headed toward what I knew to be its inevitable end: me leaving for college.

Even though Simon and I had both quit our jobs so we could spend every moment together . . . even though we were saying *I love you* . . . even though I was completely head over heels for him in a way that I repeatedly wrote in my journal I shouldn't be . . . our relationship was temporary, a fling.

*It's just fun, and you are okay with that,* I reminded myself frequently.

But then our last morning together, before I had to go home and do more of the packing and cleaning that Mia was rightfully pissed at me for leaving to her, Simon and I walked to the laundromat down the block from his apartment, and he casually said, "It's good that you're leaving tomorrow."

I watched him shove the dirty sheets that we'd been *fucking* on—not "making love," because even though we'd used the word "love," we obviously hadn't meant it—into a machine.

"Yeah, I knew that," I lied. To him. To myself.

We said goodbye then. In the laundromat. I don't remember what we said exactly or even if we kissed. I do remember walking out of the laundromat and looking at the convenience mart next door, the one we'd run to for wine and snacks so many times when we emerged starving after a full day in bed. I remember thinking that this was not how I wanted my last look at that little store to be. I'd wanted to say goodbye to Simon in his bedroom, to kiss him one last time at the door to his apartment, and then to look at it as I was walking to my car and experience preemptive nostalgia. To see it the way my future self would when she visited Wisconsin and remembered that silly seventeen-year-old who'd felt so sophisticated on the arm of her older lover buying wine in a corner store. Future me was supposed to smile, supposed to chuckle and reflect on that teenage dalliance as transformational and perfect. She was not supposed to remember feeling like she was in a slasher film and the serial killer had just ripped out her intestines with a meat hook. She was not supposed to remember that the stupid fling had actually been all-consuming love and she'd only been able to see that upon learning it was one-sided.

At least I didn't cry. Not until I got home and had to tell Mia—Mia, who as it turned out had known for a couple of weeks. Her boyfriend had let it slip and then sworn her to secrecy. That's part of the reason she'd been so cold, hoping to drive a wedge between Simon and me.

I wanted to be angry at her, but I couldn't. And I still couldn't be angry at Simon, not even when Mia showed me the phone bill with the long-distance call to the town his girlfriend was from. He'd made it one afternoon while I was in the shower. We'd had sex and then he called her.

No, I had to push that out of my head. I couldn't let this knowledge and that last ugly hour—or less, maybe it had only been fifteen minutes?—taint three months of bliss. I reiterated to myself that it was supposed to be a fling, the sort that usually happened in a vacation town or Europe in novels or on TV but, in the story of my life, had happened in Wisconsin.

And maybe it could have been my version of that, unfortunate ending and all, if I'd let go. If I hadn't taken Simon's phone calls and replied to his emails in the weeks and months that followed. If I hadn't gotten sucked in because he told me I was special, like no other girl he'd ever known, and I understood him in ways that even *she* didn't, the girl he'd thought was his one true love. If I hadn't asked, "What does that mean?" and accepted it when he said that he didn't know, that he loved me but he loved her, too. If I hadn't let him have his confusion, let him live with her while writing me love letters, in the hope that someday things would be different. If I had just walked away and never looked back like I had when I'd heard that Brandon, my last not-really-boyfriend, had hooked up with another girl.

If I had somehow managed to conjure up that sense of self-worth I'd found at fifteen, then maybe I would have had my happy memories of a three-month fling.

But I couldn't. Not after Greg. Not after all of the disappointments that had come during my last year of high school. I needed the beginning of my Real Adult story to be perfect, and since my first Real Adult romance hadn't ended the way I wanted (not that I'd wanted it to end *at all*), I nearly killed myself trying to rewrite it.

# PART 10

She's Lost Control

I met her on my eighth birthday. Flipping through *D'Aulaires' Book of Greek Myths*, a gift from a family friend, I was drawn immediately to the image of the blond girl wearing a white dress and a flower crown, her arms raised in distress as she's pulled into a dark pit by a bearded, toga-clad man in a chariot. The flowers she'd been picking fall from her hands, and four pigs that happened to be in the wrong place at the wrong time when the earth opened up tumble into the abyss alongside her. It was disturbing, but also gorgeous:

Persephone, falling, falling, falling . . .

I read that book cover to cover so many times I lost count. The cover itself actually came off and pages became loose. I carefully kept them together, though, and when my other childhood books got packed away, I kept that one out. It went from sitting alongside my Beverly Cleary books to sharing the shelf with Sylvia Plath. The inside cover bears the marks I made in my books when I played library as a kid, but the loose title page has doodles of band logos and the phone number to Ticketmaster. It was one of the few books that accompanied me to Wisconsin and to college, where it sat stacked above my desk with my Poppy Z. Brite novels and the diaries of Anaïs Nin.

Oh, Persephone. The queen of the underworld. Kidnapped by Hades. Her destiny sealed by eating pomegranate seeds. My battered copy of *D'Aulaires'* opens right to her story; my reading and rereading of that one in particular is probably what cracked the spine.

I can't say why I was so drawn to her as a child. Maybe it was because I loved stories where kids went off to strange worlds and had adventures. Or maybe I just liked her because her name rhymed with mine. ("Stephanie, Persephone. Stephanie, Persephone," Simon would murmur sometimes, eventually slurring the names together, "Perstephanie.")

Whatever it was, I internalized her. Deeply.

"One day as Persephone ran about in the meadow gathering flowers, she strayed away from her mother and the attending nymphs," the *D'Aulaires'* story reads. "Suddenly, the ground split open and up from the yawning crevice came a dark chariot drawn by black horses."

This implied cause and effect: Persephone wandered away from the ones who watched over her, and then the ground split open. (Isn't that what happened to me when I went to Scoville Park?)

"Wordlessly, she walked through the garden at silent Hades' side and slowly her heart turned to ice," the *D'Aulaires'* version goes. (And that's exactly how I became, too, with Greg. Was it where I was heading again? After all, she's really only allowed a yearly vacation from the underworld.)

Maybe I kept rereading Persephone's story because I was trying to figure out why she was made to suffer even though she hadn't really done anything so bad. (She was just picking flowers, just exploring! Certainly she did not mean to get kidnapped!)

Maybe I was trying to understand her relationship to Hades and the underworld. (Did she like it there? Did she love him?)

Maybe I just wanted to know how she could do it, go down and up, down and up, down and up and down again . . .

This wasn't just a story that explained the seasons (Persephone on earth with her mother, Demeter = Summer. Persephone + Hades = Winter); I could tell that much. There was a lesson in here for girls, especially girls like me, who wandered off because the world was vast and wide and beautiful. Who knew it would crack open like that? And you would be dragged away? And you would eat the food of the dead without being fully aware?

"Persephone, lost in thought, had eaten the seeds," the *D'Aulaires'* text reads. (Had that been me, though? Lost in thought? Or had I eaten those pomegranate seeds because they looked appetizing, I was hungry, and they were pretty and new?)

I should have known, from my many, many readings of Persephone's story, that you always have to go back down there again. To the underworld, the darkness, the icy winter cold.

You do not make that trip just once and then emerge into the sunshine to stay. It is not a onetime thing—the very special episode of a TV show. You are not a stand-alone novel or a movie or the final book/film/season of a perfectly planned series.

I wanted to be. I felt like I deserved it. After *Stephanie: The Junior High Years* and *Stephanie: The High School Years* proved to be so hard to live, especially that season about Greg, surely *Stephanie: The College Years* would be better. Maybe not perfect—I knew better than to expect that (or did I?)—but the overall story arc would be happy, fun. There would be success and love and true friendship, and above all, clarity. I would finally figure this life thing out, and when I hit bumps in the road, I would draw from my past experiences and work through my troubles quickly and easily.

I would not repeat past mistakes.

I would not make even worse mistakes.

I would not fall (fail) even further, land even harder, shatter into even more pieces.

But I did.

That was the real story of Persephone, I realized at the ripe old age of eighteen. It was a story of falling, again and again. A cycle that would last forever, and the only way to survive was to turn yourself to ice.

## II.

"Seventy percent of you won't graduate from here," our RA tells us at our very first hall meeting. She's smoking a clove cigarette and drinking a beer. "Look around this circle. Half of you won't be here next fall."

There are eleven of us sitting on the cigarette-burnt carpet in our common room. Ten freshmen, one transfer student. All girls, the majority dyed and/or pierced (I have inky black hair and five ear piercings, which will be up to thirteen by spring). Eight smoking cigarettes (I bummed a clove from the RA and then bought a pack at the gas station; they are cheaper than regular cigarettes back home). All of us drinking alcoholic beverages (the transfer student is twenty-one, so she hooked us up. Most people got forties; I got wine, which I am drinking out of a giant blue cup).

I don't try to guess who is going to drop out (aside from the girl from France who has already cried like three times), I just stubbornly tell myself, *That will not be me.*

The thought—and the need to believe it—is a reflex. Less than a week ago, I told my parents that I didn't want to come to school. Six short months in Wisconsin, three short months with Simon, had changed me. What was the point of going to *this* college if I didn't believe in the revolution anymore? And was there even a point to going to *any* college when I'd already found Real Adult Life?

My dad recited his usual "Absolutely Not." Of course I was going to college. I was smart, and that's what smart girls do. And I'd chosen *that* college and I'd gotten a scholarship to cover most of it and my loans were in place for the rest, so that was that.

My mom was softer, trying to ask, "What do you want?" But that question made me even more furious than being told I had to go. I didn't want to admit that I didn't know.

I, Stephanie Kuehnert, who had always known, had no fucking clue what I wanted to do with my life.

The only things I did know made me feel like shit: my parents were divorced; between my angry grrrl and sullen goth phases I'd pushed away most of my friends; I loved Simon, and I needed him to love me and to heal me from Greg, but he was moving to the East Coast to be with another girl. I'd gone to Wisconsin looking for a fresh start, thought I'd found one, and then it had all fallen apart. Just like Scoville. I couldn't bear the idea that college, which had been my end goal for as long as I could remember, might blow up in my face, too, but if my past was any indication, I was doomed.

However, since I couldn't answer my mother, couldn't see another path, I'd agreed to stay on the one I was on.

I let my dad drive me to college. He tried to bond with me by bringing audio recordings of female beat poets. "I am not wearing all black because I'm a beatnik," I told him, and when it was my turn to play tapes, I educated/punished him with loud industrial albums by Skinny Puppy and Christian Death. Before he left, he snapped a photo that both of my parents would frame as if it was a sweet shot of their little girl going off to college, not me, pissed as hell, stopping just short of flipping off the camera.

**August 1997, the college drop-off photo that for some reason my mom kept framed on her mantel for years**

My plan is to go through the motions. It will be High School Part Two: academic success and controlled rebellion. I'll get wasted, but still go to class. And really, I couldn't have picked a better school for it.

The RA lights another clove and begins to go over the rules. In a nutshell, there aren't any. There's no curfew; she's not going to be checking our rooms every night. We're on a smoking hall. We chose that. Since technically, this is a freshman dorm, we are not supposed to have parties with alcohol, but no one will really care if we do. The security guard will also turn a blind eye to any drug use, but, she notes, the police in town will not. The sexual consent policy is pretty much the only thing anyone cares about. *(It is one of the reasons I chose this school. I thought it was so radical, so feminist. But I'm not so sure I care anymore. I'm already broken. How much worse could any additional damage be?)* It may be awkward to be like, "Can I kiss you, can I touch your boob?" but do it. Other than that, we are advised to have fun safely, to use the basket of condoms and dental dams we'll find in the bathroom.

She prattles on for a bit about the cafeteria, the library, the wellness center, and student government. Finally, she stubs out her third or fourth clove (in one of the ashtrays that will disappear in the next few days, smuggled into people's dorm rooms, leaving us with no choice but to make the floor our ashtray) and says, "Nobody is going to tell you to go to class, and as you know, you receive written evaluations here, not grades. Classes are pass/fail. Your teachers are not here to hold your hand. They are here to teach. What you learn is on you. That's why most people don't make it. This school attracts a lot of free spirits, but it's so unstructured that a lot of those free spirits just float away." She shrugs like, *Good riddance*, and we are dismissed.

When the meeting ends, I'm still thinking, *I can do this. Power through and get out, just like high school.*

When the night ends, I'm puking off the side of the fire escape, my roommate hauling me in as it starts to rain.

Mia drops out of her college of choice before Thanksgiving break. Mia, who is smarter than me. And the world doesn't end. In fact, she's moving back to Wisconsin.

I want to do that, too. So I call my parents. Crying. Begging. Arguing that this school isn't doing anything for me. I'm not interested in social work anymore, and the creative writing classes suck. The teacher gives terrible prompts. (At least that was my excuse for why my notebook was mostly blank pages, false starts, and unsent letters to Simon.)

As usual, my dad doesn't listen, and even though they're divorced and he's living in another state with another woman, my mom still tries to find some sort of compromise—*See how you feel at winter break, and if you still hate it, you don't have to go back next fall, but don't you want to give it at least a full year?*

I don't. I can't pretend to care. I can't pretend to believe I can change the world. College was supposed to be the top of the mountain, the peak from which I could see everything and map out the rest of my life. Instead, the world is shrouded in fog.

But I've found a friend to party with, so that's what I do. Kirsten and I get drunk before, during, after, and instead of class. In our rooms, in other people's rooms, in the common room, in the boys' hall upstairs, where they make a giant hot tub out of their showering area by lining the floor with industrial garbage bags, closing off the doorway with a plank of wood that you have to step over to get into the "tub," and turning all of the showers on at once. (We joke that they should be given honorary engineering degrees even though our school doesn't have an engineering program.)

I decide that if I'm going to fail, I might as well fail spectacularly. If I'm not going to come away from college with any good stories written, I might as well come away with some to tell.

My new goal is to avoid being sober at all costs. It's the only way to deal with my feelings about school and about Simon.

## III.

Simon . . . Our relationship was just like my notebook, full of beautiful beginnings that crashed and burned. Cross it out. Try it again. Tear it out. Ball it up. Cry. Stare at the blank pages. Write more words. Also wrong. Also not good enough. (I am never, ever good enough.) Cross those out . . . And on and on again.

Our breakup—if you could call it that, since I was unknowingly The Other Woman, not The Girlfriend—shared some similarities to my split with Greg, though I didn't see that at the time. (Simon was the cure to Greg; he couldn't be *like* Greg in any way.) He'd dumped me because he wanted to see other people—or rather, he *already was seeing* another person—and I pined. The difference was that Simon pined back, and not just for the first week or so like Greg.

I was in the computer lab or the library constantly, not to do my homework, but to check for Simon's emails and write long, emotional responses. Sometimes we talked on the phone, too, when she wasn't around. He told her we were just friends, that we had a "special connection." She knew I'd slept with him, so understandably, she hated me. The feeling was mutual. Because she was rich. Because she was beautiful. Because she had him.

I told myself that she wasn't good enough for him, that their bond was not as strong as ours. If I said and wrote the right things, he would see that. Sometimes he seemed to. He told me about how bored he was with her, how she could be so cold, how there was just something about me. Then he'd feel guilty, tell me how much he loved her, that they were meant to be.

He'd always say her name with a little sigh at the end, which made me want to punch him in the face, but he always said mine in a breathless hush, which made me want to kiss him. Every day, every hour, was a seesaw; depending on our latest correspondence, I was either a blissfully happy drunk or a dark and despondent one.

Occasionally, I tried to prove to myself that I didn't care about Simon. I ended up in bed with one of the only goth boys at school a couple of times, but I'd always roll over and pass out before we progressed beyond, "Can I kiss you?" and, "Can I touch your breasts?" I told myself that it was because he wasn't really attractive.

But the guy I met at the goth club an hour away from campus was definitely hot. He was tall and thin, cheekbones and jawline so sharp I could cut myself on them.

Kirsten, who regularly went back to guys' rooms and actually slept with them, got freaked out when I wanted to go with him, though. She demanded to see his driver's license and wrote down all of his information on the paper bag from the bottle of Bacardí Limón that we passed back and forth before going into the club.

"Okay, Jack," Kirsten said sternly as she handed back his ID. "If Steph's not back on campus by tomorrow night, I know who you are and where you live and I'm calling the cops."

"Don't worry, I'll have her home," he told me before leading me down the street toward his car.

"Your friend is a little overprotective, huh?" he remarked as we walked.

I stumbled, kicked off my heels—so easy for dancing, not so much for walking—and giggled as I bent down to pick them up. "Your name is Jack."

He looked at me, confusion in his dark eyes. "Why is that funny? It's a normal name."

"It's funny because I didn't know that until just now, and I'm going home with you."

Jack shook his head, his sprayed-stiff black hair unmoving, and helped me pick up the shoe I was fumbling for.

It wasn't much farther to his car, maybe fifty feet, but I realized right away that it had been a stupid idea to take off my shoes because my fishnets did not offer any real protection from the gravelly roadside. We were in some shitty industrial part of the city . . .

Then it dawned on me:

*Wait, I'm in some shitty industrial part of the city with a guy whose name I just learned and my friends are driving off and I'm getting into his car, which has . . . What the fuck, why does he have New Jersey plates? Did he just move here from New Jersey? This place sucks. Why not move to Philly or New York? The only logical explanation is that they are stolen plates or this is a stolen car and he's a serial killer and he's going to leave my body in some ravine and when they find me, my mom is going to kill me all over again because how could I be so stupid?*

I still went home with him, but as usual I pretended to pass out because I couldn't go through with having sex with him. I told myself it was because of my serial killer paranoia. Not because of Simon. Not because I still wasn't over what had happened with Greg. Not because I was suddenly a scared, frigid prude. After all, I could still have sex with Simon.

I went to visit him over Thanksgiving break while his girlfriend was away and I fucked him in the bed they shared. He felt guilty about it later. I felt accomplished.

We hooked up again over New Year's while we were both in Wisconsin. Once again he said he felt guilty . . . but he still loved me; he wanted to be with me . . . but he was with her.

Circles. Circles. Spinning. Spinning. Spinning.

That's how I felt when I was with him and when I wasn't with him.

On Halloween, while listening to a radio broadcast of a Cure concert that Simon and his girlfriend were actually at, I drank homemade absinthe and puked all over the giant stuffed black-and-white cat that my mom had given me since Sid had to stay with her while I was at school.

After I returned from my Thanksgiving visit with Simon, I smoked opium with a hallmate, got into the shower in my nightgown, and then tried to run out to the supposedly haunted glen behind campus. Kirsten, who was only a couple inches taller than me, managed to carry me back inside, kicking, screaming, and sopping wet.

The night we returned from winter break, I drank almost an entire five-liter box of wine while watching movies with Kirsten. I felt strangely sober until I went to the bathroom to brush my teeth. Then I tossed my toothbrush on the sink and threw myself into a stall, puking like I'd never puked before.

I was wearing a necklace, Simon's necklace, and I tugged at it, sobbing, between vomiting sessions. I moaned, "I wanna die," again and again. Too often, apparently, because one of my hallmates got the RA, who called 911.

Next thing I knew there were flashing red and blue lights and uniformed EMTs chasing me around the common room.

"I didn't actually want to die! Haven't you ever said something like that when you were sick? I just want to sleep!" I screamed as I ran.

Finally, I managed to get to the pay phone and woke my mom with shouts of, "They're trying to take me away! Tell them I'm fine! Tell them I'm just drunk! Tell them the cuts on my arms are old. You saw them over break. Tell them you won't give them the insurance information. That you won't pay for them to take me away!"

To her credit, my mother managed to stay calm and instructed me to give the phone to an EMT. I did so triumphantly, thinking I'd won, but when the EMT handed the phone back, my mom said, "I believe that you aren't trying to kill yourself, but someone told them you were, and now you have to go to the hospital so they can check you out. It's the law."

So I went. Kicking and screaming and refusing to lie down in the back of the ambulance unless they put the sirens on, which they wouldn't because it wasn't an emergency. I wasn't dying. I was just an unruly, drunk college girl, who wouldn't learn a damn thing from this experience.

## IV.

New Orleans, Louisiana. March 26 *(or wait, technically the twenty-seventh?)*, 1998. Three a.m.

*("Three a.m. knows all my secrets . . ." That's my favorite line from my favorite book,* Lost Souls *by Poppy Z. Brite. It's about a boy named Nothing who runs away to New Orleans and finds himself hanging out with the vampire who is really his father. It's Kirsten's favorite book, too, now. I introduced her to it when we met, and we both reread it before coming down here for spring break.)*

No, wait, I think it's more like four or five. I left the club at three, didn't I? Didn't it close at three? Maybe not. Clubs and bars don't ever have to close here, apparently. The bar below our hotel room is open twenty-four hours. I can hear the music thumping through the floor. It's not helping with the erratic rhythm of my heart.

Maybe I should go downstairs and get another drink. Maybe that would help.

Wait, don't I have a drink? I think I have a drink. I had a plastic cup of rum and Coke when we were standing outside the club and Kirsten was kissing that dark-haired guy we'd met on the dance floor. He wasn't the prettiest guy there, and he was kind of old. Probably midthirties. But he had coke. We snorted it off some dark corner table and things got all fast and blurry after that.

I've been doing coke since . . . I don't know, either right before or right after winter break. It makes me feel powerful. Special. And it shuts off that nagging little voice in the back of my brain that asks too many questions.

*(What are you doing? Aren't you smarter than this? Are you really going to ruin your life? Over Simon? There has got to be a better way to handle this! You don't think this is* actually *fun, do you?)*

*(It's obviously fun. SHUT UP.)*

The only thing that sucks is that it's hard to come down from and I already have problems sleeping. While I was home for winter break, Mia let me try her Ambien prescription. I immediately went to the doctor to get my own after having a great night's sleep for the first time since junior high and—*bonus!*—a completely trippy experience with Mia before we passed out. We were making nests for aliens. We woke up the next morning to find my dirty laundry scattered all over my room and shaped into mounds.

You aren't supposed to take Ambien with alcohol, but I usually do.

I did tonight after Kirsten decided to go home with that guy—

*(You let Kirsten go home with that guy? What if he's a serial killer? Do you even know his name?)*

*(She wanted to go and I'm sure I can remember it . . . whatever. SHUT UP.)*

—and I took the streetcar back to our shitty hotel, located somewhere between the French Quarter and the Garden District. It was all we could afford—the kind of place where alcoholics with nowhere else to go rent rooms by the week.

The walls are scuffed, dented, and nicotine-stained. There are cigarette burns on every surface, and the stench of old smoke and spilled liquor is pleasant compared to the underlying odor of mildew. We share the bathroom with the person in the room next door. One flimsy bolt keeps them from busting in while we pee—or from busting into our room through the bathroom. I'm glad I brought my butterfly knife. I take it to the bathroom with me and keep it on the nightstand next to the bed.

*Next to my drink!* I realize triumphantly.

I suck the rest of the warm rum and Coke down, hoping it will take the edge off, slow everything down so that I can finally pass out.

There's light coming in through the curtains, though, and I can't sleep when there's light. I pull the mustard-colored blanket over my head, but it's itchy and hot and kind of stinks. God, yeah, it definitely stinks, and I can't breathe. I can't . . .

I toss the blanket off my face and then I see why I can't breathe. There are little astronauts stacking tiny chairs on my chest.

"Stop! You're suffocating me!" I tell them, but they stare blankly at me. At least it looks blank since they have space helmets on.

What is it about Ambien and outer space?

*The spacemen aren't real,* I try to tell myself. *You've just combined too many substances.*

And then I wonder, *What would one more Ambien do tonight?* After all the coke and all the booze, would it push me over? It would be kind of poetic, wouldn't it? Dying in a cheap motel in New Orleans. They'd publish my sparse short stories and macabre poetry after my death and laud me as a misunderstood genius. And Simon would feel terrible . . .

But I couldn't do that to Kirsten.

*(Where is Kirsten? What did you let her do?)*

*(She'll be fine. SHUT UP.)*

I can't let her come back, shaking her head, ready to tell me how disappointing this guy was (they always are) and find me not breathing under that gross, cigarette-burnt blanket.

So I lie awake listening to traffic coming down the I-10 off-ramp. The light seeping in through the curtains grows brighter. My mouth is dry, and I have a headache, but there are no spacemen suffocating me. The anxiety has passed. I've come down.

Someday I will write a story about this. The hallucinations, the way this blanket scratches my skin, the color of the morning light, feeling numb as sobriety sets in.

Someday I will write. I will be able to pick up journal and pen and put more than a few frustrated lines in it.

*(Not if you keep this up . . . Why do you think you have writer's block? Because*

*you are killing your brain* and *your soul. And do you really think this is a glamorous way to die? Do you really want to die? You are nowhere near achieving what Sylvia or Kurt did. And whatever happened to wanting to be Courtney, the survivor? Or maybe just Stephanie, the storyteller in her own right?)*

*(SHUT UP.)*

The door rattles. I reach for the knife out of instinct, but it's Kirsten. She kicks off her boots and, seeing that I'm awake, sighs and says, "Dude."

That's as much of a report as I'm going to get for now. She climbs into bed and immediately passes out. Now that she's here—now that I don't have keep swallowing the worry and the guilt over getting so fucking high that I let her go off in a strange city with a stranger without doing her the same courtesy she had me and asking to see his ID—I can pass out, too.

The next day we take the streetcar into the French Quarter, deciding no bars, no coke, no sleazy guys. It's our last night. We're gonna get a bottle of wine and drink it by the Mississippi, just the two of us.

On our way to the river, we pass a strip club where the girls are dancing to Nine Inch Nails instead of the usual hair-rock bullshit.

"That is fucking awesome," I say, and Kirsten concurs. "That's what I should do after I drop out. I'll come back here, work at that strip club at night and write during the day."

Kirsten nods her approval. "That sounds like a decent plan. I could do an internship out here and we could live together for a bit."

We have lots of plans like this. Our favorite is the one where we save to buy a cheap house in New Mexico and live out our lives working low-maintenance jobs like grocery store cashier. We got very serious about it at one point, spending hours in the computer lab looking at thirty-thousand-dollar properties, but we both know it will never happen.

The New Orleans stripper plan won't either, even though I get so into it that a week later I drunk-dial my mom after midnight and tell her about it. "Imma be a beauuuutiful, *angry* stripper. Isn't that, like, the puuurrrrfect job for me?"

"If that's what you want to do." She sounds cheerful and bright to me. Even though I woke her up. Even though she panicked at first and was all, "What's wrong? What's wrong?" Because usually something is. Usually, I'm crying about hating school and myself and loving Simon but hating Simon. Saying that I want to be a stripper, especially since it's a plan that I'm happy about, is a major step up from that—even if it's a major step down from the girl I used to be.

I've made the firm decision to drop out at the end of the school year, telling my parents that I still want to be a writer, but I don't need college to do it. My dad was not on board, but I didn't care. He informed us over winter break that he's getting remarried. He shared this news in his usual cool, collected manner, and in my usual outraged, dramatic one, I'd kicked the liter bottle of seltzer water that he was drinking from, splashing it all over him.

My mom has accepted my choice to leave college, but she keeps saying, "If you go back by the time you're twenty-one, I'll still help you pay for it." I ignore those comments, thinking I'll be in New Orleans or New Mexico or, more likely, dead by then.

I prattle on about the angry or sad songs I'm going strip to. "'She's Lost Control' by Joy Division—that would be perfect," I tell her.

Then I finally let Mom go because I know she's tired and we both know I'm not actually going to New Orleans. I'm going back to Wisconsin. Mia is living there again, but I'm not going there for her. Just like I'm not really dropping out of college to write.

I'm doing it all because of Simon.

## V.

Simon and I move into a one-bedroom apartment together, though he will continue to maintain that we are "just friends" because he's still in a long-distance relationship with his girlfriend, who'd also dropped out of college and moved back in with her parents, necessitating Simon's return to Wisconsin.

We are "just friends" who share the same bed most nights and definitely don't "just sleep" in it. Much to my satisfaction, most people assume that we are together. We live together, after all, and we're always out at the club together.

The scene in Wisconsin might be small, but it feels glamorous—all the dressing up, the drinking and dancing. I am someone on Simon's arm, draped in black velvet and outlined in kohl.

As long as I drink enough, the fighting and misery are just drama and intrigue—the juicy parts of our early history that biographers will one day say fueled our creativity . . . not that we are writing much of anything. With all of the partying, there isn't time for the poems we'd exchanged while I was in college, and my short-story notebook languishes untouched in a pile of books I'm not even reading.

Eventually, Simon's girlfriend breaks up with him and we go through a few weeks or maybe months—time blurs thanks to wine and rum and cocaine and MDMA—of him blaming me, of screaming matches, of him fucking other girls, of me writing notes in my own blood, of my threats to die and his threats to let me.

*(We weren't supposed to be Sid and Nancy—that was Greg and me, broken and damaged. We're F. Scott and Zelda, a little drunk, a little mad, but brilliant. We're supposed to be brilliant!)*

*(You were supposed to be brilliant and maybe you still could be without—)*

*(SHUT UP!)*

Then, finally, really, I am his girlfriend. He declares this one quiet night in bed when we are too hungover to leave the house or even draw the curtains. He's loved me, he says. He always has. He should never have tried to deny it. That had only hurt both of us. But we're together now, for real, and we won't hurt anymore.

I have won. I am triumphant.

Even though I have hit rock bottom and fallen through several times over to get here.

Even though I am an unrecognizable puddle of a girl.

## VI.

If my life were a novel, there would be a point where I faced my worst demons, lost, retreated into darkness, but then found my strength and used it to set everything right in my world.

In other words, I should have a story about an incident with Simon that made me see how unhealthy our relationship was and, after wallowing or struggling briefly, put an end to it.

I don't.

Instead, I have a series of incidents where I make an attempt to change, but always fall short of breaking up with Simon. This went on for far longer than I want to admit. For years.

I was the kind of character that disgusts me—makes me throw the book and scream, "What the fuck is wrong with you? Why can't you just get your shit together and move on?"

But this is harder to do in Real Life than it is in stories.

I'd fallen down a hole. I told myself that the free fall was fun. Then I would hit something, land on my back with the wind knocked out of me. I'd wake up, cry in pain and shame. Declare that this was it—rock bottom.

There were so many rock bottoms:

My near overdose in New Orleans.

Blacking out at the club on New Year's in Wisconsin.

Begging my mom for money after draining my savings and hitting the max on my emergency credit card.

The look of disgust on Mia's face after I missed work at the job she'd gotten me because I'd dropped acid with Simon and her boyfriend. She dumped her boyfriend. I managed to keep my job but lost her respect entirely.

The fight where Simon, so drunk that he would not remember the next day, punched me in the gut three times because I was trying to stop him from drinking laundry detergent.

The parking lot fight where Simon and I both nearly got arrested.

The many, many fights in clubs.

The many, many fights after getting home from the clubs that culminated in me slashing my own skin with my own knife and taking more sleeping pills than I should have after copious amounts of alcohol, but still waking up in the morning.

Groggy, sick, covered in blood, I would tell myself that it had to stop. I had to get it together and climb back out . . . after I rested for a minute.

I'd rest for so long that I'd get comfortable. And then the ground would begin to crumble beneath me because, as it turned out, I hadn't hit bottom, just a ledge.

Those ledges could never support my weight for long even though I tried to take up residence on so many of them. Thinking it could be a compromise—a reprieve from the falling without the strain of that upward climb that I'd convinced myself I was too weak to make.

This is the truth about rock bottom:

It doesn't exist.

You will keep falling until you die unless you choose to climb.

Climbing will not be easy. You will lose your grip. You will backslide and fall again. You will have to choose over and over again to nurse your wounds and continue onward.

The journey will be harder if you insist on carrying someone else with you, someone who is deadweight, like I did with Simon for so long.

But I climbed toward voices that I heard in the darkness, voices that I missed:

My mother's. Acacia's. Mia's.

Their outstretched hands gave me strength and helped me recover when I slipped.

On my journey upward, I found pieces of me that I thought had broken off, and they made me stronger still.

I could not pick up all of the pieces at once, but slowly I began to reassemble them in midair.

I hit the last ledge when I was just a few months shy of my twenty-first birthday. I'd been falling for three years.

There had been uglier mornings, ruder awakenings. This just happened to be the one where it clicked. Maybe it was the cumulative effect of all of those painful landings. Maybe I just couldn't ignore the voices anymore. The gentle coaching from my mom. Acacia's "subtle bluntness," as we called it. The screaming in my own head. And the meowing.

Sid was crying pitifully, and when I staggered out of bed, I found him staring into the bathroom where his litter box and water bowl were, unable to get to them across the lake of puke. My puke. All red liquid, the color of the many, *many* drinks I'd had before driving home.

(*Oh my god, what have you fucking done? It's one thing if you OD or you go home with a stranger who turns out to be a serial killer. That's on you. But do you even remember driving home?*)

(*Not really. I hit a curb at some point and I remember laughing.*)

(*Laughing? Why is that funny? It could have been another car or an animal or a person. You could have really hurt someone. You DID hurt Sid. Listen to him crying.*)

(*I know. I hear him.*)

(*He's always been there for you. He got you through Greg. He loves you unconditionally and relies on you completely.*)

(*I know. Shit. What have I done? What have I become?*)

I picked up my cat and buried my face in his black-and-white fur, telling him, "I'm so, so, so sorry," and silently thanking him for forcing me to listen to myself.

Simon was still asleep, so after cleaning the bathroom, I called Acacia. We'd been slowly rebuilding our friendship. I'd been trying to hide my drama from her since I knew it was the reason I'd lost her, but she was the only one who would understand why what I'd done to Sid was the awakening I needed.

"It's time, Steph," she told me.

Acacia knew that for the past few months I'd been dancing around applying to an art school in Chicago with a fiction-writing program. My mom's offer to help me was still on the table but set to expire that year. In some ways, my mother was more determined that I could become a writer than I was. Since I had doubts about what kind of living I'd be able to earn with a creative-writing degree, she'd promised to help me with future student loan debt if I needed it. Additionally, since this particular school was a fifteen-minute train ride from her house, she'd told me that since my brother would be going away to college in St. Louis that fall, I could live with her rent-free in order to get my life back on track and focus on my studies.

Mia had moved back to Chicago that year. She was on the opposite side of the city, but Acacia lived in an apartment two blocks from my mom's house.

I'm sure that over the course of our many conversations about That Chicago Fiction-Writing Program, Caci wanted to scream at me, *Dude, just fucking come home!* but that was not how we operated. We walked alongside. We listened. We carefully formulated responses, as I had when I saw her longing to try crystal meth at boarding school. Sometimes we had to let the other walk blindly through a field loaded with land mines and pray she'd come back alive because if we gave chase it could kill us both. That was what Acacia had just done with me. I was almost back. She just had to coax me to take the last few steps.

While I petted Sid, she made her case, acknowledging my biggest fear and turning it around on me as only she could: "I know you said you'd never come back to Oak Park, but if you let that stop you from going to a school you really want to go to, that's one more way that Oak Park hurts you. Staying away means Oak Park wins."

"Yeah, but coming back feels like a failure," I whined.

Firm, wise, and strong as she'd always been, Caci said, "Stop viewing it as a failure and look at it as a fresh start."

Deep down I knew that it should have been a fresh start without Simon, an opportunity to make a clean break and end the relationship that should have been a three-month fling and had morphed into three mostly hellish years.

I wasn't ready to do that, though. I'd fought for Simon like he was an Olympic gold medal. Even though he was really just a crappy participation prize, I had participated, and our relationship was the only thing I had to show for my post–high school failures. If I could just make it work, it would prove that those out-of-control years hadn't been for nothing.

So when I told Simon about my Chicago plan and he said he wanted to join me, instead of breaking up with him, I convinced my mom to let him move into her house, too. I believed that getting our creativity on track would fix us. We would finally have a real relationship. We'd stop drinking so much, we'd get serious about our art, and all of the dysfunctional ugliness would fade away, revealing that sweet, artistic core that I knew we had.

So I tried to ignore the bad nights, the arguments over not having enough fun, the times he got so drunk that he couldn't pull up his pants after he went to the bathroom, and my own hangovers, which left me feeling stupid and weak. Instead, I focused on the solid weekday school-and-work routine that kept me believing that Simon and I were getting better.

I kept telling myself the same lies, repeating the same fairy tales. I had always used fantasy to sustain me, to help me sleep at night.

I was a storyteller, after all.

And though I could not write the ending I wanted to my story, writing was my way of climbing back to the surface. Writing and music and writing about music . . .

# PART 11

*Altars.*  *Saviors. Rock 'n' roll. My life is best represented in verse—verse, chorus, verse. Every memory is a song or an album or a chord strummed on a distorted guitar. My favorite songs tell my story better than I can. And my favorite band . . . well, they changed my life again and again.*

There was a vigil for Kurt Cobain at the Seattle Center a couple of days after he died. I watched it on MTV through bloodshot eyes. People held candles and created altars out of Nirvana CDs and pictures of Kurt in the green grass. Kids stood in a fountain and let the water rush over them, faces turned up to the gray sky. A recording of Courtney Love reading Kurt's suicide note played over the loudspeaker.

After the note reading, MTV continued their coverage, weaving together Nirvana videos and live performances and interview clips with more footage of that gray-shingled house with the long driveway that we'd seen the gurney wheeled down, carrying his body. Later that afternoon, Courtney emerged from the house in a pale green robe and joined the fans who were camped out in the park next door. Chain-smoking, she told a group of girls, "Something good can come out of Kurt's death. I don't know what it is yet, but something good can."

*Something good can.*

That was what led me to Scoville Park. The desire to do something more than cut pictures of Nirvana out of magazines and plaster them to my wall. To light candles, close my eyes, and pretend I was in Seattle, pretend I was surrounded by people who got it. I told myself that I would find those people, and one day, we'd go to Seattle to pay our respects and then everything would be okay.

I buried that dream after Greg, after Scoville failed to live up to my expectations, after *I* failed to live up to my expectations. I buried a lot of things, a lot of broken shards of me, and ran away and swore I'd never look back. But eventually I realized that I had to.

Had to face who I was and who I wanted to be.

Had to dig things up. Get the dirt under my fingernails. Unearth those pieces of myself. Put them right.

I met Juliet's daughter, Ava, for the first time when she was nine months old. I was eighteen, home from college for winter break. Things with were strained with Acacia, so when I wasn't with Mia or up in Wisconsin during those two weeks, I was with Juliet. No matter how much time had passed since I'd seen her or how much bullshit had gone down, Juliet was always easy to be around. I might have been wearing elaborate eyeliner, white face powder and black lipstick, but I felt like the flat-chested eleven-year-old with mousy brown hair, and I was *enjoying* it. Things had been so much less complicated when I was that girl.

Juliet and I watched *Star Trek* reruns while Ava powered her way up and down the hallway in her walker. Actually, I mostly watched Ava. Beautiful, smiling, curly-haired Ava. I was entranced by her—and I felt like shit for not making time to meet her sooner. I apologized to Juliet for this, but she shook her head.

"I'm just glad you're here now, Stephie-Lou. Finally meeting your niece."

*Niece. Yes.* I looked at Ava as she zoomed back into the living room, little cheeks puffed out in determination. *Niece.* The word felt right. It matched my relationship to Juliet. More than friends. Different from friends. Sisters.

I'd planned to go home after *Star Trek*, but I'd missed my sister and she'd missed me, so we decided to hang out longer. While she put Ava to bed, I retrieved the box of wine I'd brought home from school. Juliet had always been a pothead, but recently she'd started drinking, too.

See, we were sisters. Totally alike. Okay, not totally. But the differences between us didn't matter. The love mattered more.

We were drunk, sitting at the card table in her kitchen, when Nirvana came on the radio.

"I don't hate them anymore," Juliet told me. "I think I mainly hated them because you loved them and I didn't get it and I hated that you loved something that I didn't get. But I get it now, why you loved them." She laughed. "Does that make any fucking sense?"

I laughed, too. "Yeah, it does." I thought about the beginning of freshman year, when she started smoking pot and meeting boys, and I wrote judgmental journal entries about how she was ruining her life. Because a life without me had to be a horrible one, right?

"I'm sorry," Juliet said. She'd stopped laughing. Her hazel eyes—eyes that mirrored mine, minus the orange ring that she still told me was "so cool" every time we saw each other—were serious, sober. Even though we'd known each other for a decade, even though we were sisters, this Juliet—a Juliet stripped of her protective layer, of the silly, the weird, the cynical, the sometimes mean— was a Juliet I rarely saw.

I reached across the table and grabbed her hand. "What are you sorry about?"

"How I treated you. How fucking horrible I was to you, especially that day. I called you laughing—*laughing*—that Kurt was dead even though I knew how much he meant to you."

We'd never talked about that. I'd kept it locked up. Hating Juliet wasn't something I was capable of. So I buried it deep in the recesses of my damaged heart. I ignored Juliet for a while, and then when she returned to Oak Park, I pretended it had never happened. And she had, too, for almost four years.

"I don't know if you'll remember now or if you even remembered at the time," she continued, tears sliding down her cheeks. "I don't think you did, because you didn't call me, but the day before he killed himself, that was the one-year anniversary of the day my grandma died."

My heart sunk. I hadn't remembered. I should have. Her grandma had been like my grandma, too, and more important, she was the one stable force in Juliet's life.

"My grandmother didn't want to die. Do you know what she would have given to live? But she had no choice. The cancer took her. And then this guy, this rock star with a baby girl"—Juliet jabbed her finger either at the radio or Ava's room, they were both in the same direction—"he kills himself. And I thought, *What a fucking coward*. I thought, *How could he* choose *to throw his life away when my grandma . . .*" She choked up.

I scooted around the table to embrace her. Our tears and snot and our long hair (mine jet black, hers brown with an auburn hue) blended together. Our *I'm sorry*s blended together. Then she sniffled, pushed her hair out of her face, and ran the back of her hand across her eyes.

"No, I'm sorry," she said. "Because I took it out on you. I never should have taken it out on you." Her damp eyes pierced mine, so I knew she wasn't just talking about the day the news of Kurt's death broke. She was talking about the sleepovers, the violent hair-brushing, all of those dark moments between us that we'd never acknowledged.

I curled into her again. Hugging her. Forgiving.


One late afternoon in April, a few months before I moved back to Oak Park, I lay in a fetal position on the floor of my Wisconsin apartment in front of the stereo and let Kurt Cobain's voice wash over me like a soothing wave.

Simon walked in on me singing to myself, cocked his head, and asked, "Are you drunk?"

Fair question, but I was sober. Instead of answering him, I mumbled, "They were my favorite band, and I've barely listened to them in forever because they were *his* favorite band. That's such bullshit. They're *my* favorite band."

Simon got a beer and joined me on the floor.

"I was in a liquor store parking lot when the news came on the radio," he recalled. "I'll never forget. It was like our generation's Kennedy."

I nodded, even though that was a cliché. Even though at that moment, it didn't even feel like we belonged to the same generation—I was a freshman in high school when Kurt died; Simon was almost legally old enough to buy booze. The age gap between us that I mostly ignored was suddenly glaring, but there was an even bigger chasm:

"Of course I didn't feel it to the degree you did," he said of Kurt's death.

Simon didn't get my love for Nirvana. Not really. He'd seen them in concert, on the *In Utero* tour, which my parents hadn't let me go to, but when he told me about it, the highlight for him seemed to be getting drunk in his friend's car on the way to the show.

When I started to revisit bands like Hole, Sleater-Kinney, Bikini Kill, and Rancid, Simon didn't get it at all. He cringed and said, "How can you like this? It's so . . . screamy."

Those screams had embodied my aches and my anger. They'd given me strength and power that I'd forgotten about.

I missed the music that had shaped me.

I missed the person it had shaped me into.

Though we'd been together for three years at that point, Simon didn't really know that person at all—and as it turned out, once he met her, he didn't really like her.

(Nor she, him.)

When I got back to Oak Park, back to my teenage bedroom, which was still plastered with all of my old posters and magazine cutouts, my drive to reconnect with my old passions—to reintegrate the punk girl who was as much a part of me as the writer—only got stronger. Like I had post-Greg, I found community on the Internet, this time on a message board for Hole where I talked with fellow fans about music and traded memorabilia.

As things with Simon grew more strained, he blamed the message board.

It was the message board's fault that I wasn't fun anymore.

It was the message board's fault that I was different.

I let him blame it because it was easier to do that than to explain that I was trying to fill the holes inside of me.

(That's how Courtney Love named her band, you know. People think it's dirty, but it's not. "You can't walk around with this hole inside of you," Courtney's therapist mom would tell her.)

There was the hole that had always been in me—a hole created when my family moved to Oak Park, stretched wider by my cruel new classmates, wider still when Juliet and I drifted apart. Scoville Park hadn't filled it like I'd hoped, but maybe the bootlegs of all of the Nirvana concerts I'd never gotten to see would.

There was that hole I'd carved into myself at my first college and during my time in Wisconsin—that I'd dug with pills and booze. Maybe I could fill it in with new copies of the magazines that I'd cut up and plastered on my walls as a teenager. No? Let's throw in copies of the magazines that had come out while I was too drunk to care.

There was the hole in my relationship with Simon—the one I'd thought my new college would plug. And college was going well this time around. I loved my fiction-writing classes so much. I was developing characters, creating entire fictional towns, finding my voice, but Simon said he missed my old stories, he liked my old voice better. I tried not to cry, tried not to think about the widening canyon between us, tried to fill it up by searching out cat-eye sunglasses and dresses like the ones I'd worn in high school.

Then there was the hole I kept falling into—the hole Simon called "fun." The hole I used to love. Sometimes still did. Especially with Juliet. A hole filled with wine and tequila and Malibu rum and the pills that I'd become dependent on to sleep. The message board helped me avoid the temptation of that hole, but I couldn't tell Simon that—after all, it was the place where we'd met—so I let him blame me, blame the message board, and say things that dug us into new holes.

What I couldn't trade for, I bought on eBay.

Hole's *Live Through This* on white vinyl.

The ten-inch that Kurt Cobain had done with William Burroughs.

If I collected it all, maybe it would fill me up.

The building at my new college where I take most of my classes sits across the street from Grant Park, the large, magnificent slice of green between the Loop and Lake Michigan. This is the Chicago I daydreamed about when I was seven, the Chicago I was excited to move to all those years ago.

Things are not perfect—far from it. I'm still with Simon. I'm still drinking more than I want to. I'm still figuring out how to put all of the pieces together, but when the sun is shining, when the words are flowing, I have hope.

I spend at least an hour in the park every day, preferably alone, always with a notebook. I haven't written this prolifically since I was seventeen. I'm filling a new journal every couple of months. The entries will morph from wounded outpourings to reflections with story potential to huge chunks of fiction. I'll write an entire novel before summer, a book set in Scoville Park.

It's way too autobiographical, and I know it. I must allow it to simmer, take on its own form, so the next summer I start writing about a teenage girl from Wisconsin who wants to be a musician. She is born from a journal entry that I wrote about sitting in the basement of my childhood home looking through my parents' record collection.

One of my classmates thinks that the first short story I write about her—a laughably terrible first sexual experience with a wannabe rock god—is hysterical. "You've gotta write more about that Emily chick!" he insists. And soon I cannot get her out of my head.

Emily's motivation—the mother who disappeared to follow the music, a damaged character named Louisa that I've already written about—will click while I'm waiting for the L in an underground station. I'll remember the whoosh of the train arriving at the same time the idea solidifies, as I realize:

*This is it. My homage to Sleater-Kinney and Riot Grrrl and all the music that kept me alive. This is the book I was born to write.*

When I returned to Oak Park, I worried about running into Greg, but as each month went by, I felt more certain that we wouldn't cross paths. Maybe he'd moved. Hopefully he'd died.

But no. After I'd been in town for eighteen peaceful months—and had gone

My very first draft of what would become the first paragraph of my first published novel

---

I have another YA idea of a book of letters, I was about to write about it but its too crazy to concentrate

Rock God          3/25/02

I keep an altar to rock n

Altars. Saviors. Rock 'n Roll. I brave my fears of spiders, dust plumes as thick as a bad smog day in LA & the cold smell of piss from the house's last owner's cooped up dog. I feel the cold, grey painted cement through my blue jeans like I'm sitting on ice but regardless of everything I dig, feeling the perfect square edges poke between my fingers, the slap of cardboard plastic dust covers against plastic dust cover as I flip through each album so satisfying but not as good as it will sound when I find the one I want, slip it out of its paper jacket and onto the record player, the needle skipping & skittering for a few seconds until it finds its groove, the first chord scratching its way through the speakers, a catchy chorus reverberating in my ears. Altars. Earthquakes Rock Gods. They have

---

# ROCK GODS

Altars. Saviors. Rock 'n' roll. I braved my fear of spiders, dust plumes as thick as L.A. smog, and the stench of dog piss that the last owner of the house had let permeate the basement to tirelessly search my father's record collection for my next holy grail. Sitting on that cold, dirty, painted cement floor in my blue jeans, with the Wisconsin winter creeping through the tired walls and windows of our house, I dug through crates of albums, feeling their perfect square edges poke between my fingers. The slap of plastic dust cover against plastic dust cover was so satisfying, but the best moment came when I found the record I wanted, slipped it out of its paper jacket and onto the record player. The needle skipped and skittered for a few seconds until it found its groove, the first chord scratching its way through the speakers, a catchy chorus reverberating in my ears. Earthquakes. Rock gods.

Music was in my blood. My mother left me with my father when I was four months old so she could follow the beginnings of

*I Wanna Be Your Joey Ramone*
final copy

more than five years without laying eyes on the bastard—there he was. At my fucking train stop.

His hair was short, its natural shade of dark brown. He looked like any twentysomething dude waiting for the L. But the sight of him . . . I felt like I was having a heart attack. My palms were clammy. I was dizzy. I couldn't breathe.

Simon was with me. I clutched his arm, and he looked down at me, his thin eyebrows knitting together over his black sunglasses. "What's wrong?"

My mouth opened and closed a couple of times before I got it out. "That's Greg," I finally said, jerking my head in the direction of the guy who I usually only referred to as Him or The Asshole or My Abusive Ex.

"Oh" was Simon's response.

*Oh.*

"Why's he here? He shouldn't be here. There's another stop closer to his house." I panicked.

"I don't know. You'll be fine. He's all the way over there." Simon patted my arm.

"You'll be fine"? I wasn't fine. And he wasn't *that* far away. The distance between me and him wasn't even the length of a train car. I pointed this out, but Simon simply assured me that we'd get on a different car.

We did, and I tried to forget about Greg, but then he got off at the same stop as we did, too. "It's like he's stalking me!" I hissed at Simon.

"I'm sure it's just a coincidence. It probably won't happen again."

But it did. Every day for the rest of that week. Simon did nothing. I went to the bathroom when I got to school and clawed at my arms. I hadn't hurt myself like that since I'd moved back from Wisconsin. I'd finally trained myself to pick up a pen instead. Sometimes to write words or draw lines on my skin, but more often to write in my notebook. For years, I'd stared at a fresh cut and told myself to remember it because it would be the last one. But, I realized as I looked at the pathetic scrapes on my wrist, I didn't remember the last one, I didn't want to, and I certainly didn't want to draw my own blood with my own fingernails for Greg. I had to take control of the situation somehow.

I'd gone back to therapy when I'd moved back to Oak Park, at my mom's insistence. I'd been seeing the same therapist on and off since my meltdown in high school, but after I saw Greg, I really started taking it seriously. My therapist taught me to breathe through my panic, and when Greg was on my train, I recited the names of all the stops forward and backward or focused on the names of the churches and businesses that we passed.

A few months later, when Greg invaded another part of my territory, I reacted differently.

Acacia and I were at one of our old high school haunts. Laughing, drinking coffee. Then I stopped laughing.

"What?" Caci asked.

Greg had just walked through the door of the diner. I jerked my head in his direction and spat his name.

"It was probably Caci that he was really afraid of. He always was afraid of her," I told my therapist at our next session. "But for the first time, I felt like I had the power."

He shook his head. "I want you to repeat that last part without the disclaimer."

"I had the power."

My therapist nodded. "You do."

I was so determined to reclaim my life that I finished my undergraduate degree very quickly. I took a full load of classes and summer school while working multiple jobs. If you counted only the time I was in school—ignoring the two-and-a-half-year gap between my two colleges, as I wanted to—I would graduate in three and a half years, just like I had in high school. However, during this same period, I watched Juliet spiral out of control like the pilot of a plane that lost one engine and then the other. I didn't know how to help because, successful as I might have looked, my own damaged aircraft was fragile, and I was barely keeping myself out of a tailspin.

Drinking took a toll on her marriage. She attended AA meetings and said she had to stay away from me because I enabled her. I agreed. I wasn't enabling her on purpose; I was just shitty at stopping her from making bad choices. Like when we went to our favorite Mexican restaurant to celebrate her first paycheck at a new job and she bought shot after shot of expensive tequila. I'd said, "Don't spend all your money on me," but she laughed and said she wasn't, she was spending it on tequila, so I let it happen.

I took it seriously when she started outpatient rehab, though. They put her on medication that would make her throw up if she drank. That helped for a couple of weeks. We started hanging out again sober. I told her I was proud of her and that I liked us both better when we weren't drinking.

Then she showed up at my door one night and I saw a pint of tequila tucked into an inside pocket of her coat. I snatched it from her and ran to the kitchen to pour it out in the sink because, dammit, I wasn't going to be an enabler!

She screamed bloody murder as soon as the booze splashed into the sink.

Simon joined the fray, siding with her. He was drunk, and he felt Juliet had the right to be drunk, too, if she wanted.

"You're a fucking hypocrite," Juliet yelled at me.

"Yeah! What would you do if I poured your sleeping pills down the sink?" Simon added. He blew it off whenever I worried that I might have a drinking problem, but whenever I hinted that *he* might, he liked to point out that I was taking three different drugs to get to sleep every night.

"Okay, I'm a fucking hypocrite, but I'm trying! And I can stop drinking—can you?" I challenged them.

I stopped for a few months just to prove my point. Simon didn't even try—probably because he was too drunk to remember the argument. Juliet couldn't stop. No matter what.

So she joined the Army Reserve. She did it for Ava, she said. The army would provide job training and money for school, and she could finally become the nurse or the researcher she'd always wanted to be and support her daughter. Plus, the regimented structure would help her turn her life around.

"I won't be able to drink in basic. I'll be fine after that," she'd told me.

But when Juliet's ex-husband and I took Ava down for Juliet's graduation from boot camp, she admitted she'd started up again.

She drank through the rest of her training.

She was drunk, I could tell, when she called me from Fort Hood.

The cell reception had sucked since she got there. It cut in and out. Staticky. She sounded as far away as she was about to be.

Tomorrow, she said, she was leaving for the Middle East. Forty-five days in Kuwait and then off to Baghdad. She probably wouldn't be back for almost two years. Ava—our giggling, Hello-Kitty-and-dolphin-loving little fairy princess—would be eight, almost nine.

*Nine.*

We didn't discuss that. And we definitely didn't say "if," instead of "when." I refused to even think about that.

"I'll get sober in the big sandbox," she reassured me once again. I already knew that it was another empty promise.

I didn't know if I could stand to keep worrying about her.

I didn't know if I could stop.

*(Was this how my mom felt during all of those drunken late-night phone calls from me? I need to apologize to her . . .)*

I wanted to cry through our conversation—the last conversation for an unknowable amount of time.

I wanted to pour myself a drink and get wasted with her one last time.

But I didn't do any of that. I knew that drinking, especially, wouldn't help. All I could do was keep the three promises that she asked me to make:

- First and most important, I would take care of Ava no matter what. I would be a real "aunt"—better than Juliet's blood aunt was to her. I would make sure that Ava had the future that Juliet and I dreamed of, try to protect her from what hurt us, and steer her away from the mistakes we made.

- I would "finish that fucking novel," as Juliet put it, and keep sending her the pages like I had been since she'd started basic. She said it was good and she knew that even though it was about a rock star, it was really about us. I was fairly sure she meant the girl friendships, and there was a little bit of the two of us in them, but a lot more of me and Caci. Louisa, the mother who disappears to follow the music, on the other hand . . . There was a reason for her name. Stephie-Lou. Julie-Lou. She was our alter ego. The dark shadow in both of us. The girl who'd been so badly hurt, so deeply damaged, that she had to run. I'd started out writing that book for myself—both to live out my rock 'n' roll fantasies and to remind myself why I needed to keep healing—but soon I was writing it for Juliet, as my subtle way of begging her to get better and to come home to her little girl.

- I would send her a postcard from Seattle.

I decided to visit Seattle on the ten-year anniversary of Kurt's death. I was twenty-four and in grad school then. I was still reckoning with the mess of a person that Simon was and that I had been/could be at times. I was writing constantly. But it still felt like I was missing something. If I made this pilgrimage—went to this place that I'd wanted to run to since I was fourteen years old—maybe that would do it. Make me whole. Heal the old wounds at last. Simply give me the little bit of strength I needed to fully and completely move forward.

I met up with four girls, fellow Nirvana fans that I'd befriended online. We shared a room in a hostel by the waterfront and explored the city together.

I visited Viretta Park three times during my ten days there. Though I had a huge list of things to do and places to see, I knew that tiny patch of land next to the house where Kurt took his life was most crucial to my own story.

We took a bus there, riding up and down hills from the side of the city bordered by Puget Sound to the side bordered by Lake Washington. Then we walked for a mile, following the winding road along the lake to the park.

Each time we brought flowers and candles and watched people of all ages, from all over the world, come and go, leaving their own flowers and candles, as well as pictures, letters, even a box of macaroni and cheese, on the bench in the center of the park that had become an unofficial shrine to Kurt.

On the first day we visited—April fifth, the anniversary of what was determined to be the day he died—my friends and I joined a group that had formed around a couple of people with guitars. We sat in the grass near the bench, singing Nirvana songs. Our circle fluctuated in size as fans came and went. In the sunlight we were rowdier, screaming the words at the top of our lungs, laughing at ourselves when we forgot the right line, guitarists breaking strings. It mimicked the energy of Nirvana: the chaos, the honesty, the general good goddamn time. As night fell, everyone in the circle lit white candles, which we held until they threatened to burn our fingers. The mood became more somber, our voices quieter but more powerful. I huddled closer to my friends for warmth, cupped my fingers around the flame of the candle, and closed my eyes to the darkness of the park as I sang, knowing this was the beginning of what had been ten years in the making: my goodbye to Kurt, and to the damaged girl within me who'd worshiped him.

Our second visit to the park was April eighth, the anniversary of the day the world learned he was dead and thereby the real anniversary of his death for me. It was still crowded, but only one of my friends accompanied me. This gave me more space to reflect, and by the end of that day, as we walked slowly away from the bench, out of the park, and past Kurt's house, I remembered something from a magazine that I read the year after Kurt's death. A fan had written *He was*, and I'd cut it out and taped it to my wall above a picture of Kurt.

I realized that was all I needed to say about my past: *It was*. It happened, and it was over. I didn't need to forget or to forgive, I just had to stop looking back.

On April tenth, our third and last day at Viretta Park, which was also our last day in Seattle, we found that everything had been cleared from the bench. It was a little bit jarring, a little bit like when I looked around after three years of getting numb and realized how much of myself had disappeared.

But my friends and I were prepared, armed with more flowers, and a bag of a hundred tea light candles, which we used to spell out KURT below the bench. We sat there through the afternoon. A few people came and went, but when darkness fell, there were just seven of us, and, armed with only three lighters, we lit up Kurt's name. You could see it clearly from the street; it burned with the same ferocious brightness as Nirvana's music.

As I stared, it finally sank in: what I had been seeking for the past ten years, that pure creative force, that voice that Kurt Cobain had given the world, was inside me. I had carried it with me through my destructive adolescence and my slow recovery to Seattle. Or, perhaps, it had carried me.

Before we left, we blew out the candles, each making a wish. For the first time, mine was not about a boy or about making peace with my past. It was about my future.

*Please let me make it as a writer.*

And then, maybe because I felt like I deserved a second wish or maybe because I couldn't help thinking it, I added:

*Please let me make it back here.*

I hadn't expected it, but I'd fallen in love with the city of Seattle at first sight. On the bus ride from the airport to downtown, something just happened. My blood buzzed the same way it had in eighth grade whenever I was around my first crush. I was giddy and wide-eyed. I could barely talk to my friends because I was too busy staring at the lush green hills and fir trees and the serene blue-gray of Puget Sound. My pulse raced as one thought played on a loop in my mind:

*This is where you belong.*

After Scoville and Wisconsin both failed me, I'd given up my search for that place. I'd settled for Chicago like I'd settled for Simon. But my feelings grew stronger every day I spent in Seattle. It was as if I was breathing fresh air again for the first time in, well, nearly a decade. I

could see the bright blue of the sky, smell the salt water, feel the warmth of the sunlight, taste the misty rain.

*This is where you were always headed. You are almost there, out of the hole. Just drop the deadweight and finish the climb.*

All I'd wanted was closure, but with that—or perhaps because of it—I'd found the home that my heart belonged to.

~~

5/20/05   This book is what I have right now. I need to pour my energy into it, let it thrive, finish it. Then shape & perfect. Let this story be as pure as the stories I told to myself & others as a kid. A vision I see & am eager to portray. A joy from start to finish. It is mine. I love it. This *is* fun. A game, a puzzle. I stretch my mind to create. I need to live inside this story Fuck the bullshit in the outside world. The worries about how to make ends meet. Right now I have nothing but this. I will let it consume me. It will be mine. It will be good. Fucking great. What I've envisioned since I first told stories.

This is the closest I came to writing about breaking up with Simon in my journal. Our split was so inevitable, and I'd yelled and fought and cried for so long, that when it happened, I had nothing left to say. Well, not about him at least.

When he left, I let him take whatever he wanted—the shared furniture, appliances, DVDs, and CDs. Stuff mattered so much more to him. It had only mattered to me when I was trying to fill the hole that being with him had stretched wider and wider. That hole had shrunk a lot in Seattle and more with every step I took away from him. It seemed like breaking up with someone should do the opposite—it should tear a hole, wide and painful—but for me, it finally closed one.

Or it almost did.

After Simon moved out, it hit me: my house was half empty; the person who had consumed so much of my life, gone. Both Caci and my mom offered to come over, but I turned them down. Instead, I sat down in the middle of the unfurnished living room (he'd taken the couch and the TV) and called the one person that I knew I needed to talk to in order to ensure that I didn't fill up this new blank space with the wrong things, the wrong people. The one person who could make the final stitch, tie it tight, so that hole stayed closed.

"Hi, Steph," my dad answered. He sounded far away. He *was* far away. He lived in Maine with the woman he'd married and my half brother, who'd been born a few days after my twenty-first birthday. When he'd told me that he was having another kid, I'd been so angry that I refused to speak to him for a year. After that our relationship had consisted of him buying me things, me yelling at him when I was drunk, and the occasional joint session with my therapist where Dad wished I would forgive him and I said I didn't know how.

I'd finally figured that out.

"Dad," I said. And then I lost it. "Daddy, I need you. Simon and I broke up, and it's good, but he's gone and I have this house and all of these things in it are broken and I'm broken. I'm so broken. Especially when it comes to men, and I'm afraid that I always will be unless I fix things with you."

It was something I'd been thinking since I was seventeen. Since before I met Simon. Sometimes I thought it was a little too simple, too Freudian or something. But I'd kept circling back to it. I needed to love myself, to forgive myself, and for whatever reason, I needed to forgive my dad to do it.

I held my breath. Literally. To prepare for the inevitable disappointment, the excuse about work, the . . .

"I'll get the first flight I can," he told me.

When he got there, he slept on my floor at night, and during the day we went from room to room fixing whatever was damaged or didn't work. This sort of handiwork wasn't my dad's specialty, and there were a few things not quite fixed right, but it didn't matter. He'd come. He'd helped me put myself back together again.

I didn't have to worry about that outside world "bullshit" and "how to make ends meet" for long either. When I called Mia to tell her about Simon, I learned that she'd broken up with a boyfriend, too. She was living on the north side of Chicago and was also fretting about having to find a roommate.

Of course, when I proposed it, Mia was wary at first: "The way you bailed on me after you met Simon . . ."

"I know. I'm so sorry. I promise that won't happen this time. I'm focused on my book right now, and figuring out who I am. I'm doing what I should have done back then."

"Neither of us really knew what we were doing or what we needed back then," she said. Proving why I needed her—she would hold me accountable for who I was, but not let me be ashamed of my past. I couldn't erase all that had happened since the first time Mia and I had lived together. I couldn't rewrite it or pretend it hadn't happened. When I'd moved to Wisconsin with Mia, and especially when I'd returned after my year of failing spectacularly at college, I'd been running from my problems, desperate to find something that would wash my pain away. Since I'd come back to Oak Park, I'd been facing them. I knew I needed to continue doing that. I had to stay for at least another year, and not just to finish grad school and finish my book, but to finish healing. Then I would be ready to move forward and carry what I'd learned with me to Seattle.

In the meantime, I wanted a second chance at Real Adult Life with Mia as my roommate. We went back and forth for a while, trying to determine if it would work. I only had one concern: Sid had developed irritable bowel syndrome, which I blamed myself for, thinking that the years of me fighting with Simon had stressed him out. Adding Mia's two cats to the mix might be hard on him.

"I don't know how we can assess that, Steph," Mia said. "I mean, we'll keep them separate first, introduce them slowly."

"I just don't want him peeing everywhere. How about if you bring your cats over for a night. They can stay in the basement, but he'll know they're there. We'll have a sleepover, hash the rest of this out, and if it goes well, if you feel good about living with me again and Sid doesn't pee, everything works out and you move in."

She agreed and drove over with her cats. We cooked delicious food that made my house smell and feel like a real home. We stayed up all night talking like old times, but with new wisdom.

And Sid didn't pee.

# The Writer in the Story

## Pieces of A Girl

Write it like you'd make a mixtape

### Key theme(s):

- Live a life that is story-worthy
- "There wasn't always a place to go, but there was always an urgent need to belong. — this need as a medium for self expression
- Shapeshifting until you become comfortable in your own skin

### Other Inspiration & reminders:

- Men's experiences don't require contextualizing so neither does my teenage girl life (think Hemingway / fuck Hemingway)
- More "...And Out Come the Wolves," less "Nevermind"
- Embrace the contrast in storytelling moments / modes
- Let the reader put together the pieces w/o telling them the larger whole
- It's a cycle of experiences but I was expecting the triumph of unlocking a new level
- Circles — Labyrinths — Nesting Dolls — Broken Mirrors
- Why are you still alive??? ("They want us to think that to be a girl poet means you have to die.")
- The search for Stephanie (not just generic "identity")
- Performative adulthood cut short my own healing
- Independence as lore & how it leads to being an outsider

Remember the difference between a mixtape & a greatest hits album!

`I was pieces of a girl.` *Weirdo. Grunge. Grrrl. Goth. I didn't think I was allowed to be all of it at once.*

*I was everything for everyone else and nothing for me. I gave people the pieces they wanted and hid the rest.*

*I was usually the outsider, occasionally the insider. I never had any self-esteem.*

*I measured my value by the love of others. I didn't know how to love myself. Me for me.*

*I was pieces of a girl. I was very good at cutting them out. Cutting myself down.*

*I used to be smart.*

*I was supposed to be something.*

*I might fail.*

*I did fail.*

*I am a failure.*

*I was pieces of a girl, but I had a storyteller heart.*

*Storytellers like pieces. They like puzzles.*

*Storyteller grrrls in particular like to cut and paste.*

*I am pieces of a girl.*

"Why are you still alive?" my editor, Andrew, asks in conversation about this book. I put it up on my whiteboard with other inspiration for the book, like, *Write like you'd make a mixtape.*

*Why are you still alive???*

When I tell Suzy, the illustrator of the book, about this comment, she says, "I thought the same thing!" We both laugh. Not because it's funny. It's not. Not really. But sometimes you develop a sort of dark humor as a coping mechanism.

Suzy is ten years younger than me, but we have that along with some other crucial things in common, which along with her incredible artistic talent made her the perfect collaborator for this project—we share a love of music, with punk and goth being particularly formative; zines were a creative and emotional outlet for both of us; we're devotees to astrology ("I saved all my journals in a giant Tupperware because, you know, Cancer," I confess, and she responds that hers are stored in plastic bags in a storage container because she's a triple Virgo.); and we're both survivors.

"I do that thing that I think many survivors of trauma do," I say to Suzy, explaining why the question that both she and Andrew had upon reading my story was never something I thought to ask myself before. "I think, *It wasn't that bad. Like I can name all these people who have been through worse.*"

In my head, I can see Kurt Loder from *MTV News* asking Courtney Love the question, *Why are you still alive?* It's something she has a right to and I don't.

"Even as adults ourselves who survived some shit, I think we tend to underestimate the ability of young people to survive anything," Suzy says. "That was something I kept thinking about while illustrating this. Even thinking about the way I drew the characters, I wanted the characters to look very young. You and your peers, I wanted you to look baby-faced. That was very intentional on my part."

Suzy explains how she noticed that male illustrators in particular tend to make teenage girls sexy in comics and graphic novels, when we are/were not. When we're just dorks. It's cultural to age teenagers up, to have adult actors play them, which was true when I was watching *Beverly Hills, 90210* in the nineties and is true now in shows like *Euphoria*.

"I didn't want to illustrate your story like *Euphoria*. Of course, when you start getting into the drugs and the partying and the general shit show that became your life . . ." We both laugh again. "That was harder to draw because I was like, I want her looking haggard but still nineteen."

"You pulled it off!" I exclaim, explaining that the juxtaposition between the story, the text that portrays adult situations, and the images of baby-faced kids, is an important reminder, even to me, about how old I really was.

Suzy allowed me to see my life as I always wanted to in my head—as a movie, a happening. She brought to life even the parts I didn't imagine.

"That entire Greg abuse section, I originally was like, *That is not going to have any illustrations*," I tell her. "And I think that was because in my head I was so disassociated from it that I didn't even want to see it. But looking at it now, it's perfect."

"Really?" she asks. "There were parts of it that were really hard for me to illustrate because they were so intimately familiar, just those dynamics. But because of this, I had to be really conscious of how to represent you in such a vulnerable moment and how to sensitively capture what you were going through and what I think many people who read this book may have come across or be going through without making it look exploitative or sensational. I think there's something that's really banal about abusive relationships, stuff that is easy to overlook because your sense of what's normal just erodes and it takes these different shapes. So something I wanted to try and show was how more and more extreme your life had been becoming. You were in these situations that a lot of people might see as extreme or just ridiculous, like, *How did she get here?*"

We both laugh, again in that knowing way, and I say, "Right."

"But," she continues, "a lot of teenagers, especially those of us who are rebellious, just roll with the punches. We're just like, *Oh, great, my boyfriend is having another freak-out again. I guess I am going to have to weather this. Just another day!* But that's part of what makes us tough, what makes us punk girls. I think that so many of us that grow up in a subculture—punk, anything that is male-dominated—a lot of us put ourselves through the gauntlet just to show that we can take it. That was something I really identify with.

"In reading your memoir to illustrate it, I was like, *Damn, Steph. You're tough. You're Teflon.* But do girls need to be Teflon? I don't think any kids should have to be."

"No," I say definitively.

"No," we say together.

So how does it feel to look at myself so young, surviving the sorts of things that make people ask why I am still alive?

Grateful. Whole. Seen. Part of the constellation of the human experience.

One of the girls who grew up too fast.

One of the girls who really was just a nerd, a weirdo at heart.

One of the girls who lived.

# Acknowledgments

An incredible number of people believed in this book and/or me. It and/or I would not be here today without them. Let's start with the people you met on these pages. First, to my biological family. Mom, Dad, Dan: I never had to question whether you would "let" me write this book, tell these stories, even though they would be painful to revisit. I love each of you so much. Each one of you has become a hero to me in your own way. Thank you for loving me for the weirdo/punk/sensitive artist creature that I am. Especially you, Mom. You've repeatedly seen me at my worst but never once stopped believing in me.

To protect the privacy of everyone else, I will continue to use their pseudonyms, trusting that they know who they are. My Girls, Elizabeth and Isabelle, for the zines, for the genuine girl love that allowed our friendship to weather time and my worst moments. The Little Boys, Jeremy and Elizabeth's brother, who goes unnamed in this text, for the purehearted friendship that kept me from completely self-destructing. All of my Riot Grrrls from Chicago and online. Marcy, for letting me apologize and teaching me about myself in the process. Brandon . . . fuck, I wish you were still here to see this. I loved your whole complicated self and am grateful to you for loving mine. Juliet—I love you, sister, always; weirdos and Trekkies forever. Mia, for building a home with me and helping me rebuild myself twice. You are my strength. Ava, my sweet niece, who is now one of the most brilliant, thoughtful, and compassionate adults I know. Thank you for giving me a reason to grow up, to be better. Caci, you are my person. You have been my person for nearly thirty years. (Shit, dude, we're old. How'd that happen, but also, yay? We survived, dammit.) There are no words for how much you mean to me, though that firefly comic that Suzy drew got pretty close.

Now, the people who made this book happen. Adrienne Rosado, the agent who championed me even when I wanted to give up on myself and my stories, thank you for your faith, encouragement, and the celebratory gorilla messenger. Julie Strauss-Gabel, thank you for believing in me as a writer and my "young adult zine style memoir" idea, for giving it all the time and work it needed to become what you knew it could be, which is something I couldn't even dream of at the time. Thank you to Andrew Karre, whose editorial guidance got it to that "better than I could have dreamed of" place. I needed a fellow Midwestern '90s punk who could tell me things like "write it like a mixtape, not a greatest hits album" and "more . . . *And Out Come the Wolves,* less *Nevermind.*" Suzy Exposito, your drawings not only transformed this book, but transformed my own view of myself and my story. I cannot thank you enough for being part of this project even as you were beyond busy, launching your own career. No one but you, my fellow goth-punk-zinester-witch, could have done this. Anna Booth, for a brilliant cover design and the vision that brought this book together aesthetically, again making my wildest dreams come true. Thank you to Rob Farren and Janet Robbins Rosenberg, my copyeditors, for making sure I'm consistent and sound good. Any mistakes or bad grammar (such as my insistence on adding an *s* to Ridgeland Common because that's how we said it) are mine, not theirs. And finally, thanks to the incredible Penguin Young Readers marketing team for getting this book in the hands of readers.

This book also would not exist without *Rookie* magazine. Tavi Gevinson, you did a revolutionary and magical thing in 2011. You made what I dreamed about while reading *Sassy* and making zines into a reality. *Rookie* was more than an online publication, it was a community. Thank you for creating it and for inviting me in. My voice and creativity were reborn, heightened, and challenged during my years at *Rookie* thanks to Tavi and the other incredible editors I worked with: Anaheed Alani, Lena Singer, Phoebe Reilly, Danielle Henderson, Amy Rose Spiegel, Derica Shields, Diamond Sharp, Elona Jones, and Jane Morgan. Then there was Lauren Redding, who kept us all afloat, and all of my fellow writers and artists whose genius inspired me and made me up my game. We had the best Internet Slumber Party for years where we laughed hysterically, shared our dreams and our fears, and always lifted each other up. I don't have space to name everyone, but I love you all. A couple of special shout-outs: Jessica Hopper has been such a generous mentor to all of us. She connected me to *Rookie* and also gave proposal writing guidance that resulted in this book. Esme Blegvad collaborated with me on numerous comics which not only helped shape my vision for this book, the work we did on creativity and mental health was a literal part of my healing process. And finally, all of the *Rookie* readers. You impacted me more than you know.

Other important shout-outs from various corners of my life: Thank you, Em Olson, for the gorgeous headshots and website, but most importantly, friendship and bringing me into Smarty Mommies. Thank you, Smarties! Thanks to Jeff Philpott for photographing all the bits and pieces of my life that were added to this book, but more than that, being a friend, mentor, and the kind of boss who understands the necessity of creative pursuits. Jane Hodges and Mineral School gave me the incredible gift of the time, space, and nourishment I needed to work on this book on more than one occasion. Jeri Smith-Ready is my writing ride-or-die; thank you for the Skypes, text check-ins, and always being willing to read something at the last minute. Allison Augustyn, Martha Brockenbrough, Karen Finneyfrock, Judith Graber, Kristin Halbrook, Jade Anna Hughes, Natalie Jaeger, Tara Kelly, Kate Koppelman, Melissa Marr, BethEllen McNamara, Jenny McNealy, Susan Meyers, Eryn Mulloy, Casey Paganucci, Becca Scheiblauer, Jenny Seay, Sonya Vatomsky, Carly West, and Alexa Young—you've all been there in ways big and small for me throughout this journey.

And finally, Scott, my self-proclaimed biggest fan. My partner. For loving all my pieces. For always understanding that I'm a writer to my core and knowing what that means in terms of my mood and how I manage my time. For moving across the country to the city of my heart. For being an incredible dad. This book is for you, for over a decade of gentle, consistent, loving support. I love you. And I love you, Apollo! You are my favorite piece of me and my next, biggest adventure.